Priests and Power

Dente Bosomfo Kofi Tawia (d. 1981) with staff of office, wearing Asante kente cloth

Priests and Power

The Case of the Dente Shrine in Nineteenth-Century Ghana

D. J. E. Maier

Indiana University Press
Bloomington

This book has been produced from camera-ready copy provided by the author.

Copyright © 1983 by D. J. E. Maier

Manufactured in the United States of America

Library of Congress Cataloging in Publication Data

Maier, D. J. E. (Donna J. E.)
    Priests and power.

    Bibliography: p.
    1. Krachi (African people)--Politics and government.
2. Krachi (African people)--Commerce. 3. Krachi
(African people)--Religion. 4. Dente (African deity)--
Cult. 5. Ghana--Politics and government--To 1957.
6. Ghana--Commerce. 7. Ashantis (African people)
--History. I. Title.
DT510.43.K72M34 1982   966.7   82-48582
ISBN 0-253-34602-9

Contents

Figures

Tables

Preface

The amplification afforded by oral data -- in
many cases eye-witness accounts -- was necessary
and important for this book. It was also urgent
for in 1966 the formation of the Volta Lake
inundated most of the century-old town of
Kete-Krachi, forcing its inhabitants to be
relocated about 1/2 mile from the old town.
Several other important Krachi villages were
inundated completely with the inhabitants settling
in many cases several miles away. Thus people who
not only could recall past events, but who could
recall spatial arrangements, historical trade
routes, town names, and social positions of former
towns now obliterated, were becoming rarer year by
year.

Field research for this book was carried out
primarily in 1972 and 1973 in Ghana. I returned to
Ghana in 1977, 1979 and 1982 to work on additional
projects while continuing to follow up and confirm
my earlier work. The field work involved mostly
oral interviews with members of the many divisions,
ethnic groups, and factions of Kete-Krachi. These
were conducted through an interpreter in Krachi,
Hausa, Twi, Ewe, or English, whichever was appro-
priate, almost always without a tape recorder but
with much informal socializing in my broken Twi.
This supposedly unsophisticated method was in the
end I feel justified by the many personal and
political confidences which were ultimately relayed
to me. I found oral material most useful for

amplifying with personal anecdote and insight archival materials I have also collected, and I rarely used oral sources in any other way than with archival corroboration. The oral materials and the experience of living in Kete-Krachi for almost a year also revealed to me the importance of and composition of various schisms and factions in the region which have roots reaching back at least a century and a half.

All the interviews conducted in 1972-1973 are available through purchase of Volume 2 of my Northwestern PhD dissertation, "Kete-Krachi in the Nineteenth Century," from University Microfilms International, Ann Arbor, Michigan. I would be pleased to provide copies of later interviews and letters from Kete-Krachi upon request.

Archival work was carried out in Accra, Kumase, Tamale, and Ho, Ghana, and Lome, Togo in 1972-1973, 1977, and 1979. I also researched in the London Public Record Office 1974, Basel Mission Archives, Basel, Switzerland, 1978, and the Bremen Mission Archives, Bremen, West Germany, 1980. All this plus travellers accounts, and the oral and archival materials collected by the Institute of African Studies, University of Ghana, Legon, provided the sources for this book.

A note regarding written translations is necessary here: Because a large number of quotations from German and some French materials were incorporated in the text, I felt that optimal continuity and reader understanding could be maintained only with English translations, and therefore all quotations are in English. All of the translations are my own, with two exceptions. First, Inge Killick's translation of H. Klose, Togo unter deutscher Flagge (1899) was used (available at the Institute of African Studies, Legon), though in every case the original German text was consulted. Second, Marion Johnson's translations (unpublished) of M.J. Bonnat's diaries in L'Explorateur (1875-1876) were employed as a guide, though some minor changes were made, for again the original French was consulted in all cases.

Spelling of place names has been a nagging difficulty. While the more phonetically correct spelling of Krachi is Krakye, I have chosen to use the former as it is what the Ghana Post Office, government, and people of Kete-Krachi use today. With other names such as Dwaben and Kumase less

often used in this book, I have chosen the more
academic spellings. Nevertheless, in all quotes
the original spelling of the source has been
maintained. While sometimes curious or even
confusing I trust these variations demonstrate
historical accuracy and the myriad regional
differences for pronunciation of the same place
name.

This manuscript was typed and prepared for
press through much travail by Tricia Meany.
Research grants for this work came from the
American Association of University Women, Fulbright
Hayes, American Philosophical Society, Northwestern
University, and the University of Northern Iowa.
Many Ghanainas have helped and showed me
hospitality in my field research, and many are
acknowledged in my interviews. But Horrocks Kwasi
Gyiniso has been of special assistance over the
years and our correspondence has kept me up to date
on Kete-Krachi politics. I could thank dozens of
people, but Ivor Wilks has been the mainstay,
advisor, inspiration and a colleague through all of
my scholarly endeavors in African history.

1

Introduction

Krachi was a border province of the Asante
Empire in the eighteenth and nineteenth centuries
and, as such, was carefully restricted in its
commercial and provincial privileges to the point
of being deliberately underdeveloped. Today the
Krachi people generally occupy the area in east-
central Ghana bounded by the Volta Lake (Volta
River until 1966) and the Oti and Daka Rivers.
They speak their own language -- Krachi -- a Guan
dialect, and now they number about 60,000 persons.
Under Asante domination they were mostly farmers
and hunters and were not particularly warlike,
highly centralized, or very wealthy. The Krachi
traditional religious shrine of the god Dente,
however, was known throughout Ghana and was highly
revered even by Asante. This gave Krachi a certain
unique importance and afforded some protection
against the harshest aspects of provincial subjection.
      The Krachi people resented Asante hegemony,
rebelled against it at least once unsuccessfully
(1830), later successfully (1874), and then began a
career of state-building on their own. Krachi's
next twenty-five years are particularly engaging to
an African historian, for the state-building
occurred under the leadership of the Dente priest,
known as the Dente Bosomfo. Rarely is the assertion of overt political authority by traditional
religion as explicitly and clearly documented as in
the case of late nineteenth-century Krachi.

Once free of Asante, the new capital Kete-
Krachi enjoyed a commercial boom which brought
about fierce competition among Krachi traditional
rulers, Asante traders, new Hausa/Muslim entrepeneurs, and Europeans (the British and Germans).
However, Krachi's late start at political development meant that colonial domination in the 1890s
ended only twenty years of independence. The
European powers repressed and thwarted Krachi's
dynamism, and its unique political/religious
coalition was arrested in midstream.

The present study seeks to analyse the circumstances which made it possible for African traditional religious authority to be translated into
political power in Kete-Krachi. The masters of the
Dente shrine used land, trade, and diplomacy to
supplement their religious eminence and achieve
genuine power over competitors and masses alike.
They opened new land to agriculture, formed alliances, raised armies, and acquired impressive
wealth for themselves and their state. Inextri-
cably bound up with this, and of particular interest to historians of Asante, was the way in which
Krachi as an Asante province interacted with that
central state system through various stages of
acquiescence, rebellion, competition, and aggression.

The later developments in Krachi demonstrate
how European consuls attempted to manipulate enterprising and ascendant African polities for
vicissitudinous imperial goals. Ultimately Europe
replaced Asante as Krachi's suzerain. The thorough
suppression of traditional religious control, a
fairly regular practice of the imperialists, did
alter the balance of power in Krachi. However,
colonial rule left chiefly and Muslim elites in
positions of peripheral consequence, and the final
chapter of this study will suggest that nineteenth-
century patterns of factionalism were hardly
altered. The Dente Bosomfo, despite his loss of
power, remains a prestigious figure today and the
fundamental social and economic cleavages of Krachi
still fuel political conflict.

I

On the 19th of January 1876, Monsieur Marie-
Joseph Bonnat, Governor of the Volta River from

Akroso to Yeji by appointment of His Majesty
Asantehene Mensa Bonsu, and Agent of de Cardi
Company of Liverpool, was travelling north up the
Volta River towards Krachi with a fleet of salt
canoes. The party drew near the capital, Krachikrom, with some apprehension, for the priest of the
shrine of Dente was considered "the greatest persecutor of the Ashantis." Bonnat believed that the
priest had ordered the massacre of Asante traders
and administrators in the interior the previous
year. Several shots were heard, but it was only
Bonnat's companion Robert Bannerman, mulatto nephew
of the Asantehene, "trying out his revolvers to be
ready for any eventuality." The canoes stopped
briefly for M. Bonnat to make his toilette: "I put
on a fresh turban for my head, a red cushion on my
chair. I am all in white with a violet serviette."
    At six o'clock the company reached Krachikrom,
and Bonnat saw and heard for the first time the
roaring cataracts in the river there. The bank was
"covered with natives waiting," but the grand
impression with which Bonnat and Bannerman had
hoped to confront the elders of Krachi was dissi-
pated. The chiefs, king, and priest had been
sitting in public ready to receive the visitors but
had grown impatient and gone to their houses.
Bonnat sent two bottles of gin to the authorities
with apologies, but the reception was postponed
until the following day.[1]
    Bonnat, the first European visitor to Krachi,
considered it the key to Salaga, a major market 95
kilometers further north, which was the main
commercial center for Asante and northern hinterland trade. He had learned of Salaga's importance
while a prisoner in Kumase, from 1869-1873, and was
firmly convinced that penetration to Salaga would
"open one of the richest parts of central Africa to
trade and civilization." He wrote to Governor
Strahan of the newly declared Gold Coast Colony:

> Salaga and its important native trade has
> since centuries been entirely into the
> hands of the Ashantees . . . From there the
> kingdom derived from all times the greatest
> part of its wealth.[2]

Yet in order to reach Salaga via the Volta River,
one had to pass through Krachi. More importantly,
one had to disembark and transship one's goods at

Krachikrom for here were cataracts impassable even
for canoes. One therefore had to come to terms
with the rulers at Krachikrom in order to pass,
for, as Bonnat pointed out, "the Crakey people are
determined above everything to retain alone the
transit trade which brings them enormous profit."[3]

II

In 1817 T.E. Bowdich had visited Kumase on
official business for the Company of Merchants
Trading to Africa and while there collected a large
quantity of material regarding the geography of
Greater Asante and West Africa. His books (of 1819
and 1821) and that of Joseph Dupuis (1824), an
equally astute observer sent to Kumase in 1820 on a
follow-up mission to Bowdich's, provide some of the
earliest detailed written data on the structure of
Asante and the nature of its hinterland. Both
Bowdich and Dupuis furnish the earliest references
to a town called "Odanty" or "Odentee" located on
the Volta River, due east of the town of Basa on a
branch of the Kumase-Salaga route (see Figure 4).
Odentee is described by both authors as being the
location of a ferry traversing the Volta east and
west.[4] Although between 1820 and 1876 the sources
are virtually devoid of references to that place,
it seems incontrovertible that the Odentee of
Bowdich and Dupuis is the same place as the Krachikrom of Bonnat, and the former two books thus
constitute the earliest written material on Krachi.
Detailed descriptions of both the north-south
and east-west routes through Odentee as provided by
Bowdich and Dupuis permit specification of Odentee's location. Bowdich delineated in detail the
land route to Odentee from Kumase through Kokofu, a
village just east of Atebubu, through Wiase and
Basa to the Odentee ferry, a journey of about 17
days by his reckoning.[5] Dupuis records that "the
distance to this ferry is reckoned twelve days good
travelling" from Kumase; the route "is frequented
by the traders who convey merchandize to the
markets on the confines of Dahomey for the supply
of that empire," these merchants being Muslims, he
claimed, not "heathens." He then detailed the
route from Krachi to Abomey, albeit with rather
obscure spelling, and symbolized Odentee on his map
as a major rather than a minor town.[6]

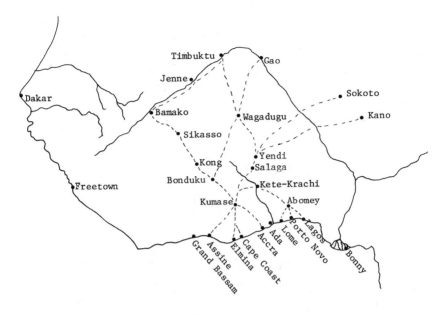

Figure 1: Nineteenth Century West Africa
with some major trade routes

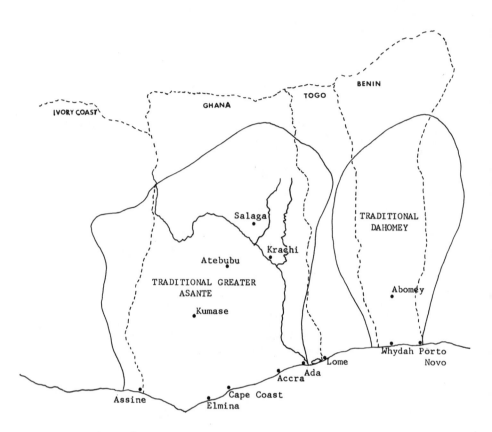

Figure 2:   Nineteenth Century Greater Asante
with Present-Day National Borders
Super-imposed

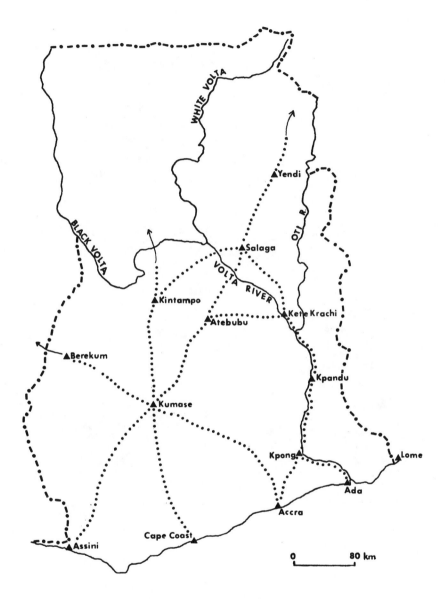

Figure 3: Nineteenth Century
Asante Trade Routes

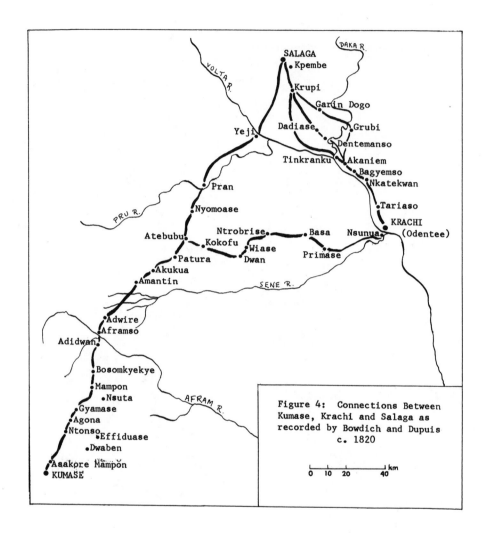

Figure 4: Connections Between
Kumase, Krachi and Salaga as
recorded by Bowdich and Dupuis
c. 1820

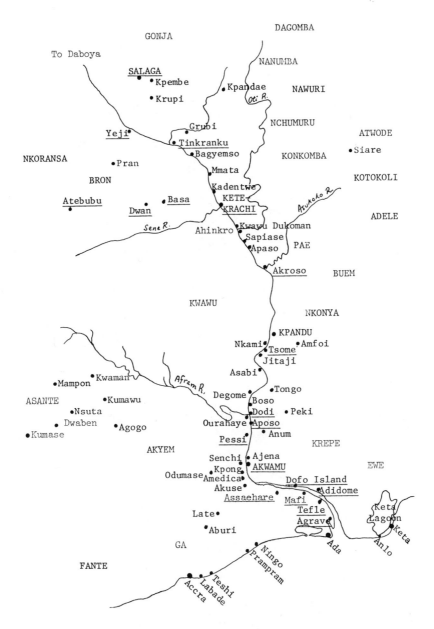

Figure 5: The Volta Valley, c. 1875.
Places mentioned by Bowdich (1819) are underlined.

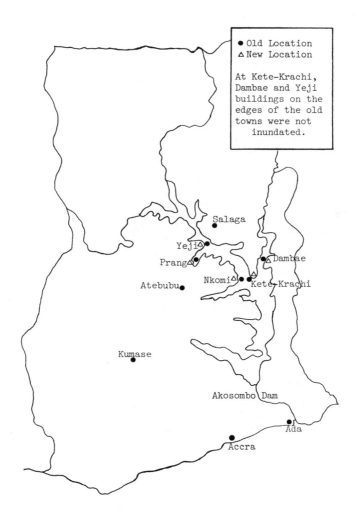

Figure 6: Post-1966 Ghana Showing
the Extent of Flooding by the Volta
Lake and Relocation of Major Towns

Figure 7:   Aerial View of Kete-Krachi and the Volta River, 1951

Figure 8:   Rapids on the Volta at Kete-Krachi, High Water, 1910

Figure 9:   The Volta at Kete-Krachi, Low Water, 1898, with the
newly-built British Krachi Station Visible on the Far Side

Figure 10:   Kete-Krachi Ferry Crossing, c. 1950

Late nineteenth-century sources confirm that the east-west route through Kokofu, Wiase, and Basa intersected the Volta at Krachikrom and was in great use in the 1880s and 1890s by traders, political embassies, armed forces, and refugees (see Chapter 6). It still constitutes a major communication link through Atebubu for Krachi today. The route is significant in that it represents the primary (though perhaps not the only) channel of contact between Krachi and Kumase, Krachi's suzerain until 1875. The Bowdich and Dupuis data indicate that the main route through Wiase and Basa was well-developed and well-known by the early 1800s, reflecting on the strength of Asante authority in the area at that time.

The "Odentee ferry" is surely the same ferry which sources from the late nineteenth century describe as being operated at Krachi by the paramount chief there, the Krachiwura.[7] The very narrow channel which accounted for the cataracts at Krachikrom also formed an ideal ferry-crossing in both rainy and dry seasons (see Figures 6-10). It was possible for one to walk across the river on the protruding rocks during very low water, and even today the Volta Lake at the point of the old Krachi ferry-crossing is less than one mile wide -- one of the narrowest sections of the lake and the passage of a modern ferry as well.

Dupuis' information suggests that Odentee was located on a route linked with Dahomey, and there is evidence today that late nineteenth-century Krachi was in contact with people living in Dahomey. Some Nchumurus (people closely related to Krachis and sometimes living under Krachi hegemony) recount a tradition of migrating to Dahomey, probably in the first half of the last century, and of maintaining contact with Krachi and other Nchumurus by sending gifts back annually. In the 1930s they chose to return to Krachi, and it was decided to settle them near Bagyemso, although many found "things contrary to their expectations [and] most of them returned to Dahomey Republic."[8] Oral evidence also suggests that at least in the early twentieth century some Krachis traded to the territory of Dahomey and were familiar with the language of some Dahomeyans. Nevertheless very little political interaction seems to have taken place between Krachi and Abomey.[9]

Bowdich gathered additional information about Odentee's position on a north-south axis. He was informed about the salt traders who took canoes north from the mouth of the Volta at Ada in order to reach the market at Salaga: "The natives who carry salt up the Volta pull . . . to Odentee the 11th [day]. Here the river becomes too rocky to proceed conveniently, and hence to Sallagha by land is 4 journies."[10] Bowdich recorded this Volta route carefully (see Figure 15), for by knowing the distance from Ada to Odentee, from Kumase to Odentee, from Odentee to Salaga, and from Kumase to Salaga he felt able to fix the location of Salaga, which he, like Bonnat later, regarded as "the great market" of Asante and the north.[11]

Bowdich was also interested in tracing the course of the Volta River inland which had not been done at that time, and in the process of doing this he acquired useful date regarding the salt trade. His information affirmed that salt was the major commodity traded up the Volta, starting from Ada, and that Odentee was the "highest point of the river to which salt carriers navigate from the coast,"[12] where the salt was then unloaded and taken on to Salaga by land. Bowdich's widow's books, drawn from the former's notes a few years later, add that Odentee was the point where "merchants of the interior purchased [salt] for the inland markets,"[13] thus indicating that a market exchange as well as a shift in the mode of transport took place at Odentee.

Until the building of the Akosombo Dam in 1966, which created the Volta Lake and flooded large areas of the watershed (see Figure 6), Krachi was located at insurmountable rapids on the Volta River. These rapids, although not the first ones on the Volta from its mouth, were the largest ones. Canoes could be paddled, poled, and pulled through the earlier rapids, but those at Krachi were too large and violent (see Figures 7-10) and, in this sense, marked the head of navigation on the Volta for canoe traffic. Although later some traders would portage their canoes and travel farther up the river, the section of the river above Krachi was quite shallow and frequently interrupted by more rapids. Bonnat's account of Krachi and Bowdich's information on Odentee make it clear that the traders unloaded their salt from canoes there and had it carried by land on to Salaga. Bowdich's

time data -- that Odentee was eleven days by canoe
from Ada -- correspond precisely with Bonnat's
experience of ten days journey from Akwamu to
Krachi and with later twentieth-century evidence.
Similarly, Bowdich's calculation that Odentee was
four days' travel south from Salaga corresponds
with every nineteenth-century account of the land
journey from Salaga to Kete-Krachi.[14]

Finally, Bowdich's brief description of Odentee
as "a fetish sanctuary of great repute, and said to
be splendidly furnished"[15] establishes the unity
of Odentee and Krachikrom beyond doubt. Krachikrom, as observed by Bonnat, possessed a religious
shrine or oracle known to this day as Dente. It
was located in a cave in the wooded bluffs overlooking the Volta gorge at Krachikrom and constituted one of the major attractions of the town.
This shrine must be understood as a resource in and
of itself, which will be discussed in greater
detail later (see Chapter 3). Suffice it to say
here, however, that the Dente shrine is somewhat
unique. It is an oracle situated in a cave, rather
than an inanimate object as most "fetish" manifes-
tations in Ghana are. An oracle, where the voice
of the god is actually heard, is extraordinary and
has a mysterious aura about it. Such an oracle is
easily manipulated. It is not dependent upon the
charisma of a priest who must, for example, go into
a trance, and whose skill and perception can bring
great fame to a shrine during his lifetime but,
logically, neglect if his or her successor is not
so gifted.[16] An oracle such as the Dente shrine
can endure successfully over many generations, and
a "fetish sanctuary of great repute" must be viewed
in Ghanaian terms as a resource to be valued in its
own right.

III

Several significant characteristics of Krachi
in the first two decades of the nineteenth century
can therefore be inferred from the evidence of
Bowdich and Dupuis. Although not on the principal
land trade route from Kumase to Salaga, Krachikrom
was sufficiently important by the early 1800s to
stimulate a minor route by which traders could
reach Salaga and the northern and eastern markets
and by which Kumase could remain in contact with

Krachi for political control. By the early 1800s,
Krachikrom was also the site of a ferry crossing
controlled by the Krachiwura, which provided income
in the form of transit fees, a means of monitoring
and hence taxing goods, and a means of regulating
the   passage   of   people.[17]   Krachikrom   was
concurrently   located   on   a   portage   on   the
north-south Volta trade route used regularly and
naturally by salt traders. Thus by the early
nineteenth   century,   whether   travelling   between
Abomey and Kumase or between Salaga and the mouth
of the Volta, or even between Salaga and Kumase,
some traders were passing through Krachikrom.

The trade and traffic on the secondary route
through Krachi at this time was probably not of
great   magnitude.   However,   the   Dente   shrine
constituted an additional feature. The shrine was
clearly well-established with "great repute" by the
early 1800s, and pilgrims from Asante and other
places must have been travelling the routes leading
to it as they do today, for apparently Bowdich's
and Dupuis' informants, travellers themselves, only
knew the place by the name of its shrine.

In addition, as will be seen, the Dente shrine
represented a considerable income for its managers
quite independent of its fortuitous or calculated
location at a transit stop on a trade route.
Dente's advice and counsel alone were worth a great
deal to those who believed and to those who ruled
over those who believed. In 1882, after Krachi's
separation from Asante, the British commissioner
Lonsdale commented that "to regain possession of it
[the Dente shrine] the Ashantis would risk a great
deal, it was in former times their oracle."[18] As
mentioned above, Bowdich's and Dupuis' informants
referred to Krachi only by the name Odentee. The
shrine and its priest were clearly the remarkable
aspect of the place; the tiny Krachi ethnic group
with its own dialect and rather insignificant chief
was hardly noteworthy.

The portage and the Dente shrine -- these then
were the significant factors at Krachikrom in 1817
and the basis of whatever importance Krachi might
possess at any point in time.. They were shrewdly
singled   out   by   Bowdich   as   the   most   notable
characteristics   of   the   place,   and,   as   such,
constitute the import of the earliest European
reference   to   Krachi.   They   starkly   confronted
Bonnat   as   key   hurdles   55   years   later.   Themes

involving these two factors will be found running throughout Krachi's history in the nineteenth and early twentieth centuries. The Krachi leaders in the later nineteenth century were able to manipulate them both in such a way that their combined significance exceeded the sum of the two parts. Other factors influenced the growth and decline of Krachi -- agriculture, slavery, invasion, diplomatic intrigue -- but all were aimed at control of Krachi's keystone location on the Volta River and its Dente shrine.

2

Salt, Yams, and Slaves

Geography, Ecology, and Demography

Europeans in Africa in the nineteenth century were quick to analyse trade potentials and hence they were quite conscious of Krachi's strategic river position. In 1894 a German administrator wrote an observation which precisely echoed Bowdich's information of 1817:

> Kratchi is intimately dependent upon its position on that great river [Volta] which forms a convenient connection with the coast . . . Her trade importance is based entirely on this favorable location, the point up to which the Volta River is navigable for canoes at all times.[1]

Thus, although the economy of the Krachi market place became increasingly diversified in the 1890s, salt, an item optimally shipped by river transport, remained the most stable item of its trade. While economic, political, demographic and military factors might influence the flow of trade goods and traders, and cause an entire shift in the land trade route system to another safer route, the Volta River always remained, and the salt at its mouth continued to be collected and transported up the river (until the introduction of lorry transport in the 1940s).

Krachi was thus more than a market on the river. It was a center for exchange of the natural resource salt. The salt had to be trans-shipped at

the Krachi cataracts, and this involved a turnover
in labor. Southern traders (e.g. Adas, Akwamus,
Krepes) and their slaves, skilled in the knowledge
of river navigation, transferred their cargo to
Muslim and northern traders and their slaves, who
were skilled in the management of head-load transport. This generated demand in Krachi for housing
and feeding strangers, though in the early decades
of the nineteenth century when salt trade through
Krachi was restricted by Asante, even a few canoes
a month could not have precipitated much activity.
However, because the labor and ownership exchange
occurred at Krachikrom, the approval or permission
of the Dente Bosomfo and Krachiwura had to be
secured, and this usually resulted in an ongoing
arrangement whereby a certain proportion of salt
was paid as a toll or tax to the Krachi authorities. This toll is said to have been one bag of
salt per canoe and this probably amounted to three
to five per cent of the salt which changed hands at
Krachi (although the Germans and British later
charged as much as ten per cent and the market was
able to endure it).[2] Being far more than the Krachi
authorities could use themselves, this salt was
then traded by them for profit. The fact that
Krachi was a pivotal point on the salt trade route
had great significance for Krachi's potential
development, and an examination of the methods and
growth of the salt trade is necessary to place
Krachi's position into some perspective.[3]

                              I

        The salt to which Bowdich and Bonnat referred
originated in Ada and neighboring towns around the
mouth of the Volta River where it was periodically
collected from salt-yielding lagoons, loaded into
baskets or barrels and shipped north on the Volta
by canoe to satisfy the demand of the interior
markets. It is difficult to determine precisely
when this salt trade became a profitable under-
taking. Sea salt was probably extracted along the
coast from the time that people were there to
extract it. However, extensive trade grew with the
increased communications and population that
developed after the sixteenth century. Dapper, in
his book based on many different sources and
published in 1668, described some early salt

industries and trade which were not necessarily
part of the Volta River trade but which illustrate
a salt supply/demand network established by the
mid-seventeenth century: "The best fired pans [of
salt] are found at Anten and Sinko [near Accra];
from there the salt is taken throughout the entire
country to be bought."[4] Villault was able to give
an eye-witness account of the industry in 1670 near
Cape Coast and also confirm that salt was traded
"higher into the country" where the merchants "make
good advantage by it."   Bosman noted as he travelled along the coast in 1705 that the salt boilers
could amass "vast riches" and "unwieldy sums"
because "all the Inland Negroes are obliged to
fetch their salt from the shore."[5]

The eighteenth century accounts maintain not
only that salt production and trade were thriving
and lucrative, but that Accra and places east to
the Volta were sites of the most productive salt
industries and were displacing less efficient
producers. Thus, by the 1730s Accra salt was being
sold even at Cape Coast.[6] In the western coastal
locations salt was secured by boiling or evaporat-
ing brine in copper pans or earthen pots' but in
Accra and points east where the coast was not so
hilly, huge artificial salt pits and natural salt
lagoons could be used far more efficiently.[7] These
pits and lagoons produced large quantities of salt
which could satisfy an ever-increasing demand in
the interior for the product -- a demand which
derived from the fact that throughout the seventeenth and eighteenth centuries the people of the
forest and Asante were increasingly trading their
gold, ivory and slaves for European goods and salt
on the coast, rather than for salt from the Sahara
as was probably the case earlier. The Asante in
fact explained to Bowdich that they used their sea
salt "which is easily procured, and affords an
extravagant profit," to purchase silks and cotton
cloths brought to their northern markets from
Hausaland.[8] This was quite a reversal of the
sixteenth century pattern of Hausaland's dependence
on the northern Sahara for salt.

The demand must indeed have been growing for by
the later eighteenth century the production of salt
near the mouth of the Volta was quite highly
developed. Isert, a Danish medical officer in the
area in 1784, observed that the people near Keta
lived "principally by salt-making," and that they

stored the cleaned salt "which can compare with our best Spanish salt" in huts containing fifty barrels or more. He counted one or two of these huts for every house.[9]

It is difficult to ascertain just when this salt began to be traded up the Volta River in the organized manner that was to be described in the nineteenth century. Seventeenth century references to river trade are scant, the chief one being by Barbot, who was on the coast in roughly 1680 and who observed some trade on the Volta, though not specifically salt trade. The Dutch Governor informed Barbot that,

> the natives buy of the Abyssinians and Nubians, with whom they have a free commerce, by means of this river running up, always very wide and large, a vast way inland, towards the north north-east: but it is choaked in some of the upper part of its channel, by galls and clifts, as the Blacks report . . . but I suppose the trade of this river is of no great advantage, since the Hollanders, who are well acquainted with the country, have no settlements there; or it may proceed from the dangers of navigating that river.[10]

Yet in 1734 the Danes did establish trading factories at the mouth of the Volta. References become more detailed and the central role of salt is underscored. The Danes for example were soon drawn into a trade dispute between the Ada to the west of the mouth and the Anlo to the east. Isert claimed this was "because of their [the Ada's] flourishing salt-works which brings them most of their wealth for they can sell the salt so profitably to the mountain-Negroes and to the Asantes."[11] In 1784 a military expedition of Danes and Adas subdued the Anlo, thus securing the Ada monopoly of salt production. The enmity and wars between the two peoples continued throughout the nineteenth century, however, being in no way minimized by Ada's pro-Asante leanings, and the Ada fairly well dominated the salt trade well into the twentieth century.

The Ada's success was partly because of their salt-bearing lagoon which was restricted, taxed, and protected by religious sanction -- all three

characteristics being common to such lagoons
throughout the pre-industrial world.[12]   A British
District Commissioner in Ada in 1922 described the
management of the Ada lagoon:

> When the lagoon is observed to be showing
> signs that salt will be available in the
> coming season (it is very far from being
> available every year) the fact is reported
> to the Fetish Priest . . . At the Priest's
> orders sticks are then placed in a semi-
> circle across all the paths that lead to
> the lagoon and it then becomes a serious
> offense to go to the lagoon at all. At
> this as well as at the later stages watch-
> men are stationed at various points to see
> that the Fetish regulations are not broken.

Salt formed by evaporation throughout the dry
season. Then a signal was given, religious ceremo-
nies were performed, and then the people collected
as much salt as they wished, piling it in a heap at
the edge of the lagoon to be taxed by the representatives of the priest before taking it away. The
salt formation does not occur in large amounts
annually. For example when the above description
was recorded the main portion of the lagoon had not
yielded since 1914; despite this there seems never
to have been an insufficient supply of salt for
trade because the salt "when collected is stored,
often years before being exported up the river."[13]
     Perhaps causing, perhaps resulting from the Ada
monopoly was the definite consumer preference that
developed in the interior for Ada salt as opposed
to other salts. The Tarikh Gonja, an Arabic
manuscript dating from 1894, makes reference to
this:

> All the people bought this [northern] salt
> except the people of Asante who did not
> like it, and prefer the salt of Idasadabude
> [Ada and Labade] which is expensive. The
> people of Asante charged taxes whenever
> they found Daboya [northern] salt with
> anybody.[14]

Paul Hutter, a Swiss trader involved in the Ada
salt trade in the early 1900s and later retiring to
Kete-Krachi, observed:

> The salt the French sell is very clean and
> the Addah salt rather dirty but funny to
> say the natives in the Hinterland prefer
> Addah salt to all other kinds, saying it is
> the sweetest . . .[15]

And the District Commissioner at Ada was in accord
noting that in the interior there was such a
decided preference for Ada salt that people bought
it whenever it was "at anything like a competitive
price with the imported article."[16]

The Asante were dependent on sea salt because
there were no natural salt deposits in the interior
south of Daboya, and their cultivation of Ada
friendship and control of the Volta trade must be
seen partly in this light. It was believed on the
coast by Fantes and Europeans in the nineteenth
century that the Asante were preparing for war when
they bought up large quantities of salt for stock-
piling and for provisioning the army, and that
Asante would not go to war until it had a sufficient supply of it.[17] The missionaries Ramseyer
and Kuhne, prisoners in Kumase from 1869 to 1873
during the Asante war with Fante, Krepe, and
(later) the British, attested to the great shortage
of salt that developed during the prolonged war-
fare. The record of their experience also demonstrates the craving that develops when one is
deprived of salt. Ramseyer and Kuhne wrote to
missionaries on the coast requesting that salt be
sent to them and continually begged the Asantehene
for salt. The latter was himself aware of the
shortage in Kumase and upon giving the missionaries
a ration of the precious item, admonished them to
use it carefully. Ramseyer wrote, "salt is rare
and expensive in Ashanti, a handful costing 4d.
and it is not generally supplied to slaves."[18]

Although the salt trade could be interrupted by
war, it usually operated in a planned and predictable fashion. River trade in Ada salt became quite
organized by the early nineteenth century, probably
in response to the increasing demand of Asante with
its developing urban areas, swelling population,
and increasingly controlled trade methods. Major
markets were to be found in some of the river towns
such as Dodi, customs collection on river transport
was efficient, and in the 1820s it was reported
that "the profit from one market to another [on
salt] was not quite 100%.[19] Bowdich's information

in 1817 indicates that the river journey was well
worked out: eleven days to Krachikrom by river,
four days more to Salaga by land.   More than 100
years after Bowdich's report, the Krachi District
Commissioner noted anew that by river to Krachikrom
averaged 11½ days, varying with the season.[20]

In 1875 when Bonnat travelled up the Volta
River to Salaga, he carried primarily salt for
trade, and the diary which he kept provides a very
useful first-hand account of some aspects of the
salt trade.   He began his expedition with five
canoes and twenty-seven hired men (later trade
accounts would indicate that even though he was
travelling at the end of the rainy season, this was
more labor than he needed, for in the dry season
there were generally three men to each canoe and in
the wet season four [21]).   Bonnat's partner, Mr.
Bannerman, was half-Asante and had apparently
transported salt on the river before, though it is
not clear how many canoes he had.   Another partner
named Mr. Sprackett (using the name Dobson sometimes) followed Bonnat a month later with thirty
canoes and sixty men.   Profit from the sale of salt
in Salaga was their goal.

Bonnat described the numerous rapids between
Ada and Krachi which in periods of high water could
mostly be traversed with loaded canoes by poling.
At more severe rapids the salt was unloaded and,
being packed in barrels, was rolled around the
rapids.   Usually the canoes were then taken through
the currents empty rather than being portaged
around which would have required additional time
and labor.   In some cases it took up to two hours
and "savage cries" to manage just one series of
rapids.   If the water was too deep for the poles,
ropes were employed to pull the canoes through.
The rapids in general became progressively more
difficult as one proceeded upriver.   Bonnat recorded a description of the most imposing yet passable
cataracts, the last two prior to those at Krachi:

> Soon we saw in front of us a line of rocks
> formed of small round stones united by a
> cement the color of iron . . . But turning
> to the right we found a very narrow passage
> where the water fell with violence.   The
> depth was so great that our poles were of
> no use . . . Higher up we met the Bee, the
> most dangerous rapid of the river and the

last before the arrival at Krakey. It is a
fall of 15-18 feet on a width of 500 meters
where the water flows past thousands of
rocks.[22]

Despite the severity of these rapids, the canoes
could still be managed through them. However, at
Krachikrom the rapids were the most imposing,
dropping fifteen meters in a quarter mile within a
channel only eight meters wide in places. The main
waterfall was four meters high.[23] Clearly a canoe
could not be pulled through them. Ramseyer,
travelling from the west and crossing the Volta on
the Krachi ferry in 1884, recorded a description of
these rapids at low water:

> . . . we arrived at the Volta which was
> very low, so that the rocks, which are
> usually hidden in September, rose above the
> water and our ferrymen were obliged to use
> great caution in crossing . . . although
> the town stands 60 feet above the river,
> the flood sometimes rises to within a short
> distance from it. [24]

As one German observer commented, "whoever, driven
by thirst for knowledge, once climbs down and up
the rocky bank, thinks quickly not to repeat this
excursion again."[25] The river north of Krachi to
Yeji (the nearest point on the river to Salaga) was
quite interrupted with rapids and veered sharply to
the northwest, away from Salaga. Hence in Bonnat's
time it was not used for commerce at all, though it
would be developed by the British in the early
twentieth century.

The salt was thus unloaded at Krachi and
reapportioned for headloading to Salaga. This
required considerable labor and, according to
Bonnat, cost not less than twenty-five dollars per
ton.[26] Nevertheless it is indisputable that labor
was saved by moving the salt via canoes as far as
Krachi rather than head-loading it all the way from
Ada to Salaga for canoes could carry anywhere from
1500 to 6000 pounds of salt which would require
fifteen to sixty carriers, while four men at most
were needed to transport each canoe.[27] Time was
also saved by utilizing the river route -- eleven
days on the average by canoe while walking from Ada
to Krachi involved about sixteen days, and the

return trip down river by canoe could take as
little as four days.[28]
    Slaves were an integral part of the salt trade.
Bosman in 1705 noted that slaves were most likely
to be bought where the salt was sold.[29] Slave
labor was necessary for paddling the canoes and
carrying the salt, and late nineteenth century
observers reported that the salt trade did not
flourish when the slave trade was not active.[30] A
participant in the salt trade of the past remembered the salt and slave market that developed at
Krachi:

> Adas, Anlos, Ga, Ewes -- when they bring
> the salt in return they buy slaves. Barter
> trade, salt and slaves. If they need salt
> they come here [to Krachi] for Ewes sell to
> Krachis and they [in turn] sell to Asantes.
> Dagombas, Gonjas came too to buy salt. The
> Mamprussis and Dagombas fought and came and
> sold their slaves to Krachis . . . If you
> need slave or salt, come here.[31]

Krachi's position on the important north-south
route to the coast acquired even greater significance when, in the later nineteenth century, the
British encouraged the development of the entire
Salaga-Accra communication complex, by land and
river, in order to circumvent the Asante controlled
Salaga-Kumase-Cape Coast route. This policy was
first recommended by Bowdich:

> . . . it would be desirable gradually to
> approach Inta [Gonja] and Dagwumba, by
> establishing a settlement up the Volta,
> which has been shown to run close to
> Sallagha, the grand emporium of Inta, and
> is navigable within four days of it [i.e.
> to Krachi]; . . . The King of Ashantee
> viewing our settlements on the Volta,
> would, I have no doubt, be reconciled by
> our undertaking to sell neither guns or
> powder to any but his own people . . . If
> the King of Ashantee were not satisfied
> with our new settlement confining the trade
> of guns and powder to himself, he would
> certainly be repressed by the alarming
> reflection, that it was at our discretion
> (depending on his behaviour) to supply Inta

and Dagwumba with both, thus to undermine
his empire;[32]

Unfortunately for Asante, it was the latter element
of Bowdich's proposal that the British would
ultimately adopt.

In the early nineteenth century the Volta river
trade was regulated by Asante. Its allies and
tributaries, the Akwamu, managed the southern
section of the river with customs officials and
tolls. Further north Asante established the town
of Ahinkro (Kingstown) close to the junction of the
Oti and Volta Rivers and less than a day's land
journey from Krachikrom, probably to monitor both
land and river routes. Officials of the Asantehene
were stationed there and in Akwamu to prevent the
passage of arms and ammunition from the coast to
the north (see Figure 5).[33] Sometimes governance
of the river necessitated a sterner Asante presence: In 1870, when the British were actively
beginning to break the Asante barriers in the
south, a British gunboat brought up the Volta
encountered (and bombarded) a garrison of thirty
men commanded by an Asante captain on the island of
Duffo (fifty miles from the mouth of the Volta).
By 1871 the British were noting a weakening of
Asante control:

> The opening of the River Volta by steamers
> has had a great moral effect. Affiliah the
> [Asante] Ambassador [to Cape Coast] has
> more than once unconsciously demonstrated
> his concern about it, the reason being
> obvious: first the Aquamoos, who have been
> for a long period tributaries of Ashantee,
> are clearly at our mercy; and again other
> tributaries of Ashantee, often glad to
> revolt, can be reached by river and can
> provide themselves with the arms and
> ammunition the Ashantees have jealously
> prohibited from reaching them up to the
> present time. [34]

Finally, following the temporary occupation of
Kumase by the British in 1874, Asante management of
the Volta route lapsed even further. The British
seized their opportunity and in 1876 sent Skipton
Gouldsbury to Krepe, Akwamu, Krachi and Salaga to
sign trade treaties and to secure promises that the

route would be kept open, and that traders would
use it rather than passing through Kumase (see
Chapter 5). From this time on, the Volta and the
paths which paralleled it were increasingly used
for trade to the interior; but the British were
successful at "opening" this route only because the
paths and river ports were already in service to
some extent, and Krachi grew in importance only
because it already possessed some reputation as a
major halting point along the route.

                              II

    Another ecological factor contributing to
Krachi's importance was the agricultural potential
of the wooded-savanna surrounding it. Krachi
headed a vast though sparsely populated area of
yam-farming land capable of producing excess food
for export to other areas or for the support of a
large indigenous non-farming population. Today
Krachi is considered one of the major yam-producing
areas of Ghana, along with Brong and Dagomba-
Nanumba, both of which border Krachi. [35]
    Relative to other African crops, yams require a
fairly large amount of labor for proper cultivation, and they must be grown in mounds on land that
is newly cleared or has lain fallow for at least
six to ten years. Normally 1700 to 2000 mounds are
cultivated per acre, and a good farmer will make
about 100 mounds per day.[36] The plants must be
staked and weeded, the latter done at least twice
during the growing season, all of which increases
the amount of labor investment. An average peasant
farmer produces two to five tons per acre,[37] and
the land is often inter-cropped with millet or
guinea corn, ground-nuts or beans.
    The yield of yams per acre in the Krachi
district is in fact quite high and it is estimated
that only 0.6 or 0.7 cultivated acres per person
are necessary for satisfactory subsistence -- a
comparatively low ratio for Ghana and is "probably
because of the high yield of yams." Krachi can
easily support a critical population density of
sixty per square mile (population density in 1970
was only thirty per square mile.)[38] The surplus
productivity of the land is used for foodstuffs to
be sold.

Quantitative records of yam exports from
Kete-Krachi date from as early as 1903. Export
figures increase consistently whenever recorded,
and in the year 1937-1938, when roads in the area
were improved, the export of yams, groundnuts, and
millet was estimated at ten times the previous
year. Krachi chiefs complained frequently in the
1930s when there were insufficient buyers for their
surplus and officials estimated the Krachi district
to be capable of producing an annual surplus of one
million yams for export to Accra in 1949. Krachi
farmers took the lead in expanding cultivation in
the 1950s wherever feeder roads were made.[39]
Today, with the facility of the Volta Lake freight
ferries, Krachi is more than ever an essential
exporter of yams to the Kumase and Accra regions.

The evidence indicates additionally that
twentieth century conditions are merely a continua-
tion of a production pattern begun in the 1870s.
The agricultural economic base and techniques of
production in Krachi have hardly altered to this
day. The farming there is rarely little more than
an extension of subsistence hoe cultivation and
bush fallow; but the area under cultivation might
be three times that of subsistence. Today, when
the labor requirements for growing sufficient yams
for sale to the south exceed the capacity of the
family, poorly paid wage labor from the north is
employed.[40] Thus the realization of Krachi's
potential for excess yam production is contingent
upon the availability of a supplementary labor
force.

In the late nineteenth century when an expanding commercial population created demands for
food-stuffs in excess of subsistence, the equivalent of poorly paid wage labor, slaves, were used.
Rather than exporting yams to other urban areas,
Krachi at that time utilized its productive capabi-
lity to supply the urban population of the growing
market at Kete -- a non-farming population that
settled near Krachikrom as a result of increased
trade opportunities there from 1874 on. Numerous
travellers observed the extensive farming developing in the Krachi district in the late nineteenth
century. In 1888 the German explorer von Francois
recorded walking for hours north of Krachikrom
towards Salaga "through almost un-broken corn and
yam plantations."[41] Another German visitor in 1894
noted:

. . . the main occupation in Krachi is
farming. It is [the Krachi's] job to feed
all the travellers and traders of Kete and
to supply the big Kete market with live-
stock and foodstuffs. The beautiful big
farms through which one walks to the south
of Krachi give evidence of the industrious-
ness of the Krachi people . . . the farms
have huge well-tended yam fields where the
yam grows either on the ground or on
sticks. Everywhere one sees people working
in the fields.[42]

It is not merely coincidence that such observations were made when Krach's population, both urban
and rural, was under-going rapid expansion. The
origin and growth of the trading town of Kete will
be discussed in Chapter 7, but it should be noted
here that whereas in 1876 Kete had probably not
come into existence, in 1877 it was a conspicuous
market place and by the 1880s had mushroomed
adjacent to the traditional town and capital of
Krachi, Krachikrom. The latter's population quite
likely never exceeded 2,000[43] but Kete grew from a
place of "zana mat huts"[44] to a stranger's town of
approximately 6000 in 1884,[45] to a booming market
of 10,000 in 1895.[46]
The rural population of Krachi was increasing
at the same time that the urban population of Kete
grew so impressively. Commerce expanded in Kete
because of the deliberate encouragement of the
British and the crumbling of Asante authority
(which previously had prevented much trade in
Krachi and drew all trade routes to Kumase). The
same factors contributed to a growth of rural
population. The collapse of Asante control in 1875
was followed by civil war and insecurity in central
Asante, which sent many refugees from north and
east of Kumase migrating into Krachi. Ramseyer and
Bonnat both noticed, for example, that the area
between Atebubu and Krachi was fairly deserted
because the chiefs and villagers had gone to live
at Krachi "and whom fear of Asante still kept
away."[47] A large number of refugees from the
Asante town of Nsuta, including the Queen Mother,
moved to Krachi for safety following the destoolment of Asantehene Mensa Bonsu in 1884. They
presumably took up residence in the quarter of Kete
already occupied by Nsutas who had fled to Krachi

even earlier, probably in 1875, after they and
Dwaben failed in a rebellion against Asante. (The
Dwabens fled into the British Gold Coast Colony.)
Many of the Nsuta refugees were settled on farms
outside Kete-Krachi by the Dente Bosomfo and
Krachiwura.[48] There is evidence that refuge or
protection was sought and found in Krachi prior to
1875 as well. Traditions of the different peoples
in that part of Ghana often make statements of
which the following Basa declaration referring to
events of the 1830s is typical:

> Truly speaking, Dente indeed proved to be a
> powerful god which caused us to seek for
> the protection of Dente and so, eventually,
> we became subject allies to the Krachis.[49]

However, it is probable that cases such as these
were more rare and less well-defined than those
recorded subsequent to 1875.

The influx of slaves was also increasing after
1875 and it is quite clear that slave labor was
used extensively for farming on the lands surrounding Krachi, specifically in a share-cropping system
whereby the slaves surrendered the bulk of their
harvest to their masters. Inspector Firminger,
sent to Krachi and Salaga in 1887 to recruit for
the Gold Coast Constabulary, observed that the
region was the "highest cultivated part of West
Africa and this cultivation is entirely the result
of slave labor. For miles beyond miles nothing is
seen but farms . . . The slaves are nearly all
Grushis who are first-rate farm hands and very
tractable."[50] Grussis and Mossis were the most
common ethnic groups to be sold in the West African
slave markets, and there was probably a market for
these slaves at Krachi in one form or another
dating from the beginning of the nineteenth century, for as mentioned earlier, salt and slave
trade went hand in hand; but of course this particular market at Krachikrom and then at Kete
expanded with the rapid increase in trade and
population described here.

Many of the slave farms and slaves were owned
by the Dente Bosomfo himself, and one must therefore assume that they were either bought by him or
given to him as gifts, tribute, or taxes. Slaves
might even be sent to the Dente Bosomfo as security
for defensive alliances, as occurred in 1892 when

Nkoransa sought military support from the Dente
Bosomfo.[51] There must also have been a certain
amount of calculated expropriation of slaves by the
Dente Bosomfo through the taxing of the trade, if
one is to account for observations such as Klose's
references to "many fetish villages which were all
populated by slaves of the priest" and to the
frequent raiding (or taxing) of caravans for goods
and slaves which were taken to the Bosomfo's
villages.[52]

In addition to being bought, sold, and seques-
tered from the Kete-Krachi market, some slaves fled
to Krachi voluntarily seeking the sanctuary of the
Dente shrine in exchange for being slave farmers
for the Dente Bosomfo and surrendering the bulk of
their harvest to him. Dickson (1969) asserts that
this was a privilege afforded by all shrines.[53]
Probably the earliest recorded case of this type in
West Africa is provided by Isert who travelled on
the coast in 1783-84, and observed at the town of
Malfi the following:

> It [the town] is also very famous because
> of the Fetish Temple there, wherein any
> slave, who can reach there, wins his
> freedom. This indeed happened to me, to my
> great sorrow. [54]

Although one of Isert's own slaves did reach the
"temple," his liberty was apparently short-lived
for Isert persuaded a baptized mulatto to enter the
shrine and retrieve the slave.

In Krachi, references to this type of sanctuary
are common in the sources after 1875. Klose
reported that in the Dente Bosomfo's farming
village of Bompata "the inhabitants are almost all
slaves who have fled from the terrible rule of the
Ashantis to this side of the river;"[55] and missionary Clerk noted on one of his visits to Krachi
that the Dente Bosomfo's village Tariaso had "just
received an increase of some 40 slaves who had fled
from their master Kwabena Panyin in Ateobu and
sought sanctuary with the Fetish Odente."[56]

The most specific case in the records regarding
slave-refugees is of a man called Kalla Grushie.
In 1888 new recruits were being sought for the Gold
Coast Constabulary by the British, and several
recruiting expeditions were dispatched to Salaga
via Kpandu and Kete-Krachi to enlist "Hausas,"

though in fact they sought to make contact with the
slave caravans coming into Salaga. At Krachi,
Inspector Williams demanded that the Dente Bosomfo
turn over a group of "refugees" known to have come
there recently. After some palaver, the Dente
Bosomfo promised to relinquish them and they were
taken off to Accra. The "recruits" themselves
however were most reluctant to leave Krachi, they
resisted, and some violence resulted.

In the subsequent investigation by the British,
statements were taken from Kalla Grushie and his
fellow recruits. Kalla Grushie testified that he,
his wife and children, and some 100 other slaves
had fled for protection to the Dente Bosomfo, who
settled them on land to continue their occupation
of farming. He stated: "We ran to Bosomfo because
we were about to be killed [at the funeral of the
Atebubuhene] . . . We Grushie people are only
farmers . . . I want to go back to Krachie." The
majority of the other recruits testified that they,
too, had been slaves at Atebubu and had fled from
there to the Dente Bosomfo when their lives were
imperiled upon the death of the Atebubuhene Gyan
Kwaku. They desired to return to Krachi, to their
farms and families, to be slaves of the Dente
Bosomfo rather than soldiers of the Queen. (Unfortunately the Governor's solution was to dispatch
two of them to Krachi to escort the wives of all
the recruits back to the coast. The two men were
not to be seen again, of course.)[57]

The slaves involved in this case apparently
genuinely believed that by coming to the Dente
shrine they would find protection. They did not
anticipate gaining "freedom" in Krachi, however,
knowing that they would simply farm under a new
master, the Dente Bosomfo. They were confident,
however, that their lives would not be as endan-
gered as whence they had fled.

The Dente Bosomfo and his elders clearly made
good use of slaves, whether they were gifts, taxes,
purchases, or voluntary arrivals. They settled the
slaves as farmers and profited from their production, just as the former masters had done. The
fact that the slaves were required to yield up most
of their harvest to their masters, and hence to the
urban population, caused them to remain at a lower
standard of living than the commercial and political ruling classes. Indeed they can be said to
have fulfilled precisely the same role as the

present-day poorly paid wage labor from the north.
Hence it will be important to remember in future
chapters that the slaves who provided the labor for
the large areas of farm land in the Krachi region
in the late nineteenth century represented a
considerable and calculated investment for the
Krachi elite and particularly the Dente Bosomfo.

In summary, Krachi possessed certain fundamental ecological elements with potential for development. They were its location on a river route with
direct access to a basic natural resource, salt,
and control of an expanse of land extremely suited
for high-yielding food-crop farming. These factors
could be manipulated and exploited by people,
enhanced or attenuated by political currents,
improved or thwarted by technological developments
(such as lorry transport or cheap English salt);
but in the late nineteenth century these were the
fundamentals on which the Krachi state had to
build, and as such they reappear often in any
analysis of political changes in the Volta basin.

3

The Dente Shrine
Of Oracles and Obedience

The geographical orientation and agricultural potential of Krachi were basic to its survival and growth. Among the surrounding people, however, including the Akan, Ewe, and Gonja, the region was best known for the shrine and oracle of the god Dente, located at Krachikrom.

I

There is no doubt that the oracle of Dente was considered powerful and accurate and that it was famous and awesome to the peoples who came into contact with it. Most striking about Dente's reputation is that it extended well beyond recognition from the Krachi people. Dente was not just a tribal god or fetish. The earliest documentary evidence available to this effect is from one of Bonnat's business companions trading to Krachi in February 1876 who commented that "the whole of the surrounding tribes" consulted the Dente oracle.[1] Considerable oral evidence also exists for the inter-tribal appeal of Dente. For example, the Ewe peoples to the south of Krachi, although never in any political alliance with the Krachis, expressed great respect for Dente:

No god is as famous as Dente of Krachi on the whole of the Gold Coast. It is known in all our local places that he is a god to

be feared . . . All places which know him
believe that he knows the affairs of every
town and for this reason they come from
distant places and ask him to advise them
concerning their sicknesses and other
troubles.[2]

Bonnat, Gouldsbury, and Lonsdale, each of whom
travelled between Krachi and Salaga in days preceding the latter's collapse as a trading center,
presumed Dente to be the god of Salaga, a Gonja
town. Gouldsbury especially emphasized that the
people of Salaga "were under the fetish of Crackey,
and that they were completely subject and obedient
to the mandates of that oracle."[3] To the north
and east of Krachi (see Figure 5) many Dagombas,
Nawuris, and Adeles recognized the potency of the
shrine. Lonsdale noted that Dente's fame to the
south and west "extended throughout Ashanti, the
Buems and Inkonyas, also the Kwahus all acknowledge
this fetish as supreme."[4]

In view of the fact that Asante was Krachi's
suzerain for some 150 years, it is interesting to
read from several sources that the Asante consulted
Dente regularly, "in sickness or family matters or
in quarrels or matters of law,"[5] for "fetish and
religions . . . divination and charms, teleology,
as well as health, wealth and disease."[6] More
significant however was the Asante government's
consultation of Dente regarding war policy.
Although advice from other shrines was also sought
by Asante prior to campaigns, Dente acquired a
reputation as a war oracle. The shrine was said to
have been beseeched for the safe return of Asantehene Osei Bonsu from the Gyaman war in 1819,[7] and
British informants prior to Sir Garnet Wolseley's
1873-74 Gold Coast campaign stated that "Carachee
is under Ashantee. . . . Here there is a grand
fetish which the Ashantees always consult before
going to war." The informants even recommended to
the British that they make use of Dente themselves:
"At Carachee you must consult the fetish, which is
powerful, otherwise it will stop your progress.
This fetish is always consulted by the Ashantees,
and if it is gained over then the Ashantees must be
destroyed."[8]

Although it is unlikely that the British
followed this advice, Asante definitely consulted
Dente prior to Wolseley's invasion. The British

agent Lonsdale and his interpreter talked to the
Dente Bosomfo themselves in 1881 about this event
and the priest told them of his reply to the Asante
messengers:

> Then Denty charged the Ashanti messengers
> to return back and to say to their King
> that it was much to his regret that from
> what he had foreseen he had to let the King
> understand that there were visible omens of
> evil and want of success on his part, and
> that the fact was so obvious that if the
> King had given it his careful consideration
> he would have saved himself the trouble of
> sending any messenger to him.[9]

Instead, the Dente Bosomfo advised the Asantehene
to "make arrangements for peace" or else purchase
"stout sandals" for himself and his army so that
they could escape "with facility and not have their
toes sprained or their feet bruised when routed and
pursued by the English."
   A corollary of the generally accepted belief in
Dente as an accurate war oracle was that it could
also prevent war. Smaller groups in the vicinity
of Krachi sought its "protection" much as the
slaves and refugees mentioned in Chapter 2 sought
sanctuary at it. Basa traditions referring probably to eighteenth century events maintain that "the
Krachi Lartes had a powerful god that could protect
us against the constant tribal warfares and any
kind of misfortune."[10] Another example is that of
the Praman peoples:

> . . . as a matter of fact [the Pramans] saw
> for themselves the wonders and miracles
> displayed [by Dente] and how it could help
> in time of war. Being convinced, the
> Pramanhene promised to the Fetish that if
> it could help him so that there might be no
> other war within two years or any other
> troubles in the area, he would thank the
> Fetish with one live sheep.[11]

The sheep was duly delivered.
   Following the Volta region's break with Asante
in 1875, the Dente shrine undertook a role of
leadership in organizing a defensive alliance to
which many small groups subscribed in the belief

that Dente could protect them somehow from a
punitive Asante attack (see Chapter 6). Despite
this political separation however, Asante itself
never rejected its confidence in the accuracy of
Dente's counsel. In the 1880s Lonsdale observed
that "to regain possession of the shrine the
Ashantis would risk a great deal." In the middle
of the Nkoransa War of 1892, when Asante was
preparing to fight Nkoransa's ally Krachi as well,
the Asantehene still consulted the Dente branch
shrine in Kumase, sacrificed a fat sheep and said
he was "a firm believer in the cult of Dente," that
he knew he was attacking the shrine's custodians,
but that their allies (the Nkoransas) were his
subjects, they had offended him, and he hoped Dente
would be willing to see justice done.[12]   In 1921
the Omanhene of Old Dwaben was consulting Dente
once again, and in 1925, upon the Asantehene's
return from exile in the Seychelles, Asantehene
Prempe I sent messengers to salute Dente and thank
the shrine for helping to keep him safely.[13]

                               II

    The Dente shrine's time and place of origin is
obscure. The British colonial officer Cardinall,
who collected folklore in all the Gold Coast
districts to which he was posted, recorded several
non-Krachi traditions of the origin of Dente, one
being that Dente was established in a cavern on the
Volta by the Asante, and another that Dente came
from the Bruku shrine at Siare (in Atwode).[14]   A
fairly standard Krachi version of Dente's first
arrival at Krachi was recorded by the District
Commissioner Cooper in 1930:

    It first appeared in the guise of a small
    boy suffering from yaws. He asked one
    woman for some water, and she . . . brought
    the boy water mixed with ground corn in a
    good calabash. The boy took the calabash
    and said "I hold, I sit down." --
    "N'de-n'te" -- from which the name Dente is
    derived.

When the boy finished drinking he led the woman,
named Mayensa, to an area of rocks, presumably the
site of the Dente shrine, where a voice was heard

speaking a strange language. The boy "stuffed her ears with some medicine" and she was able to understand the voice. However, as Mayensa could not serve Dente during her menstrual periods, the custody of Dente was given to her brothers at the time of her death, and it has been under male control ever since.[15]

The general theme of this tradition, that the god appeared at Krachi and spoke a strange language which the custodians of the shrine were blessed to be able to understand, is often repeated in different forms. A very simplified version told to the British officer Furley in 1915 (immediately after Krachi was liberated from the Germans) was that Dente originated with "a man called Dente who found medicine and cured himself" at the site of the grove and cave of the oracle.[16]

In contrast, another whole body of traditions claim that the name Dente is a mispronunciation of "Lente," which in turn is a perversion of "Late," the name of a town in Akuapem whence many Krachis claim to have migrated. The transferral of the god from Late to Krachi is in these accounts hopelessly confused -- some maintaining that Dente was left at Late, others that it travelled with the migrants, settling at various halting places such as Agogo, Dwan, and/or Ketakpande, and others that the god reappeared later at Dwan or Siare and finally arrived at Krachi (see Figure 5).[17]

Many Krachi traditions agree on the point that the Krachiwura and Dente Bosomfo divisions of the Krachi people migrated from Late in the Akuapem Hills (a part of the Akwamu Empire, 1650-1731) at about the time of an Akyem Abuakwa Queen Mother named Dokuwa, who harassed the Lates with excessive taxes. The date of this migration is often stated to be 1733, the supposed year of the Akyem conquest of Akwamu.[18] However, Akuapem traditions mention a destruction of the thirty towns of Late at the beginning of the second half of the seventeenth century, and it appears that the Akwamus and Akyems invaded the Akuapem Hills about 1660.[19] This latter date seems to be much more reasonable than the oft-mentioned 1733 for the beginnings of the migration of that segment of Krachi who claim Late origins. These Krachis relate that they stopped in many places (a journey of more than seven years surely) before arriving at Krachi where, judging from other sources, they were well-settled by 1740 (see Chapter 5).

The central question of interest here, however, is whether the Dente shrine originated at Late, being brought on the migration, or whether, as other traditions assert, the god appeared for the first time at Krachi on the Volta. Biases in oral data and feedback from written sources cloud this issue. In 1895 C.C. Reindorf, a Ga Basel Minister, published his History of the Gold Coast and Asante based largely on Ga and Akuapem traditions which he recorded in the 1860s. In this history he related the story of the god Konkom who lived in a cave at Late: Some "naughty fellows" resolved one day to see what was in the cave and discovered a one-eyed, one-armed, one-legged figure which they dragged from the cave. "This [so] offended Konkom that he entirely left the Lates for Karakye" where he was given the name Lente or Odente, having come from Late. Unfortunately, Reindorf's tradition is somewhat confused for he implies in an addendum to this story that Konkom also accompanied, on a journey to Krachi, Lates who were escaping from famine.[20] However the tradition was accepted by other Basel missionaries who must have been familiar with Reindorf's unpublished work, completed probaby by 1870. The Rev. David Asante repeated the part about Krachis coming from Late in a travel report of 1877, and a version of the Konkom story was published by the missionary Rottman in 1895.[21]

In addition to relating the Konkom story, Rottman asserted that the Late people attempted in c. 1885 to call Dente back from Krachi: "The [Lates] more than anyone else wanted Dente to return again, and they did not care what it cost." In this case, according to Rottman, a human sacrifice was required and duly carried out. Rottman in all likelihood misinterpreted this event. Dente was a deity to whom small "branch" shrines were erected throughout Greater Asante in towns that so wished it. The symbol or marker of such shrines was (and is) a clay, conical mound approximately 1½ meters high (see Figure 11):

> On top of the mound is placed a clay dish or bowl with lid to contain gifts such as cowrie shells, eggs, money (silver and copper coins) offered by individuals, and

Figure 11: A Dente Branch Shrine at the Entrance to Abetifi, 1899

the blood of the animals sacrificed to
Krachi Lente.[22]

The German administrator Klose recorded in the
1890s that it was necessary for any town desiring a
branch shrine to go to Dente in Krachi to receive
permission from the oracle there and to obtain "for
a high price" a piece of consecrated earth from the
priest.[23] Klose claimed further that human sacrifice was required, the remains being mixed with the
clay prior to erecting the mound at the chosen
site. He added that "in want of a person, however,
as I had explained to me in Kratyi upon my first
journey of 1894 the priest should be satisfied with
an ox or a sheep for sacrifice."[24]
    The Late people were probably only establishing
one of these branch shrines when the above incident
cited by Rottman occurred. An Akuapem missionary,
Peter Hall, gave an account of the same incident
which would support this latter interpretation, and
Hall further stated that Dente was only first
established in Akuapem around 1880 when the road to
Salaga and down to Accra was opened to trade:

> Some natives of Akropong travelled as far
> as to Krakye and there they were introduced
> to the famous fetish, Odente, which was
> supposed to know all secrets. On their
> return home they spoke highly about this
> fetish to the Omanhene [Kwame Fori]. The
> Omanhene was impressed. He made it plain
> to his subjects that any of them who would
> like to go to Krakye to be apprenticed to
> Odente would be allowed to do so. They
> were free to participate in the worship and
> to introduce it in Akwapim if they wanted.
> And so several people from Akropong went
> and apprenticed themselves to Odente.
> These people returned to Akropong after
> qualifying as Odente priests.[25]

It was shortly after this, continued Hall, that the
chief of Late decided to try to establish Dente in
Late and committed the human sacrifice as Rottman
had related.
    Thus it appears that Rottman misconstrued the
erection of a branch shrine at Late as an attempted
"re-establishment" of Dente there and hence his
oft-quoted account of the flight of Konkom or Dente

to Krachi must be critically examined. It is
surely based on Reindorf's tradition which was
collected in the 1860s from non-Krachi informants.
There is a possibility that Reindorf's tradition is
spurious and the existence at Late today of both a
Dente and a Konkom shrine supports this.[26] Yet
Reindorf's history is reliable in most cases and
hence cannot be disregarded. Certainly, owing to
the fact that it was written down (even before
publication), it received wide verbal circulation
via catechists and travelling missionaries. This
publicity may then account at least in part for the
fact that traditions collected in the 1960s by
J.E.K. Kumah and in the 1970s by the author often
maintain that Dente was brought from Late. Most
oral accounts collected by early colonial officers,
however, as quoted at the beginning of this section, do not mention the Late origins of Dente.

    In summary, then, although some Krachis are
almost surely of Late origin (by no means all of
them however, see Chapter 4) and although they may
have brought some sort of ancestral god with them
to Krachi when migrating, it is just as conceivable
as well that they found a local god at Krachi upon
their arrival. Indeed, the Krachiwura stated
categorically in 1920: "We do not believe that
Dente originally came from Late, Akuapim."[27] The
controversy, owing to the nature of the sources
which have generated it, does not lend itself to
resolution.[28] There is little doubt, however, that
the Dente shrine in the character that it came to
be known in the nineteenth century, i.e. as an
oracle with some political and social influence,
was bound up with and dependent upon its physical
location at Krachikrom. Hence, the origin of that
Dente shrine was whenever it initially became
active in the cave of the sacred grove overlooking
the Volta River -- regardless of whether a journey
from Late or Agogo or any other place occurred or
not. As the present Krachiwura explains, "Dente
was always with us but we really realized he was
with us when we came to this place [Krachikrom]."[29]
It can only be said with certainty that by the
beginning of the nineteenth century, Dente was
well-established in Krachi (according to Bowdich);
and traditions of Asante conquest, which will be
discussed in subsequent chapters, suggest that
Dente was well established at Krachi by 1740.

III

Descriptions of the Dente shrine (the original
site now being under the waters of the Volta Lake)
leave one with no doubt that its physical attributes were awesome. In 1876 the merchant Dobson
was informed that the oracle was "supposed to dwell
in a rock about twenty-five feet high, two miles
inland from Clachie."[30] Missionary Fisch, who
visited the shrine in 1910, provided perhaps the
most complete account, as well as a photograph (see
Figure 12):

> The route to the grotto goes along the left
> bank of the Volta atop a river bluff for
> about 1 km. down stream. There stands a
> gallery-like forest into which a broad road
> has been cut. The shelf of the bluff is
> formed of powerful grey granite rocks . . .
> Between these granite rocks are many big
> and little natural caves and crevice-like
> gaps. One such gap which has the advantage
> of three exits, one towards land and two
> towards the river, is claimed to be the
> habitation of the Fetish, according to the
> sly Fetish priest. The nature of the room
> and its entrances gives the opportunity to
> appear or to disappear mysteriously at all
> time, whatever the situation requires.[31]

Fisch explained that the shrine's supplicants stood
on what he called the "auditorium," i.e. a plateau
of the bluff which overlooked the river. The main
entrance to the shrine was above them, it being
covered with a white cotton cloth, and thus Fisch
derogatorily likened it all to the "spell of a
Punch and Judy show." He and his companions
entered the cave and found "countless large bats .
. . a pile of empty Schnapps bottles, a pair of
rusty iron bells, and in one bell lay concealed a
pair of bones of a young baboon."[32]
In 1912 the Acting German Bezirksleiter von
Rentzell at Kete-Krachi looted and dynamited the
shrine. His description concurs with Fisch's as to
the white sheet covering the entrance and the
cave's occupation by thousands of bats. It adds
that the interior was filled with calabashes of
food and money, as well as ceremonial drums, (which
he sent to Lome).[33] The dynamiting made apparently

Figure 12: The Dente Shrine, 1911

little difference in appearances, however, for the
Duncan-Johnstone in 1930 (and in 1915 R.S. Rattray)
found the shrine quite similar and surely in the
same place:

> It is approached down a wide and well kept
> glade in the forest. As we entered the
> glade we came on a small herd of kob
> feeding and they were unaware of our
> presence for quite a minute, a very pretty
> sight. With some difficulty we scaled the
> cliff and arrived outside Dente's resi-
> dence, a small cave, the entrance being
> covered by a white curtain. This was all
> the guide allowed us to see.[34]

The shrine, according to David Asante, was
quite successful because it operated as an oracle
where supplicants could actually hear a voice
emanating from the cave's interior,[35] and all
sources agree that the shrine functions in this
fashion today. Some accounts maintain that the
oracle does not speak a known language, and only
linguists of Dente can understand it after a
"special medicine" has been put into their ears.[36]
In addition, only certain days were and are "good"
days for consulting the oracle, normally every
eighth day.[37] In the past when the Dente Bosomfo
was not in Krachikrom (he often visited his own
village or "country seat"), supplicants were forced
to make extensive stays in Krachi awaiting his
return.[38]
There were certain taboos associated with
Dente. Various missionaries noted in the 1870s and
1880s that lights were not permitted in the vicinity of the shrine (or possibly throughout Krachikrom) at night.[39] This prohibition has persisted
to the present day, as described by a witness of
the removal of the Dente shrine from its place by
the river when the Volta Lake flooded it in 1965:

> The removal, at least of the physical
> paraphernalia such as the Black Stools and
> other sacred emblems, took place at dead of
> night with not a light showing. . . . As it
> happened the procession was obliged to pass
> the DC's bungalow on the higher outskirts
> of Krachi. [The DC] was again entertaining

friends and the bungalow was ablaze with
lights as the procession approached.

At first, when requested, the District Commissioner
refused to extinguish his lights, presumably in
jest.

This time a more resolute member of the
group marched up to the bungalow and, angry
at the turn of events made it clear that,
if the lights were not extinguished, the
procession would return to Krachi and,
after that, anything might happen . . .
[so] the amusement over and before he was
taken too seriously the DC told his servant
to turn all the lights off, and he stood
there in the darkness with his friends as
the procession silently passed by. 40

Monkeys in the grove surrounding the oracle
were considered sacred, though this reverence seems
not to have been unique to Dente. 41 However, Dente
is reputed by some traditions to have been able to
assume the form of a monkey when appearing to
people, and there are those today who claim to see
Dente in the form of a large monkey occasionally
near town. 42

Of concern to more people, however, was Dente's
forbidding horses and donkeys to be kept in the
town of Krachikrom. This created severe problems
for traders who needed to pass through Krachikrom
with their goods and animals to reach the ferry.
Klose observed that a special caravan path was
therefore built around the town to the ferry. 43
David Asante encountered the same difficulty upon
returning from Salaga through Krachikrom with some
newly purchased donkeys and a horse for the mission
in Kibi. He ridiculed the Dente Bosomfo's threats,
defiantly boarding the animals in Krachikrom
overnight. They all died shortly after their
arrival in Kibi. 44

People consulted the Dente oracle regarding the
usual matters of fertility and sickness; but as has
been shown, governments also sought its counsel
regarding war and possibly other political or
semi-political issues. The visiting catechist
Opoku, for example, listed the "nations" which came
to Dente -- Asantes, Kwahus, Akyems, Akuapems,
Paes, Buems -- and added that the Akuroponhene

proceeded with the custom for his predecessor's
funeral only when Dente had advised him that it was
the correct time to do so.[45] The people of Tekyiman today maintain a Dente branch shrine which they
acquired in the nineteenth century to help their
town prosper. It is located at the edge of the
town, and is moved each time the town border
expands.[46] The Dwabenhene could not perform some
funeral customs without "saluting the Great Fetich
Dente." As mentioned before, Asantehene Prempe I
sent greetings and thanks to Dente upon return from
exile in the Seychelles in 1924.[47]
     These examples demonstrating the political
advices of Dente indicate that the shrine did not
operate entirely as a healing shrine. It appears
as well that it did not operate as a witchcraft
shrine and did not administer "ordeal" (semi-
poisonous drink, which when drunk before a court,
kills a person guilty of witchcraft and spares the
innocent). Von Rentzell, a German administrator at
Krachi, claimed that Dente did in fact fulfill this
role, and for this reason he felt obliged to
execute the priests and dynamite the shrine in
1912.[48] Krachis today acknowledge that after a
person died, the Dente Bosomfo could declare
whether or not that person had been "killed by
Dente" (in which case ownership of that individual's property was assumed by the shrine), but
they deny that "ordeal" was administered or that
witches were deliberately sought out for punishment
by Dente.[49] Given the extent to which witchcraft
is interwoven with West African society, there is
no reason to doubt that Dente must indeed have been
consulted concerning witches and must have been
considered capable of removing witches from a
community. However, there is no evidence to the
effect that the Dente shrine engaged in witch-
findings or the administration of "ordeal" on the
mass level practiced by more specialized cults such
as Tigare, Kunde, or even "The Prophet," whose sole
purpose is to rid communities of witches.[50]

                              IV

     The organization of control of the Dente shrine
varied over time. The chief priest is known by the
title Dente Bosomfo (bosomfo meaning priest). He
must be a member of the Dente division of Krachi, a

clan or lineage called the Dentewiae, and he must
come from one of the "royal" Dentewiae towns:
Kadentwe, Ofuase, Noboagya, Tworeso, or Tariaso. A
list of Dente Bosomfos compiled from various
sources is given in Table 1, including estimated
dates of office-holding and the respective towns of
origin of the priests. As shown in the Table, five
of the twelve Bosomfos have come from Tariaso,
which acquires significance when the importance of
Tariaso as a control town on the route from Kete-
Krachi to Salaga is recognized. Almost all of the
Dentewiae towns were situated on the Krachi-Salaga
road, but Tariaso was the largest and most important and was described as a resting place by almost
every nineteenth century traveller on that route.
Additionally noteworthy is that, unlike the case of
the Krachiwuras, there is no evidence of a Dente
Bosomfo being destooled or removed from office by
traditional means, either in the past or in the
present.

Table 1

DENTE BOSOMFO OFFICE LIST

Dente Bosomfo	Village	Dates of Office
Akenten	Kadentwe	-1833
Luafwe	Tariaso	1833-1840
Ntsafo	Tworeso	1840-1845
Adjae (Onyenebolo)	Ofuase	1845-1850
Kwasi Mpajelente	Tariaso	1850-1877
Kwasi Gyantrubi	Noboagya	1877-1894
Kwabena Kuri	Tariaso	1894-1905
Abrekpa	Kadentwe	1905-1912
Interregnum		
Kwabena Okoewane	Tariaso	1921-1932
Kwasi Bawiya	Noboagya	1932-1945
Kwame Akate	Tworeso	1945-1950
Kofi Tawia	Tariaso	1950-1981
Kofi Akenten II	Kadentwe	1981-

The identities and functions of the assistants
and linguists to the Dente Bosomfo are not so
well-defined. When the Germans executed Dente
Bosomfo Gyantrubi in 1894, they also killed "his
evil helper Okra," whom the Germans considered
equally if not more unscrupulous than the priest
himself.[51] No name other than Okra or Okla is ever
given for this individual, but it is known that he
was a Grussi slave. Klose described him as "the
special confidant of the Fetish Priest . . . he
was, so to speak, the highest executive of the
gruesome despot;" and regarding Okra's political
position Klose commented that "he is not much less
esteemed than the Fetish Priest and certainly more
than the King [Krachiwura]."[52] One of the defini-
tions of okra given in Christaller's Twi-English
dictionary (1933) is:

> a male slave chosen by his master to be his
> constant companion and destined to be
> sacrificed on his death . . . a boy or man
> attending on the king; page;

The word was often used in this sense in Krachi,
i.e. it was applied to slaves and "one who helps a
chief," and this may explain why there is little
recollection today of the Germans executing "Okra"
along with Dente Bosomfo Gyantrubi. Nevertheless,
some Krachis remember Okra as being Gyantrubi's
slave.[53]
    In 1912 the Germans arrested another Dente
Bosomfo, Abrekpa, along with his three linquists:
Chief Yaw Gyankrubi of Adamkpa, Yaw Sakyi from
Kantankofore, and Asetena also from Kantankofore, a
royal town which supplies candidates for the
Krachiwura stool. The latter two were royals and,
as such, represented the Krachiwura at the shrine.
Adamkpa is a town also owing allegiance to the
Krachiwura, though it cannot provide a candidate
for that office. For this reason, "everyone knows
a man from Adamkpa cannot be powerful . . . Only a
man from Adamkpa is the mouthpiece of the Dente
fetish."[54] Krachis explain the reason for having
linguists of the shrine so closely linked with the
Krachiwura division (rather than the Dente Bosomfo
division):

> The Dente fetish is for Krachiwura.
> Krachiwura must have his representative

there because if not, maybe the Dentewiae
people will not tell everything to the
Krachiwura. So Krachiwura's representative
is the Adamkpa chief. Always the chief
from Adamkpa goes to the fetish. He is the
first linguist. Without him no one else
can go. There are two other linguists
also. [55]

It is the Adamkpa linguist who has "medicine"
placed in his ear to enable him to understand the
strange language of the oracle.

Conceivably the use of linguists "representing"
the Krachiwura was a development or at least an
altered emphasis following the execution of Dente
Bosomfo Gyantrubi, for as seen above, Gyantrubi's
linguist in 1894, far from being a royal, was a
slave. Indeed the assertion by some Krachis that
the shrine is "for Krachiwura" must be critically
examined. There is, for example, no mention in any
of the pre-1895 sources of the Dente Bosomfo's
sharing the proceeds of the shrine with the Krachiwura, and Okra is said to have "demanded extra
tribute for himself" from villages.[56] In 1930 the
District Commissioner Cooper learned from the Chief
of Tariaso,

that Okusipu, the Dente fetish-priest, was
not getting his share of the tribute
(Tariasu is the chief town of the
Dentewiyae which is under the Okusipu). On
going further into the matter he went on to
say that Okusipu, before the Europeans came
to the country was the Chief and that the
Owura was merely the head of the Chobwei
division . . . Previously I had thought
that the Owura was connected with Dente and
that he and Okusipu were in with each other
but this alters things. [57]

Recent accounts maintain that "Dente Bosomfo had no
land, and even the fetish is for Krachiwura."[58]
However, even today, the Krachiwura does not
himself participate in the daily operation of the
shrine, and this was assuredly the case in the
nineteenth century, as the District Commissioner
Burn learned:

The Krachiwura, or Odikro as he then was,
was simply the mouthpiece of the Bosomfo.
He was never allowed to go to the Fetish
and the country was more or less ruled by
the Bosomfo in this way. [59]

It is possible that the present-day practice of
sharing the proceeds of the shrine with the Krachiwura stems at least in part from the imposition of
the Native Authority Treasury by the British in
1931. At that time the British fixed the idea that
all income from the Krachi state, specifically land
dues but other incomes as well, was to go into a
common Krachi state treasury controlled by the
Krachiwura and his elders, who would then be
responsible for the redistribution of the money to
all elders and projects for the benefit of the
Krachi Native Authority in general (this was
"indirect rule" in practice). There was considerable resistance to this idea when the British first
imposed it, with the Dente Bosomfo protesting as
follows:

Statement of Kwasi on behalf of Dente
Obosumfo: The dispute we have with Krachiwura is two: Dente Fetish belongs to us we
have always been its priests but nowadays
the Krachiwura takes all the fees. The
other dispute is because we have an oath of
Kwasida which we used to hear [and collect
fees for] but now the Krachiwura has
forbidden any oath to be heard except in
his tribunal.[60]

Nevertheless the Native Authority and Treasury were
enforced by the British.
The exact balance of power between the Krachiwura and the Dente Bosomfo in the past is a complex
puzzle which may never be resolved. The sources
are quite clear, however, that Dente Bosomfo
Gyantrubi was superior in authority to the Krachiwura during the 1880s and 1890s:

The king of the town, an aged man . . . has
less influence and consequently less
respect and less honor than the priest.
The priest is a man of consequence in the
country because in all hard cases where the
kings of these countries fail to decide in

judgment, he is always referred to, to be
consulted as oracle of the nation through
Odente, and his word is the judgment by
which all must abide.[61]

The above was written in 1878, and in 1894, over
fifteen years later, Klose made a very similar
observation:

The King has little influence and is
completely dependent on the fetish priest
and his moods. The Krachi people like all
heathens are completely under the spell of
the fetish priest and have to fulfill his
demands without a murmur. [62]

The British in 1869 had been warned that they "must
consult the fetish" (not the chief or king) in
order to pass through Krachi, and Bonnat in 1876
presented his impressive quantity of gifts to the
Dente Bosomfo (not the king) in his effort to gain
permission to pass through Krachi to Salaga. [63] In
1830 and again in 1892, as will be seen in Chapters
5 and 6, the Dente Bosomfo personally led an army
of Krachis to war, the Krachiwura apparently not
participating. Moreover with regard to economic
affairs, the Dente Bosomfo seems to have had
decisive authority. Muller wrote in 1884:

The main point is that the Fetish priest in
Krachi dominates the King . . . and gets
hold of the custom money which is on all
articles transported to the interior
especially on salt.[64]

In 1894, Lieutenant Doering was also quite clear as
to who was responsible for plundering (or taxing,
depending upon one's point of view) the Kete
market:

Mossomfo the fetish man of Kratji is the
source of all the trouble. He has built a
house in the middle of the Kete market and
here has established a kind of market
sentry . . . Further Mossomfo has built on
the road to Lome from Salaga a fence and
two huts and every Haussa coming is
plundered here.[65]

The Germans in fact always referred to the Krachiwura as "King Odukru," which suggests in accordance with Burn's information above that the Krachi Chief was not an owura or omanhene (a paramount chief over numerous towns or a large group of people) -- but an odekuro, a clan or village chief. the oath sworn for important judicial purposes was the Dente Kwasida oath, not the Krachiwura's oath. Indeed Burn elicited this confession from the Krachiwura:

> The Krachihene admitted that in olden days he was called Odikro, he then realized what he had said and try [sic] to make out that Odikro and Omanhene were synonymous.[66]

It is therefore tempting to conclude that the Dente Bosomfo held full political control in Krachi throughout the nineteenth century until Gyantrubi's execution in 1894. Yet the "King of Krachi" is invariably mentioned and remarked upon by travellers and government representatives prior to 1894, and "the King of Kratchi" is the first signature on Gouldsbury's trade treaty of 1876. Moreover, although Bonnat negotiated with the Dente Bosomfo, it was the King, "an old man of seventy" who formally received him. The division of responsibility between the two figures is never clear and surely varied over time anyway. A possible explanation for the presence and confusion of the two authorities is that the Dente Bosomfo was basically the traditional religious authority for the Krachi people while the Krachiwura, or Krachihene as Asantes called him, was selected by Asante following its conquest of the territory in the 1740s to be its political representative and channel of communication (see Chapter 4). Asante might well have preferred not to work through traditional religious leaders who, as indeed happened, tended to lead local rebellions against Asante control. This tentative explanation would account for the persistant recognition of the Krachiwura in the nineteenth century in an otherwise low-income office, and for the delicate balance of power between his office and the more traditionally powerful office of the Dente Bosomfo. It is supported by at least one oral account:

In the past we were under Krachi Dente.
The stools we are on are fetish, under the
Dente fetish. We took the Fetish Priest as
chief. There was no Krachiwura. Even at
that time Asantes came to the fetish. In
the past we took [the Dente] fetish as
head, but Asantes have been coming regularly yet when anyone comes there is no one
to attend them [because the priest is busy
at the shrine] so we took Twoboae chief
[Krachiwura] to be head. This happened
before Europeans came.[67]

Even in colonial times the power base of the
Krachiwura, according to District Commissioner
Cooper, lay "amongst the strangers who have come to
live on Krachi land," that is, Hausa, Ewe and
Asante as opposed to Krachi peoples. In this light
it is more understandable that the Dente Bosomfo
was to be found fighting in the Asante rebellions
of 1830 and 1892 while the Krachiwura was not; that
the Dente Bosomfo would become the leader of the
1875 withdrawal from Asante rule and take a leadership role in the anti-Asante defense pact of the
Volta region while the Krachiwura became weaker,
"less honorable," and "completely dependent" on the
Bosomfo by the 1890s; and that with the Dente
Bosomfo eliminated from the power structure in 1894
by a coalition of Muslims and Germans (all
strangers) the Krachiwura would begin to take on
increasing responsibility.

V

Regardless of who possessed the greater political control, the Dente shrine itself represented an
impressive intake of money, food, and labor
(slaves). One could not consult the shrine without
bringing gifts and payments. The German explorer
von Francois, in Kete-Krachi at the time of a
smallpox epidemic, noted for example that it was a
"tiring but lucrative" time for the Dente Bosomfo
because so many people were coming to the shrine
with sacrifices to ensure their health.[68] Bonnat
had to spend three days in Krachi negotiating with
the Dente Bosomfo and only after he had presented
the priest with a "450 lb. barrel of salt, a
magnificent basin, a silver bracelet, a necklace, a

briefcase, five bottles of gin, four flasks, two liquor sets, one lemonade set with glasses and carafes all painted and gilded," was he permitted to continue on to Salaga.[69]   Hunters brought the Dente Bosomfo portions of their kills, including the tusks from elephants, partly in recognition of those whose land they were hunting on and partly to ensure continued good fortune.   The missionary Awere met such a hunter:

> He made me know that he lately killed a wild animal of unusual size and was bringing a portion to the fetish Odente (its priest) that the priest may favour him with a kind of medicine which will enable him to kill some more . . . In this way the fetish priest is in every week visited by many a man from all directions with parcels of sometimes venison, skins of wild animals and ivories, etc. [70]

Moreover, the shrine's income was not limited to sacrifices for specific requests and consultations:

> Since this god is considered as the king of all gods he also has an oath which one swears, and if somebody swears his oath falsely, he must pay a heavy fine . . . If the priest or also any inhabitant of the town is owed money, he brings the matter before the god who becomes the creditor.[71]

The oath mentioned in this account was the Dente Kwasida oath, and all those who swore it in order to settle a dispute had to pay fees.   Those who failed to pay this fee or court tax, as was the case with some Nsutas living under Dente's protection in the 1890s, were shortly expelled. [72]   The shrine also collected death duties by confiscating the property of anyone whom it claimed had been "killed by Dente," as indicated earlier.   For example, the crisis in 1912 which motivated von Rentzell to execute Dente Bosomfo Abrekpa involved the death of the owner of a substantial yam farm, over which the shrine attempted to assume control. The Dente priest also established and collected trade taxes which provided him with much income, particularly during Krachi's zenith as a market center on the trade route to Salaga in the 1880s

and 1890s. For example, 100 nuts per load of kola
were collected: one load averaged 2000 nuts,
making the duty about five per cent.[73] The large
profits accruing from the tolls on the salt trade
have already been discussed. Gifts and payments
were also sent to Dente for permission to establish
branch shrines. Estimates of how much payment was
involved suggest that it was appreciable at times:
one missionary recorded that a "native King gave no
less than £100 to the Dente Bosomfo for a consecrated stone for establishing a branch."[74] The
shrine received slaves as taxes and as remuneration
for services, and gained runaway slaves seeking
asylum. The Dente Bosomfo settled them on farms
and then received a portion of their produce. As
noted in Chapter 2, these slave villages
constituted a significant investment and income.

Although some travellers found the people at
Krachikrom "untidy" and the town fouled by "stench
and filth,"[75] others placed emphasis on the town's
wealth. David Asante noted that "the roads leading
from the Krakye villages to the capital [Krachi-
krom] are kept clean just as they are in Asante."
Missionary Buss commented that "by the way they
look, the people of Krakye are quite well-off," and
missionary Muller grudgingly admitted:

> In Krakye we were presented, by the chief
> together with the chief priest, with 70
> yams, sheep, 12 eggs, and a jar of local
> beer upon which we and our people were able
> to live on for four to six days. In this
> bigoted fetish town we were presented with
> the greatest presents and indeed [this was]
> before we gave something to the chief and
> before they knew that they would receive
> something from us.[76]

The opulence of the Dente Bosomfo was recorded most
colorfully by Klose who observed a procession of
the Bosomfo and his retainers, and which seems
remarkably like those of major chiefs in Asante:
"Thousands of people" had gathered to watch the
procession preceded by musicians and drummers and
the "fetish emblems," probably pans, stools and
swords. The priest himself was carried by slaves
in a sedan chair which was lined with red silk, and
surrounded by priests and attendants. "As his
advisor and marshall who would, with his armed

slaves, ensure that all his master's orders were
executed, the Grussi-slave Okla walked beside the
sedan chair . . . the military troop consisted of a
large mass of slaves who were armed with rifles."
Among the attendants were Hausas in their white
burnouses and blue robes. The Bosomfo was dressed
in "fantastic but rich clothing," green silk
trousers and yellow silk stole around his
shoulders. Okla wore a valuable embroidered blue
Hausa robe.[77]

Thus the economic benefits of being the Dente
Bosomfo in the late nineteenth century simply
cannot be ignored. In the preceding chapter it was
proposed that the fundamental resources of Krachi,
regardless of who controlled that region, were its
geographical position on major and minor trade
routes and its encirclement by fertile farming
land. A third important factor now emerges in the
composite picture of Krachi's resources and significance, that being, the presence of a religious
shrine which, when operated successfully, earned
recognition and respect throughout Greater Asante
and was feared and obeyed within the Krachi district. The Dente shrine had great potential for
achieving ideological control over people and hence
economic and political control over the land, labor
and important trade routes through Krachi. This is
what the shrine, operated by the Dente Bosomfo and
various other elders, attempted to accomplish in
the late nineteenth century. The degree to which
this was successful, though considerable, was not
complete, for the process was halted in the peak of
its momentum by the ruthless measures taken by the
German government.

4

Krachi Origins and Organization
Incorporation and Patronage

Some understanding of the kinship organization
and group identity of the Krachi people is useful
for determining what social foundations the Dente
Bosomfo built on in the nineteenth century and for
evaluating his success at manipulating, controlling, and leading the Krachi people. The social
structure of Krachi seems, like many African
kinship systems, to have been remarkably flexible
and adaptable. It was and is in a constant state
of flux, and was not immutable and tradition-bound
as some anthropological, colonial, and oral accounts might imply. Skilled leadership took
advantage of this characteristic, and thus fundamental economic, social, and political restructuring in Krachi proceeded for some time without
the whole system fracturing.

I

The Krachi people are probably best defined as
those who speak Krachi, a Guan language. The
elders, when asked about the origins and composition of the Krachi people, invariably bring into
the discussion references to "clans" to which
Krachis belong. Anywhere from six to ten clans
might be listed by an informant and they are
defined essentially as exogamous patrilineal social
units whose general territorial aspects are

demonstrated in Figure 13. Each clan possesses its own royal and subservient towns and villages (see Tables 2 and 3), its own political office or stool, which in most cases today is subject to the Krachi-wura's stool, and its own theoretical role or position in the Krachi state structure.

The term most commonly use for clan is the Twi word nton -- the patrilineal unit of the Akan. However, sometimes the word ammusu, a perversion of the Twi abusua (pl. mmusua: Akan materilineal clans) is used. The mmusua have a more significant political dimension in matrilineal Asante than the nton; thus in all characteristics except the matrilineality, Krachi clans resemble abusua more than nton. The Guan word awu can mean a simple lineage and thus the suffix to different clan names is sometimes awua (or awiae) as in the Dentewiae clan. The Krachi word kobridjito meaning family, is sometimes used for clan, but the general feeling is that clans are much more than families or groups of families. Hence the fact that Krachis commonly use a Twi word, nton (and not the Krachi word for family), strongly suggests that the elements of clans which transcend family ties were acquired partly from association with Akan political ideas.

In his 1960s study of the Guan town of Late in Akuapem, David Brokensha found a similar phenomenon. Lates are organized around brongs or wards of the town in a manner which suggests an urban likeness to the more rurally based Krachi clans. That is, brongs, like Krachi clans, are "social units with both kinship and territorial dimensions which are central to the social organization." The word brong comes from a Twi word meaning street and is extended by the Guans in Late to mean a quarter or neighborhood of the town, and like nton "there appears to be no Guan equivalent for this term."[1]

The Krachi nton developed over time to encompass groups of villages with people who were not related by blood to each other. Slaves, strangers, and villages of emigres and refugees were apparently incorporated into the nton, and hence, though not members of the lineage, they were still considered members or subjects of the clan. Because of the political, juridical, and geographical dimensions of nton in Krachi, and the lineage connotations of the English word clan, the English word "division" in its most neutral sense will be used throughout this chapter to represent the nton and the peoples and villages associated with each. Table 2 presents data regarding the seven most frequently mentioned divisions: their names, offices, and corporate villages. Three other significant office holders are listed in Table 3. In Figure 13, in addition to the seven major divisions, a few groups and towns are included which are not Krachi divisional members but which owed various levels of allegiance to the Krachiwura and Dente Bosomfo at various times in the past.

The traditions of origin of the Krachi divisions are often contradictory. A general theme is perhaps discernible, namely that the "clans" each arrived in the Krachi region at different times and were assigned to or settled in different areas. Only the Asasewura (sometimes referred to in other parts of Ghana as Osuriwiya, Tindana, or land priest) claims to have "always been on the land" (some divisions dispute this claim) and to have descended from heaven in a brass pan.[2] The Krachiwura and his relations, the Twoboae division, maintain that they emigrated from Late, travelled through Kwaman and Agogo (see Figure 5) where they participated in the Atere Firam wars (seventeenth century), and finally settled on the west bank of the Volta at a site called Ketakpanda. There they were "much troubled by the Ashantis and in fear of their lives [so] they sent their chief and their stool with his family and a few retainers across the river."[3] Traditions collected from the Twoboae at other times maintain variously that they conquered the Nchumuru peoples living on the east side of the Volta, that they found the east side of the Volta uninhabited, and that they moved to the east side because they became used to consulting the Dente shrine which was already on the east side of the Volta.[4] The Dentewiae (the Dente Bosomfo's division) usually claim to have arrived from Late with the Twoboae and to be matrilineal nephews of the latter, i.e., sons of the sister of the founding Twoboae ancestor.[5]

In the early 1930s a major dispute over land arose in Krachi, the records of which both add to and cloud understanding of Krachi origins.[6] In the dispute the Asasewura claimed to be the priest of the land and to have given the Twoboae permission long ago to settle on the land east of the Volta at the time of the latter's move from Ketakpanda. The Twoboae claimed, rather, that the Nanumba, under

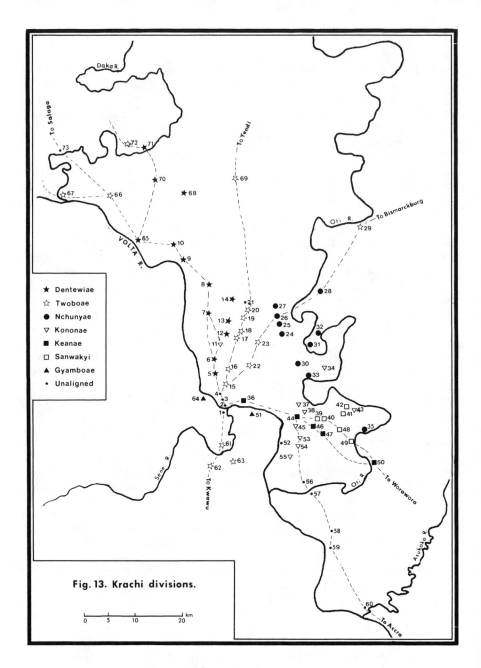

Fig. 13. Krachi divisions.

Figure 13:   Krachi Divisions

Guide to Figure 13

1. British Krachi (Nsunua)	37. Kyantae
	38. Dobiso
2. Krachikrom	39. Kpubuae
3. Kete-Krachi	40. Makokwae
4. Kete	41. Kpomfri
5. Kadentwe	42. Bomadefo
6. Ofuase	43. Atefie
7. Tariaso	44. Dadiase
8. Mmata	46. Yabeng
9. Nkatekwan	46. Krenkuase
10. Buafri	47. Adjanae
11. Woreto	48. Ayirae
12. Noboagya	49. Okrakodjo
13. Gyase	50. Beposo
14. Tworeso	51. Nkomi
15. Kantankofori	52. Osapae
16. Adamkpa	53. Kenyinemo
17. Dadekoro	54. Dentemanso
18. Brenwiase	55. Kofisu
19. Kwaku	56. Ahinkro
20. Monkra	57. Otisu
21. Osramani	58. Apae
22. Genje	59. Apaso
23. Abudjuru	60. Akroso
24. Chiriahen	61. Abokono
25. Ntewusu	62. Odeafo
26. Yawborae	63. Burae
27. Kpetchu	64. Somi
28. Adiemra	65. Bagyemso
29. Dambae	66. Akaniem
30. Tentu	67. Tinkranku
31. Mposato	68. Chinderi
32. Odumankuma	69. Boare
33. Akprinpeto	70. Okrandente
34. Banka	71. Grubi
35. Lotri	72. Papatia
36. Gyanekrom	73. Lentemanso

Table 2

MAIN KRACHI DIVISIONS AND THEIR VILLAGES

Division	Twoboae	Dentewiae	Nchunyae	Kononae	Keanae	Sanwakyi	Gyamboae
Head	Krachiwura or Krachihene	Dente Bosomfo or Okusipu	Amankrado or Kponowura	Adontenhene or Kononaewura	Benkumhene or Akpawia	Kyidomhene or Pawia	Asasewura
Villages:	*Kantankofore	*Tariaso	*Mposato	*Kyantae	*Adjanae	*Makokwae	*Nkomi
	*Monkra	*Ofuase	*Kpetchu	*Kopotrase	*Krenkuase	*Okrakojo	*Somi
	*Kwaku	*Tworeso	*Odumankuma	*Dentemanso	Dadiase	*Bomedefo	
	*Genge	*Kadentwe	*Tantu	*Owureto	Gyanekrom	*Kpebuae	
	Abudjuru	*Noboagya	*Ntewusu	*Kotonkrae	Beposo	Ayrikom	
	Adamkpa	Gyasae	Lotri	Banka			
	Odeafo	#Bagyemso	Akprinpeto	Dobiso			
	Burae	#Dormabin	Yawborae	Atefie			
	Abokono	#Akroso	Chiriahen	Yabeng			
	Dadekoro	#Apaso		Kanyinemo			
	Akaniem	#Otisu		Konkronja			
	Dambae	#Tapa					
		#Basa					
		#Kponfri					

* designates a royal village
# nineteenth century attachments now autonomous

their leader called the Bimbila Na, offered them
the uninhabited land in exchange for military aid
against the Kotokolis and Konkomba (widely scatter-
ed autochtonous groups in the area).

The general consensus among the British colonial administrators involved in this case was that
the Asasewura's claims to being the original
guardian of the land were probably reliable, his
title alone being fairly convincing. But they
concurred that this did not establish his political
seniority, as the Krachiwura had been recognized
politically as "king" of Krachi since German times.
Ferguson had reported in 1894 that the "Asasiwula,
a very influential Chief of Kraki" had been
"slighted on two occasions when presents were made
to the native Chiefs by the Germans."[7] The British
after 1914 (when they took Krachi over from German
rule) persisted in the pattern set by the Germans,
administered through the Krachiwura, and never
encountered objection until they began to inquire
into land ownership for the establishment of the
Native Authority (which would involve chiefly
control over land taxes). The British authorities
concluded that after forty years of European
colonial approval the position of the Krachiwura as
political leader was incontrovertable. Having
failed to receive the recognition he believed he
merited, the Asasewura in 1933 withdrew with his
people to the west bank of the Volta and severed
himself from all participation in Krachi politics.

The Asasewura of course did not claim to be
superior to the Krachiwura during the dispute in
1931. He simply maintained that he was custodian
or priest of the land as his title indicates and
indeed, he referred to the Krachiwura as an Omanhene (Twi term for paramount chief of a large group
of people):

> Since the foundation of the Kratchi town
> and the arrival of [the Twoboae] myself as
> Asasewura and the Omanhene stayed harmoni-
> ously, worked hand in hand, did everything
> peaceably, until the installation of this
> present Omanhene. My contention is that:
> He said he is both Omanhene and Asasewura,
> that I am his slave and only bear the title
> of Asasewura. He had therefore stopped all
> my rights and advantages. His predecessors
> used to give me one bullock every year but
> during the days of slavery they used to

give me men. . . As I take no fees or tolls
from them for ploughing and occupation of
my land hence the yearly bullock or man.[8]

The controversy is significant first, because
antagonisms were still running high 45 years later.
Second, it clouds any attempts at collecting
unbiased information today about the arrival of the
Krachi peoples because many groups try to claim to
have been the first on the land. Third, the court
information does make it fairly clear that the
Asasewura and his dependents, despite their separation today, were indeed probably the more ancient
occupants of the region. Just who his subjects and
dependents were is another question, but many
traditions suggest that the Nchumurus (people
speaking the Guan dialect of Nchumuru) were the
people occupying sections of the region east of the
Volta before "the people of Late" arrived. "Twoboae" in fact was a name purportedly given to the
Krachi immigrants by the Nchumurus when they saw
the Twoboae settling where the "grasscutters"
lived, "twoboae" being the Nchumuru word for
"grasscutter", a groundhog-like animal (thryonomys
swinderianus) which does indeed abound in Krachi.[9]
    The Nchumuru peoples and culture seem to
predate most peoples in the whole area. The Basas,
living well west of the Volta River and Krachi
area, admit that when they arrived at their present
town they found the Nchumurus.

Owing to the inter-marriage and Nchumurus
having much larger community than we the
strangers, we were influenced by their way
of life which made us to adopt the culture,
customs, traditions and even had to use the
Nchumuru language as our principal dialect
up to the present day. [10]

At some point in time, perhaps the 1600s, the Basas
drove out many of the Nchumurus, who then settled
on the east bank of the Volta.
    During the next decades the Dente shrine
probably began to function, for in c. 1740 it had
already gained a reputation. At about that time
the Asantehene Opoku Ware attacked the Basas
because they were disturbing the trade (by killing
Asante merchants) at Salaga which Opoku Ware had
recently conquered. Osubri, "the king of

Ntshummurus who resided in Basa" was attacked and
defeated by the Dwabenhene to whom Opoku Ware had
assigned the campaign. "Numerous prisoners were
taken, but most of the fugitives fled to Karakye,
seeking protection from Odente, the far-famed
fetish of the place."[11]

Thus although Krachi traditions maintain that
at least half of their divisions migrated from
Late, there are indications of a strong underlayer
of Nchumuru and Nchumuru-influenced peoples and
customs in the Krachi area pre-dating the arrival
of Late immigrants. Linguistic data bears this
out. A stylized geographical chart by Colin
Painter is given in Figure 14 which shows 25 highly
correlated Guan idiolects and supports the historical data to the effect that some dispersion of
people, probably Nchumuru, occurred at Basa, and
that Krachis are linguistically more closely
related to Nchumurus and Basas than Lates. The
idiolects of two Krachi villages surveyed, Nkate-
kwan and Tshantai, were closely related to Basa and
Nchumuru idiolects (much more so than to the Late
idiolect), though of course they were most highly
correlated with one another (sharing 92 out of 100
words). However, the Basa idiolect is shown to be
significantly related to the idiolects of eleven
other sample sites -- the highest for any site on
the chart.

The Asasewura's predecessors in office were
most likely among the early Nchumuru inhabitants.
The numbers of Nchumurus on the east side of the
Volta grew when many fled there from Basa, perhaps
in the 1600s. The numbers would have swelled even
more in the 1740s when many of the "Nchumuruized"
Basas were forced to flee there by Asante attacks
under Asantehene Opoku Ware, but according to all
accounts the Dente shrine was already functioning
by the time of Opoku Ware's attacks in the area.
As suggested in Chapter 2 the Late migrants,
probably the Twoboae and perhaps the Dentewiae
divisions of the Krachis, left Akuapem 1640-1650.

Tentatively it can then be proposed that they
settled on the west bank of the Volta at the
now-vanished Ketakpanda in the late seventeenth
century with Basa neighbors to the west and Nchumuru neighbors to the east, and acquired the
dialect and some of the customs of the indigenous
Nchumurus. By 1740 they had spread into the
sparsely settled region east of the Volta and the

A stylized geographical chart showing all correlations of 65
or over out of 100 among the 25 Guan idiolects.

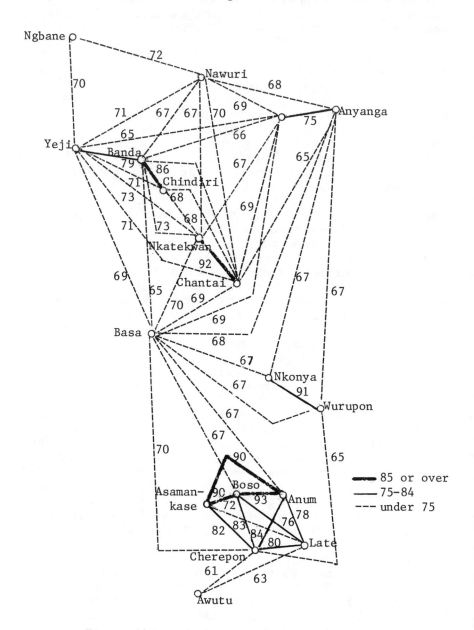

Figure 14:   The Distribution of Guan in Ghana
As Found by Painter, 1967

Dentewiae peoples were controlling the shrine with some success. They established political sovereignty when they moved to the sparsely settled east bank of the Volta, and Twoboae traditions maintain this move was accomplished militarily through the aid of the Bimbila Na.

It is equally possible that the Twoboae were confirmed in their political sovereignty by the Asante who acquired control of the east bank of the Volta without conquest in 1745 (for the campaign against the Basas had been sufficient to precipitate Krachi's surrender, see below). Certainly the various other Krachi divisions often define themselves in relationship to the Krachiwura according to traditional Asante military positions, albeit somewhat simplified, when they state for example that the head of the Kononae is known as the Adontenhene (captain of the center), head of the Keanae is known as the Benkumhene (captain of the left-wing), and so forth (see Table 2). Thus, it is tentatively proposed here that the Krachiwura may have been charged with the responsibility of organizing the Krachi peoples for recruitment to Asante military campaigns and hence this Asante organizational overlay.

All this is even more supported by several accounts which maintain that the Twoboae were among the last group of Krachis to arrive in the region.[12] In Krachi traditions there is a strong theme of numerous waves or layers of people arriving and being incorporated into the geographical and political landscape by being relegated and attached to various divisions or forming new divisions for channels of representation. One of the first divisions to arrive is said to have been the Kononae, and it is claimed that these people are of Nchumuru origin.[13] The spatial dispersion of their villages (see Figure 13) reinforces the contention that the Kononae were some of the earliest inhabitants of the region (perhaps preceded only by the Asasewura's ancestors). Traditions claim that the next groups to arrive were people of the Keanae division, migrating from Pran because of persecution by the Atebubuhene.[14] The Nchunyae people purportedly arrived next, possibly the first group from the south for they claim to have come from Efutu near Winneba on the coast.[15] They were followed by the Sanwakyi, Dentewiae, and Twoboae from Late in that order.[16] If indeed the Twoboae

were the last group to arrive it could well mean
that the Twoboae had had the greatest opportunity
to experience sophisticated Akan political and
military systems (perhaps en route through Asante
Agogo and Kwaman where they claim they fought in
the epic Aterefram wars). Hence they were either
the most familiar with means of establishing
superiority over the more autochtonous groups or
they were the most reliable selection for the
Asante who, after conquest, needed a chief or
faction through which to give orders.

                              II

     More important than the temporal and geographi-
cal origins of these divisions however is the
concept that the "clan" or divisional organization
of the Krachi people is an acknowledged process of
incorporating new peoples. As one Krachi elder
commented, "clans were made because long ago we all
came from different villages and fathers, but came
here to settle."[17] It is a never ending process of
fluctuating absorption and fission. For example,
what are apparently the oldest divisions seem to
have been gradually absorbed by stronger and
perhaps newer groups (see Table 3). The priest of

                          Table 3

                   SUB-DIVISIONAL CHIEFS

Office	Village	Division	Duty
Firao Bosomfo	Osapae	Otapoae	Volta River priesthood
Kachipa	Osramani	under Kononae	prepare food for New Yam festival
Bruwia	Okurae (Benynae)	under Nchunyae	prepare food for Dente festival

the Volta River, called Firao Bosomfo (Firao is a
Guan name for the Volta) must surely hold one of the
older priestly offices of the region. He is said
to have once had many villages under him, but they
all are known to have been out of existence by the
time of colonial rule except for his own village
Osapae. His division, Otapoae, is sometimes now
considered to be part of the Nchunyae division.
The Kosuwiae division is headed by the Kachipa
whose ritual role of supervising the annual new yam
festival and purification of certain stools (characteristic Akan rituals) suggests that this office
is one of long-standing in the community, at least
since the eighteenth century Akan influences. The
Kosuwiae division consists of only one town today,
however, which is subject to the Adontenhene, or
Kononae division.[18]

The divisions are capable of expanding as well
as atrophying. Many of the inhabitants of the
royal Twoboae town of Kantankofore moved across the
Volta to the British (west) side during the period
of German rule (1894-1914), where they formed
farming villages, the three largest being Burae,
Abokono, and Odeafo. People from the royal families in these towns nevertheless considered Kantankofore "their village" and retained their
eligibility to succeed to the Krachiwura stool. At
times these three villages are mentioned in lists
of Twoboae royal towns; otherwise the informant
assumes that by listing Kantankofore, the three
west-side villages are automatically included.

Nineteenth century arrivals can be accurately
reconstructed and this aids in revealing the system
of incorporation in operation. Some already
well-organized communities requested the protection
of Dente without moving into Krachi territory (e.g.
Pae and Akroso) presumably gaining for themselves
military and spiritual protection. The groups were
placed under the suzerainty of the Dente Bosomfo
who settled their disputes when necessary and
protected them in return for tribute in money,
crops, and manpower. The case of the Pae can be
dated quite accurately to the 1875 defeat of the
Kwawu Dukoman by the Buems, all former Asante
subjects living to the southeast of Krachi. The
Kwawu Dukoman and the Pae had allied with Asante in
1869 in an attack on the Buems. After Asante's
defeat by the British in 1874, the Buems turned on
their former enemies. Kwawu Dukoman were defeated

and driven from their homes, and the Pae reasoned
it was only a matter of time before their turn for
a Buem attack. Although the Pae were subjects of
the Omanhene of Kwawu (in Asante), the latter's
inability to protect them from Buem attacks resulted in the Pae turning to Dente for protection. The
Dente Bosomfo gladly guaranteed their security
against attack and, among other payments, received
from the Omanhene of Kwawu yearly "40 atiri or £3
cash to the Krachi Dente as a remuneration for
taking charge of his people." Pae and the villages
it comprised (Apae, Otisu, and Apaso) were then for
a time considered Dentewiae towns, though none
would ever say they were actually members of the
Dentewiae "clan". In the more secure times of
colonial rule, Pae became independent, that is, it
ended allegiance to both Dente Bosomfo and Kwawu. [19]

This "protection of Dente" which attracted so
many people to seek association with Krachi (an
accelerating process in the insecure 1870s and
1880s) was described by the colonial officer
Cardinall in the 1920s as a means of "neutralizing"
one's country, and labelled Krachi a "pagan Switzerland." Even later, impressed with the presence
of such a variety of people, he also called it an
"African League of Nations." [20] The incorporative
aspect of the division organization in Krachi was
manipulated by the Dente Bosomfo to facilitate the
settlement of refugee peoples who physically moved
on to Krachi land and were asismilated more fully
than the loose affiliation which the Pae case
represents.

Refugees were assigned and distributed among
the divisional leaders to farm and build their
villages, and for judicial and revenue purposes.
Thus, for example, Dadiase and Gyanekrom in the
Keanae division are settlements of Dwabens who came
to Krachi after the 1874-1875 Dwaben dispute with
Kumase. Although they cannot succeed to the
Akpawia (Keanae) stool, they do owe allegiance to
the Krachiwura through Akpawia, the latter being
their representative in Krachikrom and recourse for
hearing their disputes. [21] Nchumuru immigrants from
north of Krachi who became subjects of Krachi in
the nineteenth century were similarly distributed
as they arrived or as they requested protection.
Thus the Bagyemso people, probably the first
northern Nchumurus to shift their allegiance from
Gonja (Kpembe/Salaga) to Krachi, sometime before

1830 (see Chapter 5), served the Dente Bosomfo.
However the Akaniem people (an Nchumuru village
near Bagyemso) served the Krachiwura through the
Adamkpa chief. They "bring the thigh of any animal
they kill [to us]. Adamkpa looks after them. The
Adamkpa chief brings them to Krachiwura. When they
come to Krachikrom they will lodge at Adamkpa."[22]
     Somewhat later the villages of Tinkranku and
Burae were placed under the Krachiwura when they
moved into Krachi territory from Gonja (across the
Daka River). The village of Banda was assigned to
the Dentewiae division, the village of Adiemra to
the Amankrado's division, and Atafie and others
were placed under the authority of the Kononae
division.[23] Similarly, whole villages were sometimes made up of slaves who had fled to Krachi for
asylum, such as the village of Bompata, though
these villages almost always belonged to the Dente
Bosomfo for it was the shrine which guaranteed the
slaves' safety.[24]
     The immigrants represented a source of wealth
for the divisions of Krachi. They comprised a
labor pool for communal activities and military
draft, and they provided annual tribute, regular
contributions of food and meat, and fees from the
settlement of disputes. To some extent the more
villages in a division, the more wealth it controlled, though geographical location was a factor
was well. In this light it is important to take
note of the divisional control of communication
routes (see Figure 13). The Dentewiae division
controlled the major towns along the road to
Salaga. Similary the Amankrado division controlled
the Oti River crossing at Kpetchu; Krachiwura towns
were clustered around the road to Bimbila and
Yendi; Kononae villages were situated on the road
south to Accra and Lome; and Keanae and Sanwakyi
towns marked the route to Worawora and Buem,
controlling the lower Oti River crossing at Okra-
kodjo.
     These patterns, like every other politically
loaded situation, were subject to change over time.
For example, the Germans established a new town in
the early 1900s -- Dambae -- at the Oti River on
the route to their headquarters of Bismarckburg.
Dambae was planned as a major market town and
administrative link between Bismarckburg and
Kete-Krachi, and as a ferry crossing of the Oti
River (which eclipsed the Amankrado's town of

Kpetchu). Thus, consistent with German policy of
supporting the paramountcy of the Krachiwura,
Dambae was placed under the Krachiwura's jurisdiction.[25] Similarily noteworthy is that the Dente
Bosomfo traditionally had no towns on the southern
route to Accra. Yet when this route grew in
importance in the 1880s, and the Pae and Akroso
towns requested affiliation, they were quickly
placed under the Dente Bosomfo's supervision.

Not all Krachi divisions then were or are equal
in size, population, revenue, and influence. Among
the Krachi divisional chiefs there has emerged a
hierarchy of seniority which was first set down in
the British records in 1932. According to the
District Commissioner then, the Krachiwura was
considered paramount chief, followed in order of
seniority by the Dente Bosomfo, Asasewura (until he
withdrew), Amankrado, Firao Bosomfo, Adontenhene,
Akpawia, Pawia, Kachipa, and Bruwia.[26] This rank
ordering was doubtless subject to some fluctuations
and political shifts. For example, some Krachi
elders maintain that in the past the Adontenhene
came before the Amankrado in seniority but that the
Krachiwura in colonial times chose an Amankrado who
would support him in the disputes with the elders.
Thus the British District Commissioners were led to
believe that the Amankrado was highest in seniority
below the Dente Bosomfo.[27] Again, Firao Bosomfo is
rarely mentioned today in the hierarchy of chiefs,
if at all (he is fifth in the DC's list) except as
one of "the small ones", perhaps because an extremely old and ill chief held the stool for a long
time (he died in 1976 at age 98), or perhaps
because many of his villages have simply disappear-
ed over time.[28] It can be concluded then that the
rank ordering of the divisional chiefs is roughly
correlated with the size and strategic location of
the divisional villages, factors which varied over
time.

III

Considerable evidence supports the contention
that the "incorporative" feature of Krachi organization described above operated in a representative
mode for peoples in varying degrees of association
with and within Krachi. Krachikrom was described
as a "capital" by travellers, and the divisional

chiefs such as Akpawia, Amankrado, Adontenhene, etc. "represented" the villages under them by going to Krachikrom for enstoolments, consultations, litigations, and rituals. Each of these chiefs was required to maintain a house in Krachikrom. In 1882 the British observer Graves overstated this phenomenon somewhat by commenting that "each house at Krachi represents one town or village" in Bron (the latter term referring to Krachi and peoples west of the Volta). Another English observer explained that Krachikrom "is only the residence of the Elders and all the others live in plantations which is considered their real abode."[29] The missionary Clerk also commented that "Krakye is a town for the elders only," and Muller noted that "people say that only notables have huts in Kracky-[krom] and to possess one is an honour."[30] Today as well Krachikrom is a separate quarter of Kete-Krachi in which only the divisional chiefs have houses.

Although even the Dente Bosomfo was not continuously present at Krachikrom, frequently travelling to his own villages to hear disputes and to supervise his farms,[31] Krachikrom was the site of government and council, where visitors were received, representatives gathered, and decisions were made. Everyone who would be affected by policy emanating from Krachikrom apparently had the right and obligation to maintain a representative there. Lonsdale was in Krachi in 1882 at the time of the expansion of the Bron Confederation (see Chapter 6) and observed that the several groups -- many of which were not members of any Krachi division -- allying themselves with Krachi merited this representation:

> I was received by the Chief Priest of Denty, the Chief of Kratshie, the representatives of the chiefs of all the surrounding towns, the Insutahs and the Buem representatives . . . ambassadors from any of the neighbouring countries who reside permanently in Kratchie, and through whom all business is done with those various countries.[32]

It is evident then that people desiring any level of relationship with Krachi had to achieve it via representative or patronage channels. Buems

and Nsutas, although not desirous of land to settle
on and hence not attached to a Krachi division,
established a formal relationship with the Dente
Bosomfo and maintained ambassadors at Krachikrom.
Yet there is nothing particularly unusual about the
organization itself in Akan or border Akan regions.
Provincial towns in Greater Asante approached the
Asantehene via an _adamfo_ (Twi: friend; patron) or
intermediate administrator.   Incorporation   by
adoption into a clan was similarly not unusual.
The colonial anthropologist Rattray, quoting his
own diary from when he was collecting data for The
Tribes of the Ashanti Hinterland, commented:

> I am becoming more and more convinced that
> here (in the Northern Territories) a man
> acquires his clan, not because of any
> physiological process, that is, not because
> he is the son of his father, or because he
> is the son of his mother, but by a purely
> artificial process of adoption into a
> particular clan by his participation in
> clan sacrifice and "by eating clan medi-
> cine."33

The data in this chapter suggest even that
participation in clan sacrifices is merely a
formalization of a political and economic (land and
labor) process that is necessary when populations
are shifting. This process of incorporation and
representation in Krachi must surely have evolved
through trial and error and through exposure to
similar Asante practices. The process accelerated
after 1874 when Krachi became autonomous and the
Dente Bosomfo utilized the process more inten-
sively. Simultaneously, Krachi's towns, trade, and
prestige grew.   Its   military,   juridical,   and
financial services developed and hence increasingly
distant peoples requested alliance or incorporation
into the loose structure. Ramseyer in 1884 observed an aspect of this when he encountered near
Atebubu "a delegation from different Asante towns"
on their way to Kete-Krachi "to put themselves
under the fetish there as several Asante states
have already done." These towns had found they
could not do without the economic services
Kete-Krachi had to offer for their "motive was
surely to enable them to trade with Salaga and the
interior," which the Dente Bosomfo had forbidden to

any towns who remained allied with Asante after
1874 "on pain of death."[34] Numerous examples have
already been cited of individuals, slaves, and
groups of refugees who also came voluntarily to
seek the protection of Dente and other services
which Krachi could provide.

The leaders of Krachi in the 1880s probably
perceived the added strain on their capabilities
that these supplicants created and hence made the
effort (to be discussed in more detail in Chapter
5) to contact the British government on the Gold
Coast with the intent of substituting British
protection for that which Kumase had ceased to
provide in 1874. Thus they thought in terms of
extending the incorporative, patronage system
another level higher, or another concentric circle
beyond. This effort to find distant patronage with
the British failed when Krachi was put under German
control by European imperialist decisions. The
Germans' policy, for various reasons, came to be
disruptive rather than supportive of Krachi,
particularly of the Dente Bosomfo's authority.
Thus it is impossible to determine whether the
incorporative/patronage feature of Krachi's structure could have withstood the pressures of its
growing population, trade and responsibilities.

What is clear, nonetheless, is that as soon as
Krachi's importance began to decline in the late
1890s -- caused by manipulation of the Volta trade
by European policies, and the destruction of Krachi
religious prestige when the Dente Bosomfo was
executed -- the more peripherally allied groups
began to withdraw from Krachi relationships and to
establish their own autonomy or seek new patrons.
Indeed, by the 1930s the Pae, Akroso, Buem, Nsuta
and Dwaben peoples who had become affiliated in the
1880s had all removed themselves from any political
allegiance to or reliance upon Krachi. The recent
withdrawal (1973) from Krachi paramountcy of
Bagyemso, a chieftaincy which had been subject to
Krachi as early as the 1830s, and which had even
held a ritually significant position in Dente
shrine activities, is evidence of this process
continuing through to the present.

5

Asante-Krachi Relations

From Political Anonymity to Political Awareness

Asantehene Opoku Ware (reign 1720-1750) cam-
paigned to the northeast of Asante in the 1740s and
there secured for his dominion territories which
included major towns such as Yendi, Salaga, and
Atebubu. As noted earlier Basa was defeated at
this time, and from Basa the Asantehene's army
moved east to conquer Krachi where many of the
Basas had sought sanctuary. Reindorf's narrative
implies that a military encounter of great
magnitude was not necessary:

> . . . most of the fugitives [from Basa]
> fled to Karakye, seeking protection from
> Odente, the far-famed fetish of the place.
> The king dispatched his son, prince Adu
> Kwanfeni, and Konadu Anim, and the linguist
> Damang Safo of Dwaben to demand the deliv-
> ery of those refugees from Odente, who told
> the messengers, that he would never have a
> quarrel with the King, but was under him;
> the refugees must be given back. This
> brought Odente into connection with Asante,
> but chiefly with Dwaben to which province
> Karakye was attached.[1]

Both Basa and Dwaben traditions concur that Krachi
surrendered without a fight, the Dwabens even
maintaining that the Dente shrine, acting as a war
oracle, predicted that the Krachi would have no
luck if they tried to fight the powerful Dwabens.[2]

One thousand prisoners of war were paid to Dwaben to avoid bloodshed. These prisoners settled in a quarter of Dwaben and served as a guarantee that Krachi would not rebel. Because of its coopera- tion, however, the remaining Basa "refugees" were "given" to Dente.

That Krachi was placed under the control of Dwaben and not the direct control of Kumase is not surprising. Most of the territories acquired by Opoku Ware at this time were distributed among the various chiefs who had helped in these campaigns. Such chiefs included the Mamponhene and the Dwaben- hene who, next to the Asantehene, were two of the most powerful Akan chiefs, or amanhene, at that time. The Mamponhene was awarded Atebubu, Krupi (including Salaga) and Yendi, while the Dwabenhene was given Nchumuru, Basa, Krachi, and Nanumba. This somewhat fief-like distribution of conquered territory of course only strengthened the power of these already powerful chiefs. It expanded a system sometimes referred to as Asante's "sub- imperial" system, which was management of distant provinces through intermediary powers (sub-imperial powers) rather than through the center, Kumase.[3] It set up the dynamics of a situation encompassing alternative power bases, which resulted in considerable competition and jealousy between the sub-imperial powers and the center. Ultimately it led to secession.

I

Thus, probably through negotiation and surren- der rather than through war, Krachi came to be under the suzerainty of Dwaben by 1745. When discussing their past relationship with Dwaben, Krachis refer to Dwaben as their adamfo -- meaning literally "friend" in Twi, but sometimes translated explanatorially as "landlord;" the best English equivalent is perhaps "patron." The role of Dwaben as a sub-imperial power, with the Dwabenhene as adamfo, was rather strictly defined, and to Dwaben's advantage. Any Krachi matters requiring relations with the Asantehene, in other words the central government, had to be conducted through the Dwabenhene. These included legal matters, the payment of annual tribute, and delegations ac- knowledging allegiance. Similarly, at least

according to Krachi traditions, the Asantehene
could not deal with the Dente shrine without the
go-between of Dwaben:

> When Krachis want to go to Asantehene, they
> pass through Dwaben chief before they can
> see him. Asantehene sends Dwabenhene to
> Krachi Dente when Asantes want to make war
> with people [i.e. consult the shrine on
> matters of war]. Krachis go to Asantehene
> with drink [tribute and taxes] . . . but
> Krachis must go through Dwabenhene first.[4]

The years between Krachi's intial encounter
with Asante (c. 1740) and its first attempted
rebellion against Asante (1830), almost one hundred
years, are virtually blank in Krachi traditions and
Asante history offers nothing supplemental. This
was the era in which, according to even Krachi
royal traditions, there followed "many kings whose
names are not remembered."[5] Similarly in the Dente
Bosomfo office lists there is a conspicuous gap
between mention of the founders of the shrine and
mention of Dente Bosomfo Akenten (d. 1830). Such a
gap in the traditions is not surprising if one
accepts that political consciousness must have been
very weak. Krachi was subservient to Asante and
had debilitating obligations of providing annual
tributes of slaves, money and food to Dwaben and
the central government. Slave raids, if not
carried out on Krachi itself, were conducted on its
fringes in the region between Asante's far eastern
and Dahomey's far western borders, by both Asante
and Dahomey in order to meet the European demand
for slaves which peaked in this period. It is true
that the salt trade on the Volta increased greatly
in the latter eighteenth century in conjunction
with the slave trade (see Chapter 2). Indeed, it
was Krachi's role in the salt trade which resulted
in the earliest documentary reference to the place,
in Bowdich (1817). However, Asante maintained
strict supervision over the trade as well as over
political activities in the area, forcing all trade
from the coast and the northern hinterland, except
for some salt, to pass through Kumase. Thus the
salt trade was probably insufficient in the face of
Asante domination to precipitate any political
consciousness or activity.

However, in the early 1800s the increasing complexity and wealth of the northern (Salaga) trade system, the decline of the European slave trade, Asante's focus upon problems with Fante and the coast, and a consequent policy disagreement between Kumase and Dwaben, all led to a play by Dwaben for more independence. Dwaben's action, though ultimately unsuccessful, accomplished two results: it drew Krachi into political activity, and it disrupted Kumase's trade monopoly over the northeastern Volta region.

Sometime in the early nineteenth century the tribute arrangement negotiated in the 1740s between Krachi and Dwaben was altered. In a political sense, and for purposes of formal approach to the Asantehene, the adamfo relationship between Krachi and Dwaben continued until 1874; economic and moral support continued between the two until well into the 1880s; but equalization of the relationship began in the early nineteenth century when tribute to Dwaben was commuted and the descendants of the hostages from the 1745 campaign were returned to Krachi. According to traditions this occurred because the Dwabens one year tried to keep as hostage the Krachi drummers who came annually to honor the Dwabenhene (part of the 1745 settlement). Dente punished the Dwabens with thunderstorms, man-eating leopards and elephants, bleeding plantain trees, and talking yams. Finally the Dwabenhene returned all hostages, Dwabens were sent to Krachi to drum in honor of Dente, and a state sword and umbrella were awarded to Dente "as a gift of the Dwaben people."[6] This incident, however stylistically embellished, certainly represents a modification in Dwaben-Krachi relations and a symbolic political acknowledgment of Krachi.

Dwaben's reasons for admitting a more equitable relationship with Krachi (and perhaps other of Dwaben's dependencies) must be viewed in the context of its overall effort to secure trade routes for itself and to enhance its position of power vis-a-vis Kumase. In 1831 a civil war broke out between Dwaben and Kumase, the dispute being ostensibly precipitated by a case of adultery involving one of the Dwabenhene's wives.[7] Other acknowledged causes of the conflict were the general rivalry between the two regions, and Kumase's accusation that Dwaben had stolen treasury money when the Dwabens retrieved the Golden Stool

at the disastrous (for Asante) Battle of Katamanso
(1826) against the British. [8] The missionary Riis,
who was in Kumase in 1839 at the time of the
reconciliation between the two parties, provided a
more integrative interpretation. He explained that
Asante theoretically held a monopoly of trade with
the interior, which included restrictions on the
importation of guns and ammunition, the regulation
of prices, and control over who was permitted to
pass along the trade routes. Fantes, for example,
were not allowed north of Kumase, nor was Riis; and
Hausa merchants were not permitted south of Salaga.
The Gonja and Bron living in these interior regions
were similarly restricted in their movements and
actions. [9] The Governor of the Gold Coast also
believed that the peoples along the trade routes,
which would include the Krachi, being under Asante
rule, "were allowed to do nothing which could have
the effect of diverting trade from Kumase." [10]

Riis maintained that in reaction to these trade
policies Dwabenhene Kwasi Boaten had planned his
rebellion for some time, had place himself "in
close relation with these people in the interior,"
and had "drawn away from Asante" the "profitable
trade with the people of the interior." Thus he
had "prepared himself to establish himself in the
interior and as chief of that people cut off the
route to the interior to Asantes and so after a
while found his own nation." [11] Thus competition
for the control of trade and profits was the most
underlying root of the dispute between Kumase and
Dwaben.

In the end, Dwaben's bid for independent power
failed. Throughout the 1820s several "test cases"
of litigation between Dwaben and the central
government went in favor of the Asantehene. [12]
Finally, in 1831, with the Dwabenhene refusing to
abide by various court orders, Asantehene Osei Yaw
attacked Dwaben and Dwabenhene Kwasi Boaten was
forced to flee with some followers to Akyem. The
town of Dwaben was destroyed. Even in Akyem,
however, Riis claimed that Kwasi Boaten was able to
draw trade from Asante "unrestrained as before,"
using routes untravelled by Asantes, and even
trading in "flints and powders as the most sought
after and profitable articles."

Dwaben's initial and continued abuse of Kumase
trade restrictions could only have been possible
with the cooperation of Dwaben's client provinces.

At least some of these peoples saw it in their best interest to side with Dwaben on the trade issue for they were doubtless eager to break the Asante monopoly on European goods, arms and ammunition, and other potentially profitable items. Clearly the dominant groups in Krachi at this time supported Dwaben. Their traditions claim repeatedly that it was then that Asante ordered them to serve the Asantehene directly and not through Dwaben as intermediary. The Dente Bosomfo Akenten is said to have replied, "I would rather serve a pawpaw tree in Dwaben than a king in Asante."[14] Apparently the Gonja, Nchumuru and Nanumba shared Akenten's feelings. Certainly Gonja refused to send a quota of fighting men for the 1823-26 Asante campaigns in the south.

II

Krachi's and Gonja's defiance and the whole region's cooperation with Dwaben's trade policies forced Kumase finally to send a punitive expedition against these northeast provinces. The ensuing conflict is known as the Krupi war, the name being taken from the location of the first major battle (a town about six kilometers southeast of Salaga). The details of the war are still difficult to reconstruct, but it lasted several years, involved at least two and perhaps three Asante campaigns, and ranged from Krupi in the north to Pae-Akroso in the south (see Figure 5). It resulted in the death of an Asante general and a Dente Bosomfo, but in the ultimate success of the Asante army.

The Krupi War marked a coalescence of consciousness for Krachis which has persisted to the present day. Akenten and Otebrebre, the names frequently given for the first Dente Bosomfo and Krachiwura respectively, were the office holders at the time of this war. Dente Bosomfo Akenten is said to have led the military force to the Krupi and Pae battles personally.[15] Nana Bisam, the Krachi Adontenhene who led forces to Krupi likewise often heads the Adontenhene office list.[16] Specific participants and the details of their being wounded or killed in these battles are frequently remembered.[17] The Dente Kwasida oath, the most powerful oath one can swear in Krachi, originated at the time of the Pae war, arising from the death of the Dente Bosomfo (see below). Kantankofore, the major royal town of the Krachiwura division, is said to have been founded at that time as "Akenten's camp," or more exactly, "Akenten's rock" (kofore being the Krachi word for rock).[18] Probably for the first time Krachis were armed with guns and powder (perhaps provided by Dwaben) and were formed, along with Gonjas and Nchumurus (perhaps under the direction of Dwaben advisors), into organized and effective fighting forces.

Fortunately a contemporary account of the campaign in Gonja survives in the journals of the Lander brothers.   In September 1830 the Landers, travelling in western Nigeria, encountered at Busa on the Niger River a Hausa caravan which had just returned from Salaga bearing kola nuts. The leader of the merchants informed the Landers about the early part of this war and its causes. His account maintains that the Gonjas were being punished for failure to send recruits to the Asante wars of the 1820s and in this sense differs somewhat from the oral sources which emphasize refusal to accept Asante suzerainty.[19]   However, all accounts agree that the first Asante expedition was ambushed and defeated. This was in all likelihood at the Krupi battle itself where "the combined forces of the Krachis, Gonjas, Basas, Nchumurus, Pais, Akroso, Adjade and the Nawuris" sent the Asantes retreating back across the Volta.[20]   Krachi informants acknowledge however that, "we fought at Krupi and Asantes were short of gunpowder so they went back. Then we thought we had won, not knowing the Asantes were only short of gunpowder."[21]   The Landers' informant related that a second expedition was quickly equipped and dispatched by Asante and that on this occasion the Gonjas, rather than resisting, "deserted their dwellings and dispersed themselves through all parts of the adjacent countries." Since these battles were over by the time Lander's informants left Salaga for Nigeria, presumably spring 1830, the Krupi battle must be dated in the dry season of late 1829-1830.

Whether the Asante General Enuben Akyaw was in charge of the Gonja offensive is not entirely clear. However, he was certainly commander of the subsequent campaign to quell the resistance, that continued in the Krachi region, perhaps perpetuated by refugee Gonjas,. A Danish report of early 1833 referred to the Krachis "having lately been

attacked and driven towards Akwamu [south] by the
Asantes," thus dating what is known as the Pae war
somewhat later than Krupi, presumably the dry
season of 1832-1833.[22] It is conceivable that war
was incessant from 1829-1833, but the military
defeat and exile of Dwabenhene Kwasi Boaten in 1831
surely helped precipitate the Asante mopping up
operations among the Dwaben allies, including
Krachi, in 1832.

Anantahene Enuben Akyaw crossed the Volta with
the Asante army north of Krachi and turned south.
The Krachis retreated to Pae beyond the Oti River
and, in their own words, "here is what happened:"

> Asantes attacked up the Volta near Akaniem
> called Kofi Asusu, the place dried up.
> There are some rapids there which you can
> walk through during the dry season. The
> Asantes walked through the river to attack
> the Krachis. They were walking along the
> river. Fortunately an old lady who no one
> knew saw them and came to Krachikrom and
> informed the leaders that they should be
> ready, Asantes are coming to fight you.
> They are at your door. Then Krachis moved
> and crossed the river Oti and prepared,
> waiting for the Asantes.[23]

Reindorf's version adds:

> The general [Enuben] now marched to Krakye.
> Many of the people were taken prisoners;
> the rest fled across the river Oti. The
> grove and cave of Odente were plundered and
> desecrated.[24]

Apparently General Enuben moved his army on to Pae
to extinguish the Krachi resistance there, but in a
moment of carelessness, "passing the day in merri-
ment and dance," sitting in an <u>asipim</u> chair and
being fed groundnuts by his women, a Bagyemso
patrol discovered him and decapitated him -- an
onerous conclusion to any Asante military career.[25]
His head was taken to the Krachis by the Bagyemsos
and the latter honored greatly for their bravery by
later being awarded certain ritual honors in Dente
festivals.[26]

It is this slaying of the Asante General Enuben
which enables traditions to speak of the Krupi-Pae

war as if the Krachis and Gonjas had been entirely
victorious. However, Reindorf points out this was
not entirely the case:

> . . . suddenly an army of Bagyam people
> appeared and attacked the unsuspecting
> party [of Enuben]. The general and several
> influential men and people were slain on
> the spot. This forced the Asante army
> which had gone to plunder to return in
> haste and drive the Bagyams back. 3000
> captives were taken from Karakye and
> Bagyam. [27]

Colonial accounts from the 1920s and 1930s support
this interpretation also, one even stating that the
"Atabubus followed up and beat the Krachis and
regained the body of their dead leader [Enuben]."[28]
    In fact, it is most likely that the Dente
Bosomfo Akenten himself was killed in the Pae
battles of 1832-1833, for the great Dente Kwasida
litigation oath of Krachi was created at the time
of the Pae war, the oath's sanctity deriving from
Akenten having been killed on a Sunday (Kwasida in
Twi). [29] This is in perfect accord with the Akan
practice of basing oaths on extremely odious events
such that if you swear the oath and are lying,
something similarly odious may happen to you. Thus
the sacred oath of Asante, Memeneda Akromanti,
derives from the death of an Asantehene in battle
at Akromantin on a Saturday (Memeneda), his body
having never been recovered.[30] The Gonjas also
swear a lesser oath called Apae, deriving from the
serious defeat at Pae and which some sources argue
is the same oath as the Krachi Dente Kwasida,
though it would be less significant to the Gonjas
since it was a Dente Bosomfo who was killed. [31] At
any rate, the establishment of the Dente Kwasida
oath following these Krupi-Pae wars constitutes
additional evidence that they were traumatic for
the Krachis and induced a political consciousness
in Krachi not acted upon before.
    The Krachis probably attempted to take on an
Asante army because they were expecting aide from
allies -- the Gonjas and Nchumurus did help -- but
Krachi also must have received some support from
Dwaben.[32] Following Krachi's defeat at Pae,
Dwabens even attempted to perpetuate the resistance:

. . . the destruction of the Karakye and
Bagyam people was reported to Boaten, and
he forthwith sent a large supply of ammunition by a captain of Atipini to Karakye
to support them against the Asantes. But
being weakened by the late battles, the
Karakyes did not venture to take the field
against their enemy. [33]

Dwaben was finally reconciled with Kumase in
1839-1840. The new Asantehene Kwaku Dua I negotiated with Dwabenhene Kwasi Boaten and sent the
latter large gifts of money, made judicial conces-
sions to the exiles, and ordered the execution of
several important Asante chiefs who had offended
the Dwabenhene, in order to persuade him and his
followers to return to Asante in peace. [34] It is
quite likely that the restoration of some of
Dwaben's dependencies, including Krachi, was one of
the terms of this reconciliation. Krachiwura Okuju
Dente, in his 1920 statement to British colonial
officers, said that the Dwaben/Krachi relationship
was re-established not long after the Krupi-Pae
War. The specifics of tribute were established
again (six sheep, six loads each of millet and
groundnuts, hippo and bush-cow hides, and calabashes)[35] and the fealty gift of three slaves,
three sheep and £2 worth of cowries was remembered,
if not practiced, even in German times. [36] Thus
Dwaben retained Krachi as a dependency through at
least the first three-quarters of the nineteenth
century, until 1875 when Dwaben was driven permanently from the Asante union.

                         III

In the years following the Pae war, Asante
control (whether emanating from Dwaben or Kumase)
persisted over Krachi and the Volta trade route.
Krachi seems to have remained docile throughout
most of this period, and was acquiescent even
through the Ewe war of 1869-1871 -- a war which
came very close to Krachi territory. The Ewe of
Krepe had rebelled in 1868 against their Asante
sub-imperial power, the Akwamu, and an Asante army
under the General Gyasewahene Adu Bofo was sent to
quell the outbreak. Despite their sympathy with
the Ewe, [37] the Krachis did not participate in the

rebellion. Rather, when the disturbances spread to the Buem, north of Krepe, and reinforcements under the Asante Akuroponhene Kwame Agyepon were sent to control them, the Asante army crossed the Volta at Krachi and marched south without a whisper of any Krachi resistance, and possibly with Krachi assistance.[38]

Although there may have been other factors involved, the Ewe war definitely derived from Asante's desire to maintain control over the Volta trade. By the late 1860s this control was being threatened not by Dwaben subterfuge, as in the past, but by British penetration and by defiant British clients from Accra and Ada. In 1868 the British steamer Eyo successfully traversed the Ada bar (the sandbar created at the mouth of the Volta, previously impassable for all but canoes) thereby opening the Volta to steamer traffic. The implications of this did not go unnoticed to the Asante whose representative to the British in Cape Coast expressed repeated concern about it (see p. 29). As British presence in the Volta mouth region increased, the British clients became more and more confident, defying traditional Asante authorities like the Akwamu and Anlo, "really Ashanti provinces," from which the Asantehene imported large quantities of powder, lead and salt.[39] Indications of the increasing importance and tension that was growing over the Volta trade in the 1860s were the armed garrison of thirty men under the Asante captain stationed on Duffo Island in the Volta (about fifty miles from the mouth and fifty miles south of Akwamu), and the increasing number of internecine squabbles between the Anlo and Ada over which the British presided. The Ewe war indicates a final awareness on Asante's part of its slipping influence in the area, of the importance of re-establishing that influence, and of a conscious policy decision to accomplish this by war if necessary.[40]

The growing significance of the Volta trade thus made Krachi's acquiesence an important factor in Asante's economic policies and prosperity. Krachi cooperated with these policies throughout the relatively peaceful years of Asantehene Kwaku Dua I (reign 1834-1867) and into the more turbulent years of Asantehene Kofi Kakari (1867-1874). But its cooperation was apparently only via its relationship with Dwaben, for in 1874-1875, when Dwaben

began again to waver in its loyalty to Kumase and
the Asante state, Krachi unhesitatingly sided with
Dwaben.

In 1874 Sir Garnet Wolseley occupied and burned
Kumase in a forty-eight hour raid on that town, and
within months Dwaben had declared its independence
from Asante and began separate peace negotiations
with the British. Dwaben had actually fought with
Asante against Wolseley's invasion and a group of
Dwabens was with the Asante peace embassy at Cape
Coast in July 1874 when the news arrived that
Krachi had "thrown off" its allegiance to Asante.
This left the Dwaben delegation in no doubt as to
what was happening at home. They "rose up" and
said to their leader, "if the people of Krakie have
done so [thrown off allegiance to Kumase] the
people of Juabin have done so; speak to the Governor that we may go back to Juabin."[41]

Indeed, the vehemence and coordination with
which the Bron, Krachi, Gonja, and Nchumuru groups,
simultaneously with Dwaben, threw off the symbols
and restrictions of Kumase control gives strong
support to the contention that Dwabenhene Asafo
Agyei had continued the policies of his predecessor
Dwabenhene Kwasi Boaten, cultivating alliances with
the peoples along the Volta between Dwaben and
Salaga at the expense of Kumase. A traveller on
this route in 1877 wrote:

> They are so faithfully attached to the
> Dwaben King, to whom they have sworn an
> oath of allegiance, and cherish such a
> bitter hatred against the Kumases, whose
> yoke they have thrown off their necks, that
> any messenger coming from Kumase to them is
> under pain of death and any one from
> themselves who is convicted of smuggling
> powder into any of the Kumase territories
> is liable of meeting the same fate . . . It
> is all through the intrigues of this Dwaben
> King with the priest and elders of Krakye
> whom he has used as his right hand in this
> revolt that those nations were brought to
> one mind.[42]

Bonnat, meeting Dwaben refugees in Krachi in 1876,
referred to them as "these rogues who had massacred
thousands of Ashantis two years earlier," and
labelled the Dente Bosomfo "this rogue of a fetish

priest" who was "the greatest persecutor of the
Ashantis and it is by his orders that they were
massacred in the interior."[43]   Gouldsbury also was
informed that Dwaben had instigated the peoples on
the northeastern trade route to rebellion.[44]

The revolts took the form of killing Asante
officials or settlers who were living in these
northeastern regions.   The traveller Opoku maintained that in several towns, and "especially at
Salaga", "many hundreds of Kumases, who resided
there and acted as consuls, weavers, traders, etc.
etc. were all executed in one day."[45]   At Bagyemso
in 1884 he saw "the skulls and bones of the murdered men [that] were still partly to be seen
strewn in the waste or on the steppes where the
corpses had become booty for jackals."[46]   A decree
was issued by Dwabenhene Asafo Agyei and the Dente
Bosomfo that any Nchumuru caught smuggling powder
to Asante was to be executed.[47]   The Kwawu Dukoman,
who were Asante settlers along the Oti River and
who held jurisdiction over the Buem, were attacked
and "annihilated" by the Buem.[48]   In general
Asantes were prevented from trading at Salaga.

                              IV

Thus the rebellions from Buem to Salaga along
the Volta in 1874 and the simultaneous attempt by
Dwaben to make a separate peace with the British
affected Kumase seriously.   Initially Asante made
some efforts to persuade Krachi (and presumably
other groups) to place itself once again under
Asante.   Messengers were sent from the Asantehene
to bring "his refractory vassals to their senses,"
but these and the second round of Asante messengers
were all killed.   "Since then no Ashanti messengers
have been sent to Kratshie."[49]

Kumase subsequently attempted an alternate
approach to deal with the northeastern provinces.
The French trader Bonnat, who had been captured in
the Ewe war by Asante and held prisoner in Kumase
with the missionaries Ramseyer and Kuhne from 1869
to 1873, returned to Kumase in 1875 with grandiose
plans for tapping the interior trade.   He had been
impressed with the commercial importance of Salaga
while residing in Kumase and, after much delibera-
tion and with many conditions, the Asantehene and
his advisors decided to permit Bonnat to travel to

Salaga. A concession was signed on 31 July 1875 by
the Kumase Council and Bonnat. It gave him a six
year monopoly on the import-export commerce of the
Volta River from ten miles south of Akroso north to
Yegi. It also gave him "jurisdiction" of this
region, as governor and representative of the
Asantehene "to extend our relations" and "our
commerce." Bonnat was to pay three per cent on all
goods he imported and collect a five per cent sales
tax in the region in the name of the Asantehene,
proceeds from both of these being sent to Kumase.[50]

Bonnat set out for Salaga by land from Kumase
through Mampon and Atebubu, intending to travel
down the Volta from Salaga. At Atebubu however he
and his Asante guides and carriers were arrested by
the Atebubuhene, and a large contingent of Dwabens
were quickly sent to Atebubu to help with the
arrest. Dwaben had by this time made a separate
peace with the British and was behaving towards
Kumase most obstructively, though a military clash
had not yet occurred. The Asantes with Bonnat were
killed in Atebubu and Bonnat was taken to Dwaben,
though only after protest from the Atebubuhene who
wished to await orders from the Dente Bosomfo at
Krachi. Bonnat himself requested that he be taken
to Krachi, reasoning that from there he could
proceed down the Volta and salvage at least some of
his plans. However, the Dwabens refused. Bonnat
was held prisoner in Dwaben two weeks and then
returned to Cape Coast, and the roads to the north
remained closed to him.[51] His failure to reach
Salaga shattered his trading monopoly plans and the
Asantehene's plans for re-establishing some authority in the region via a European intermediary.

Thus the arrest of Bonnat, an official Asante
representative, and the murder of his Asante aides,
was viewed by the Asantehene as the final act of
insubordination and obstruction that could be
tolerated of Dwaben by Kumase. A council was
called and all the "great chiefs" including the
Bekwaehene, Mamponhene, Nkoransahene, Kokofuhene,
and Agonahene, "agreed with one voice . . . The
only remedy which will save this country and bring
it progress in commerce, and to stop disturbances,
is the removal of that one man, Asafu Agai, and we
have determined to do it."[52] Two weeks later in
October 1875 an Asante force was despatched,
Dwabenhene Asafo Agyei was defeated, and he and his
people once again went into exile in Akyem, now

part of the British Protectorate, settling at
Koforidua.

Shortly thereafter Special Commissioner Gouldsbury spoke to Asafo Agyei in an effort to determine
why the latter had arrested Bonnat and killed his
Asante guides. Asafo Agyei maintained it was
simply because Bonnat "was a partisan of the
Ashantees and wanted to bring Juabin again under
the Ashantee yoke." However at the next village
two Dwaben guides told Gouldsbury a different
story:

> . . . that the great Fetish at Keratchie
> had sent word to King Asafojay, directing
> him to stop M. Bonnat and to kill some of
> the Ashantees who accompanied him, and that
> the King sent messengers to the Chief of
> Attobo. . . as the Fetish at Keratchie had
> given orders to that effect. That in
> obedience to these orders of their fetish,
> the Attobo people stopped M. Bonnat and
> killed ten of the Ashantees who were with
> him.[53]

Although probably not entirely balanced in attrib-
uting responsibility, this account indicates that
at least some Dwabens were beginning to perceive
the Dente Bosomfo as a power equaly to the Dwabenhene in the intensifying crisis with Asante. In
early 1882 when the British representative Lonsdale
and his assistant were collecting background
information on this northeastern secession from
Asante, they were told also by participants that
"the Djuabins readily acquiesced" with Krachi's
"wish to rebel against Asante," thus perpetuating
the belief that Krachi and the Dente Bosomfo had
dominated Dwabenhene Asafo Agyai in many policy
decisions at this time.[54]

Bonnat, however, was not to be discouraged by
the Atebubu arrest and, emboldened by Dwaben's
defeat, planned to attempt Salaga once again, this
time by going up the Volta. He accompanied a
trading party led by Robert Bannerman, a nephew of
the destooled Asantehene Kofi Kakari. Bannerman's
party was even "more imposing" than Bonnat's five
canoes, twenty-seven men, six needle-guns, six
flintlocks, five revolvers, two pistols, and two
sabres.[55] As representative of the Kumase government and having an Asante companion, Bonnat was at

once unpopular with the Volta peoples and yet
respected and obeyed.

Initially all went well, as Bonnat everywhere
"laid bare the purpose of my visit, all of peace
and of trade."[56] As both a European and an Asante
official Bonnat was grudgingly accepted by the
inhabitants of the territories through which he
passed, but as he progressed further north his
Akwamu laborers were increasingly viewed as Asante
allies and greatly resented. At Wusuta the people
"trembled with rage" at the sight of them, and only
Bonnat's authority and several bottles of gin
prevented difficulties.[57] Indeed, from the middle
Volta region on everyone seemed to be in constant
concern over what was in their minds an inevitable
Asante reprisal. Bonnat encountered at Nkami four
messengers from Krachi en route to Sokode where
they hoped to obtain powder and guns to defend
themselves against the Asantes. Just south of
Krachi a simple village chief "lets out the fear of
his tribe for the Achantis, of whom they have
killed a great number and from whom they expect
vengeance."[58]

Bonnat fancied that he might be able to serve
as a mediator and thereby "perhaps, with the grace
of God, halt the flow of blood."[59] Nevertheless,
he was determined not to be frustrated in achieving
his original goal, as had happened at Atebubu, and
he was thus prepared with guns, body guard, the
security of Bannerman and his followers, and both
English and French flags. Indeed, Krachi messengers were sent to Bannerman to ask the meaning of
"all these flags with so much red in them." Bonnat
recorded that Bannerman replied, "these flags were
not at all a sign of war, but that in any case we
were ready for any eventuality. And the pile of
arms which gleamed in the center of the camp added
weight to his words."[60]

Four days of negotiation and numerous "dashes"
were required before Bonnat and Bannerman were
permitted to pass through Krachi to Salaga. Bonnat
did observe Dwaben elders at Krachi counseling the
Dente Bosomfo and maintained that they were the
same chiefs he had met at Atebubu: "They judge
seeing my following that my position has indeed
changed since before." However none of Bonnat's
Akwamu or Ewe followers was permitted beyond
Krachi, and for one who despised the "rogue of a
fetish priest," Bonnat took this injunction quite

seriously, reporting to the authorities some Ewe
traders who attempted to infiltrate his group.[61]
It is difficult to establish precisely the
extent to which Bonnat was viewed by the Krachis as
an Asante official. Dwaben had been attacked by
Kumase partly in retaliation for blocking Bonnat's
(hence Asante's) access to the Salaga market and
routes to the north. In this context, it is
significant that Bonnat was finally permitted to
pass through Krachi. However, there is no evidence
indicating that Bonnat flaunted the concession he
had received from the Asantehene for the governor-
ship of the region in an attempt to coerce the
Krachis into permitting him transit. It is purely
speculative as to whether Bonnat and the Krachis
believed the former's concession to be more of an
asset or a drawback with regard to his achieving
his aim of trading to Salaga through Krachi.
Bonnat's experiences do indicate, however, that
the Krachis must have perceived a change in their
position from 1875 to 1876. Having rebelled
against Kumase with both violence and diplomatic
insults, apparently encouraged and aided by their
longstanding ally Dwaben, they were now confronted
with the possibility of reprisals. Dwaben had
recently been defeated and dispersed, and the
British, whose actions had originally precipitated
the rebellions with their 1874 defeat of Kumase,
now not only failed to follow up their victory with
plenary conquest and administration, but failed to
come to the aid of the secessionist Dwabens who had
actually made a separate peace with the British.
Nevertheless the presence of Dwaben advisors in
Krachi indicates that the Krachis were still
anticipating Dwaben support, perhaps from Dwabenhene Asafo Agyei's base in exile, in the event of
an Asante attack.
Moreover, within two weeks of Bonnat's passage
through Krachikrom, the Krachis received an encouragement that would herald a new surge of security
and prosperity. This was in the person of V.S.
Gouldsbury who arrived in Krachi, having been sent
as Special Commissioner by the British through
Asante to Salaga and down the Volta (exactly the
route which Bonnat had originally intended to
follow) for the express purpose of "opening up the
roads and trade between the former place [Salaga]
and the Coast."[62] Gouldsbury's success at making
the journey without Asante cooperation or any

overtones of Asante association was significant.
Indeed the Asante were "grieved very much" with
Gouldsbury for "travelling up in their country with
soldiers" without informing them of the object of
his mission.[63] Gouldsbury represented only the
British, and his journey marked the initiation of a
British policy claiming the benefits of, though not
the responsibility for, the interior trade. Most
importantly it served to confirm Asante's forfei-
ture of absolute control over the northeastern
territories.

6

The Bron Confederation
Religion and the Politics of State-Building

Throughout the preceding chapter the role of
the Dente Bosomfo in the rebellion against Asante
appeared to be supplemental. The priest, however,
came to take an extremely prominent leadership role
following the open declaration of independence of
the trans-Volta provinces and Dwaben's military
defeat at the hands of Asante in 1875. He began to
assert political authority not only over the Krachi
people, but over a whole defense alliance against
Asante known as the Bron Confederation. The 1880s
and early 1890s were the zenith of the Dente
Bosomfo's political power in both external and
internal affairs. This chapter analyses the
logical progression of events that occurred between
Krachi and Asante in this era and hence focuses on
external relationships, while the following chapter
will examine the Dente Bosomfo's internal power.

I

As described previously, V.S. Gouldsbury was
sent by the British government in the dry season of
1875-1876 to travel through Kumase, Atebubu, and
Salaga, then south down the Volta through Krachikrom in order to open up the Volta trade route.
The King of Salaga agreed with Gouldsbury that this
needed to be done, for as the King explained it,
Salaga's importance as a market place depended on
the kola trade which had been completely disrupted

since the 1874 war. The road from Asante through
Atebubu had been closed to Asantes, who controlled
the source of the kola, and the Volta route had
apparently never been used for kola, probably
because it was the longer route and because Asante
had never permitted its use. The Salaga Chief
assured Gouldsbury however that "rather than have
the Ashantees back again in my country to rule it
as they did formerly I and my people would sooner
that Saharah [Salaga] should cease to have any
trade at all."[1] Gouldsbury assured the chief that
the British had no intention of encouraging Asante
rule but intended to encourage expanding trade,
open roads, and a free Volta between Salaga and the
coast. The Salaga chief replied:

> I and my people would be glad to hear the
> road open to the Coast and to trade with
> your people, and if our fetish Dentie
> allows free passage through Crackey we
> shall take advantage of such concession.[2]

Gouldsbury, already aware "that the people of
Saharah were under the fetish of Crackey, and that
they were completely subject and obedient to the
mandates of that oracle and that it was principally
this fetish of Crackey that closed the roads
between Saharah and the Coast," set off to Krachikrom where he arrived 6 February 1876, about
fifteen days after Bonnat had passed through going
north (they had crossed at Salaga). In Krachikrom
Gouldsbury met with the authorities and he claimed
that the Dente Bosomfo (most likely Kwasi
Mpajelente at this time) then promised to do
"whatever I told him, and to say whatever I wished." Gouldsbury rather smugly claimed that,

> the means I adopted to propitiate the
> oracle and its priest were not those
> usually in vogue on the West Coast of
> Africa. Suffice it is to say however that
> the priest became pliable under my line of
> argument and the result was that Crackey
> for the first time was opened up for trade,
> so that either by land or by river the
> passage was now open and free.[3]

It was not entirely true that Krachi was open for
trade "for the first time," as we have already seen

that Bonnat had been allowed through, and the salt
trade through Krachi, trickle that it might have
been, dated back at least three quarters of a
century. Nevertheless, Gouldsbury probalby did get
across the point that, unlike the Asantes who had
preferred controlled and monitored trade, the
British wanted free trade in the complete nineteenth century sense of the phrase.

Pleased with his success, Gouldsbury returned
to Salaga where his announcement concerning open
trade at Krachikrom was received with "a general
expression of satisfaction and congratulation." He
then travelled to Yendi where the local officials
"expressed themselves as much pleased with what I
had done, and said that it would do great good to
their country."4

On the 8th of March Gouldsbury was again in
Krachikrom en route to Accra and on this occasion
he signed an official treaty with the Krachi
leaders in which they swore "by our great fetish
'Dentie'" to offer "no impediment" to the passage
of free trade and traders through Krachi and to use
"zealous efforts to maintain the roads" in a safe
condition. They signed this because, according to
the treaty, it was

> . . . our earnest desire to cultivate
> friendly relations and intercourse with the
> subjects and allies of Her Majesty Queen
> Victoria, and to encourage and foster free
> trade between the interior and Her
> Majesty's possessions on the coast . . .5

Regardless of how Gouldsbury and the British
Governor construed this piece of paper -- perhaps
only as an economic pact with no further implications -- the Krachis must surely have viewed the
Special Commissioner (Gouldsbury's title) and the
treaty as indications of British recognition and
support in a political as well as an economic
sense. If not the treaty itself, the opening and
closing of roads was, as with borders today, a
highly political issue. It was one of the major
factors in wars, rebellions, and peace settlements
between conqueror and conquered in West Africa,
usually one's nationality or ethnicity determining
whether one was permitted to cross or not.

It is not surprising therefore that in early
1877 the missionary Opoku, travelling through

Krachi, encountered hints and allegations of British complicity in the revolt against Asante of 1874-1875. Dwaben's separate peace with the British, and Dwaben leadership in the rebellion are evident. It is more difficult to establish whether the British-employed agitators played a role in the 1874-1875 acts of violence, or if the statements recorded by Opoku in 1877 stemmed entirely from Gouldsbury's journey. Opoku was told that the Dente Bosomfo claimed that it was Dente's "cooperation with the Queen England" which "brought about this wonderful deliverance of these nations from the yoke of the formidable foe" (Asante). Further, he was told that Dente and the Queen of England had "contrived together" to deliver the whole Asante kingdom into the hands of Dwabenhene Asafo Agyei. Opoku was most shocked by the metaphysical proposition current among the northeastern provinces that Dente and the Queen were so "uniformly conformed together" in their persons that only Dente and the Queen knew which was which (or who was who). Later Opoku was stopped at Bagyemso to have his bags searched for powder -- there had been a spate of powder smuggling to Asante and the Chief of Bagyemso had been ordered by the Dente Bosomfo to examine every box and bag passing through. Opoku was informed that Dente Bosomfo received these orders through Dwabenhene Asafo Agyei who had received his orders through the Colonial government! 6

Certainly if not before, then following Gouldsbury's visit to the interior, friendly relations with the British were considered by the Krachis and northeastern provinces, including the Dwaben refugees who had settled in Krachi, to be important to cultivate. Thus Opoku, when first setting out on his journey, met an embassy to Accra from the interior led by "a son" of Asafo Agyei consisting of "representatives of the different interior towns who have been allied to Asafo Agyei," including Krachi. They were carrying gifts of ivory and ostrich plume to the British Governor, an act referred to in Twi as me ko to aban mu ("I go to supplicate at the fort" -- or on the government) and long considered a token of allegiance. 7 Early Krachi traditions were clear on this issue:

Besemuna [Krachiwura in the 1870s] sent a present of ivory to the English Government

at Accra. After Besemuna's death, he lived
long, and Kwaku Badumeja succeeded him; the
brother Badumeja decided to carry on in the
foot steps of his brother and sent a
present of ivory to the English Government,
Accra . . . He said, "my elder brother put
himself under the British. I have done the
same."[8]

Thus by 1876 or 1877 it was clear that Asante's
attempt, via Bonnat, to retrieve the northeastern
provinces for trade and control had been finessed
by the British. Until Gouldsbury's arrival, the
people along the east bank of the Volta were in
constant fear of an Asante reprisal for their
rebellion, and "every day there were rumours of the
Ashantees coming."[9]   Following   Gouldsbury's
successful negotiations, the Asante undertook their
own outflanking measures and established a new kola
market at Kintampo which by 1888 was reportedly
prospering and more significant for kola than
Salaga.[10]   As for Bonnat, he was dismissed from
service by his European employer de Cardi for
breach of contract, and although he continued to
publish great plans for expanding trade "at the
eastern frontier of Ashanti," he never returned to
the Volta. It is possible he was "dissuaded" by
the British Colonial Government, for he later
turned up with a Government gold mine concession in
the Gold Coast Colony.[11]
Gouldsbury's journey must then be considered a
success in terms of its opening trade for the
British. One month after Bonnat and Gouldsbury
passed through Krachikrom, the English trader
Dobson encountered none of the difficulties experi-
enced by his precursors there, "meeting with no
trouble from the natives other than their usual
delay of 'ready tommorow' which took a long time to
come."[12] The Volta route prospered and became
exceedingly important for European trade goods,
salt, slaves, shea butter, cattle, leather goods,
and palm oil.[13] Control of the route was no longer
so strict at any point, and Hausas, the primary
medium in the kola trade from Salaga to Nigeria,
who previously had not been permitted to trade
extensively south of Salaga, now began to ply the
land route which paralleled the Volta. By 1877
three hundred "northern traders" had visited Accra
via the Volta route[14] and by the 1880s permanent

Hausa trading communities were established at Krachi (Kete), Kpandu, Kpong and Accra.

Asante made one last attempt to control the Volta trade. In 1879-1880, when Asante was recovering much of its internal cohesion under the policies of Asantehene Mensa Bonsu, groups of Asante-sympathizing Hausas and northerners were organized into police regiments (modelled on the effective British Gold Coast Hausa Constabulary), and some were sent to the Volta between Kpong and Akroso to collect tolls on the trade. Governor Ussher wrote in alarm:

> This border country is the true destination of the bands of Houssa deserters who were . . . formed into two regiments by the King of Ashantee. These men hang about, and rob and murder travellers between Salaga and Pong, and lay embargos, with the aid of native petty chiefs, upon all goods and produce passing to and fro. This is a serious matter, as it is most desirable that the great road through Salaga into the heart of Central Africa should be rendered safe. [15]

The Asante Hausa police on the Volta were a short-lived phenomenon, however. British pressure on Kumase, internal problems in Asante, British Constabulary forces sent to halt the "robbing" on the Volta, and the success of the Kintampo market as an alternative for Asante, were all factors which combined effectively to bring an end to this late Asante attempt to control the Volta route. British plans for securing the route and circumventing Asante power, and hence striking a blow at Asante with a minimum of military expenditure -- proposed as far back as the time of Bowdich -- therefore became a reality.

Asante's only alternative was to re-conquer the northeastern provinces with military force. Asante had suffered considerable internal dissension following Wolseley's brief occupation of Kumase in early 1874. Events and attitudes in Asante during that time have already been examined in great detail by others. [16] Of particular relevance here, however, is that on 21 October 1874 Asantehene Kofi Kakari abdicated under pressure from the court, and was replaced by his brother Mensa Bonsu who

initiated a vigorous policy of recovering the allegiance of wavering regions, chiefly through diplomatic means, though by force if necessary.

As already mentioned in October-November 1875
the recalcitrant Dwabens were attacked and driven
into the Gold Coast Colony, but many also fled to
Krachi. The Dwabens did have support from some
Asantes, specifically factions in Nsuta, Effiduase,
Asokore, and Kwawu.[17] Among these peoples those
who were willing to re-affirm their allegiance to
Kumase as the central authority following Dwaben's
defeat, were permitted to remain in Asante; but
large numbers of secession-minded Nsutas also
sought sanctuary in Krachi, including the "sister"
of Nsutahene Kofi Asianowa (probably Queen Mother
Gyama Poku).[18] The Nsutahene was not so fortunate.
He went to Kumase to submit to Asantehene Mensa
Bonsu and was kept there, presumably to be watched,
until his (Asianowa's) death in 1878.[19] Oral
sources today recall well the Nsuta immigrants to
Krachi and even credit the Nsutas with inspiring
the name of the strangers' town of Kete, which came
into existence between 1876 and 1877 next to
Krachikrom. The Nsutas were said always to be
performing an Akan dance called "kete", and so the
place where they were settled came to be called
this.[20]

II

With the defeat of Dwaben then, Krachi quickly
came to be recognized as the leading member of the
newly forming alliance of northeastern peoples.
The alliance was stimulated by fear of Asante
reconquest, thought to be possible at any time, and
hence the need for some sort of organized, mutual
defense was perceived. By 1884, European accounts
referred to the allies of Krachi as the Krachi or
Bron "Confederation" -- Bron being a term used
widely and loosely for non-forest dwelling Akan.[21]
Actually, as early as 1875 Bonnat had commented on
the authority of the Dente Bosomfo over other
regions, stating that "Atebabo and all the north .
. . obey the fetish priest of Crakey." Opoku
referred to Krachi as "Odente of the Nations" in
1877, and the observer Ferguson, writing in 1893,
also claimed that the alliance dated back to 1874:

When however the British forces entered
Kumase in 1874 . . . Atebubu with the
members of the Bron tribes, except
Nkoranza, threw off their allegiance to the
King of Kumase and formed a Confederation
with the priest of the Fetish Dente of
Kraki at the head.[22]

The British Captain Lonsdale writing in 1882
maintained that the alliance was formally sworn in
1881:

Not very long ago, as near as I could
arrive at the time about May 1881, a great
oath was sworn and a defensive alliance
entered into between the heads of the
people of Gwandjiowa, Kratshie, and Brunfo
generally, Buem, Insutah, and Kwau, to
protect themselves against any attack from
the Ashantis.[23]

This oath of May 1881 could well have been a
reaffirmation of the alliance in face of renewed
strength and belligerent threats from Kumase under
Asantehene Mensa Bonsu, who had recently restored
Asante to much of its previous prosperity. In 1884
one finds reference again to more Nsutas and
Mampons renewing their oath or swearing anew to the
alliance:

Here [crossing the Sene River at Nkubem] we
met a delegation from different Asante
towns, particularly Mampon and Nsuta, as
well as from Asante-Akem, on their way to
Krakye to put themselves under the fetish
there as several Asante states have already
done.[24]

The Bron Confederation appears, then, not as a
static allianace but as one constantly changing,
sometimes weakening when the need for it was less
apparent, ofttimes expanding in scale and reviving
in visibility.
The oath that bound the alliance together was
certainly based on the Dente shrine. There is no
record of the exact words sworn, but it was probably the Dente Kwasida oath used in this case for
allegiance/loyalty rather than for litigation.
According to Rattray, oaths of allegiance

restricted the swearers from making war at will
with each other, and from the right of inflicting
capital punishment in certain cases, required them
to appear before their superior on call, and gave
their subjects the right of legal appeal to the
superior in custody of the oath (in this case the
Dente Bosomfo as representative of the Dente
shrine). In order to reinforce spiritual nemesis,
heavy fines and even execution could be imposed on
persons found guilty of invoking an oath falsely or
of breaking an oath of allegiance. [25]
     All the above elements are found in the evolv-
ing structure of the Bron Confederation. In the
1870s the Dente Bosomfo could order the execution
of smugglers throughout the Confederation, and
summon members for consultation. By the 1890s the
Dente Bosomfo could order his allies to produce
armed forces for mobilization against Asante (see
below). In 1891 he even threatened war against the
member Buems, but ultimately only fined them, for
attacking neighbouring Domaben without his approval. [26] Oral data confirms that the Dente Oath could
be sworn in a legal dispute in an allied town like
Atebubu and the case would be forwarded to Kete-
Krachi. By the 1890s the Dente Bosomfo clearly
expected much litigation to be conducted by Bron
allies through use of the Dente oath with court
fees and fines forwarded to himself.[27] Thus the
Bron Confederation was bound by an oath based on
the Dente shrine and the ultimate sanction or
retribution for a member betraying the alliance was
the religious wrath of the god Dente, but this
might be augmented by any physical or financial
force that could be brought to bear by the Dente
Bosomfo on the wavering member.
     The Confederation did maintain a certain amount
of representative character, as confederations and
defense alliances often try to do:

> I [Lonsdale] found here [in Krachi] what I
> had not met with at any other place on my
> journey, that is, ambassadors from any of
> the neighbouring countries who reside
> permanently in Kratchie, and through whom
> all business is done with those various
> countries. I was received by the Chief
> Priest of Dente, the Chief of Kratchie, the
> representatives of the chiefs of all the

surrounding towns, the Insutahs and the
Buem representatives. [28]

Nevertheless, all commentators from Bonnat in 1875
to Ferguson in 1894 considered the Dente Priest in
Krachi to be in a position to issue orders concerning trade, taxation, and political arrests and
executions to his various allies, including Atebubu, Salaga, Buem and even Dwaben. These sources
may have been incorrect in assessing the Dente
Bosomfo's ability to enforce these orders, but
there is no doubt that the idea of Dente Bosomfo's
power over allies and Asante dissidents was widely
circulating at the time. Even Lonsdale, when
frustrated that the Atebubuhene hesitated to make a
trade agreement without consultation, admitted that
all the Bron chiefs were "under the Fetish Denty at
Kratshie, that is under the Chief Priest of Dente,"
and that "before taking any step even of minor
importance the Brumfo invariably consult the Fetish
Dente." [29] Ramseyer went even further, commenting
in 1884 that the Dente Bosomfo threatened to become
a "second Asante Despot." [30]

Aside from being a mutual defense alliance, the
Confederation manifested itself most obviously by
providing a place of refuge for dissidents from
Asante. Dwabens, Nsutas, and Brons took up residence in and near Kete-Krachi in large numbers.
Bron peoples from east of Atebubu towards the Volta
vacated their villages after 1874 and moved towards
Kete-Krachi in fear of Asante reprisals. [31] Nsutas
were probably the largest contingent of dissidents;
they lived in their own quarter in Kete-Krachi, and
their numbers included important persons like the
sister of Nsutahene Kofi Asianowa, and an Nsuta
"Prince" who had "run away from Ashanti." In the
1880s the "Princess Abna Epuo," a Queen Mother of
Nsuta (probably Abena Siabura II), was noted as
being the head of the Nsutas in Kete-Krachi. After
1887, following armed conflict in Asante proper,
the Mamponhene Owusu Sekyere II and Nsutahene Kwaku
Dente also took refuge in the Confederation, just
outside Atebubu. [32] Many peoples, such as
Nchumurus, Gonjas, and Buems, had no need to flee
their lands for refuge from Asante since Krachi
separated them geographically from Asante; but they
still feared Asante reprisals enough to join in the
mutual defense alliance.

The refugees and dissidents in Krachi in the 1870s and 1880s contributed greatly to Krachi's image as a center of opposition to Asante and added to the Dente Bosomfo's political power and to his independent economic base. In return for protection, the emigrés contributed slaves and indentured pawns for the Dente Bosomfo's expanding agricultural base, which was now producing a surplus for the thriving Kete-Krachi market (see Chapter 2). They also gave tribute and some recognition of personal dependence, if not direct political loyalty. Some of the more important fugitives may have been hostages, or seem to have been treated that way occasionally, such as when Kumase would try to negotiate for their return (see below). Safe refuge and arable land were probably the major benefits the Confederation was able to provide for allies fleeing from Asante.

The Dente Bosomfo also gained control of significant aspects of trade and commerce. With the successful independence of the peoples along the Volta and in the northeast, the Accra-Salaga route developed rapidly, as already noted. The Dente Bosomfo could now tax and control the increasing amounts of foodstuffs, northern trade goods, and European manufactures, including arms and ammunitions, available in the Krachi market. An unambitious Dente Bosomfo might have levied some taxes on the traders and left them to organize their own market place. In about 1877, however, a new Dente Bosomfo, Kwasi Gyantrubi, took office, and his strong personality and ambition fortuitously meshed with the political and economic opportunities of the next few years. Locally he tried to tax excessively, regulate stringently, and extract slaves from the caravans using the Kete-Krachi market. Surely, however, the lucrative trade base, the strategic location of Kete-Krachi, and Gyantrubi's aggressive personality complemented the Dente shrine's religious power and prestige. Religious legitimacy thus strengthened his leadership and further ensured the success of the Confederation.

As mentioned previously, the Dente Bosomfo in 1875 organized an arms embargo on Asante that was in effect for at least several years. Opoku's experience over powder smuggling indicates that it was a capital offense in the Confederation, by order of the Dente Bosomfo. In 1893 the Dente

Bosomfo again closed the roads to Asante from
Atebubu and Bron, even preventing messages to the
coast from those whom he wished to obstruct, in
order to "prevent surprise attack" as well as arms
smuggling. [33] In the intervening period, although
an arms embargo is not specifically mentioned, the
records indicate that the Dente Bosomfo was very
much in control of the trade routes through the
Confederation which affected Asante. Ramseyer
claimed that one of the major motivations for many
of the Mampon and Nsutas "putting themselves under
the fetish" Dente was to "enable them to trade with
Salaga and the interior which had been forbidden
[by Dente Bosomfo] to all towns remaining under
Kumase since 1874 on pain of death."[34]

On the other hand, the evidence also indicates
that the Dente Bosomfo's claims for taxes and
tribute on lesser members of the Confederation
reached levels of excess similar to those he was
being accused of in Kete-Krachi itself. Perregaux
noted that the Dente Bosomfo claimed ivory tusks
and one leg of a hunter's kill from the Afram
Plains (west of the Volta) and that this "rapacity"
of the Priest, along with the Asante wars, caused
much of the area to be uninhabited. [35]

The Dente Bosomfo planned mobilization of armed
support for his allies at least twice (Nsuta-Mampon
crisis, 1888; Nkoransa crisis, 1892). This will be
examined in more detail below but does confirm the
significance of the Bron Confederation as a defensive alliance. At times the Confederation was more
than defensive, however, for Kete-Krachi often
served its allies as a place for plotting and
organizing political interference and aggression in
Asante. [36] For many allies, a preferable approach
to outright secession from Kumase was advocacy of
particular political parties and factions within
Asante which might have platforms promising less
stringent central control of outlying states,
amnesty for rebels, and no active policy of re-
conquering the seceded Bron states. As a result,
the strength and visibility of the Bron Confederation often fluctuated with and even mildly influenced the vicissitudes of political stability in
Asante proper. The behavior of Nsuta, Mampon, and
Nkoransa during various Asante crises demonstrates
this point and provides much insight into the way
the Confederation operated and the extent of Dente
Bosomfo's power over it.

III

Nsuta in 1874 had been very sympathetic to the rebellious Dwabens and had even considered declaring itself independent from Asante, but it resubmitted to Asante rule following the enstoolment of a new Asantehene, Mensa Bonsu, and his successful demonstration of force against Dwaben. The Nsutahene Kofi Asianowa went to Kumase to declare allegiance and was kept there by Mensa Bonsu. Stability and consensus quickly returned to Asante under the early years of Mensa Bonsu's reign, and by 1880 the Asantehene felt strong enough to consider regaining the lost northeastern provinces and to demand from Dente Bosomfo the return of the Nsuta "Prince" still living there. Lonsdale, in Kumase at this time, commented:

> The tone of the Coomassie Chiefs and people towards the people of Abruno, Salagha, and Kratshie is aggressive and domineering in the extreme. At one time they were openly boasting that they were going with me to these countries and that they were going to free all the Ashanti slaves detained in them, and punish persons who had given them offense. [37]

It was surely in this context of renewed aggressiveness on the part of the Asantehene that the great oath of May 1881 forming an official or renewed Bron Confederation took place.

In about 1882, however, for reasons too complex to deal with here, Mensa Bonsu's rule began to reveal itself as repressive and unreasonable, and he was destooled amid great violence and political strife in 1883. Civil war broke out over the election of the next Asantehene, with two candidates, Kwaku Dua Kumah and the destooled Kofi Kakari, competing. The Mamponhene and Nsutahene both supported Kofi Kakari, perhaps because Kwaku Dua Kumah appeared to be the candidate of the Kumase political clique which was advocating stronger centralized control and a reduced role for the aman (member states). By August 1883 several battles had been fought, in the course of which the Kakari supporters were defeated, Mamponhene Kwame Adwetewa was killed, and Nsutahene Yaw Akoma committed suicide rather than surrender. [38]

During this period of political unrest more
Nsuta refugees fled to Krachi for protection, and
observers found Nsuta "mostly in ruins and very
scantilly populated."[39]   Kwaku Dua Kumah was
enstooled, and the new Nsutahene Kwaku Dente agreed
to go to Kumase to take the oath of allegiance to
the Asantehene. But Kwaku Dente's mother, Abena
Siabura, was apprehensive and went to Kete-Krachi
for safety until it was clear that the civil war
was really over.[40]   This was probably wise, since
Kwaku Dua Kumah died on 10 June 1884 after only
forty-four days of rule, possibly from smallpox,
and on 24 June Kakari died also. Once again civil
strife developed over the election of a new Asantehene, and two new contenders for the stool emerged,
Yaw Atwereboanna and Agyeman Prempe. Major factions in Mampon, Nsuta, Agona, and Kokofu supported
Yaw Atwereboanna's candidacy, and fighting broke
out briefly with Prempe's supporters in early 1887.
A truce was quickly agreed to in July 1887; after
some negotiation the disputants seemed to agree to
Agyeman Prempe as the Asantehene-elect. [41]

Matters appeared to be settled, and, as a
British observer in Kumase at the time commented,
"Ashanti now is as peaceful as it can be till a
King is on the stool."[42]   Consequently, in September 1887, an embassy from Nsuta appeared before the
British Governor in Accra asking for the repatria-
tion of Abena Siabura and stating that 100 shillings had already been sent to Dente Bosomfo
Gyantrubi for her release. The Dente Bosomfo,
however, had refused to permit the Queen Mother to
return to Nsuta. The reasons for his actions are
not entirely clear, but the British Governor sus-
pected that the Nsuta messengers were not telling
the whole truth and perhaps the Queen Mother did
not want to return to Nsuta at that time.[43]

If the latter were the case, the Queen Mother
had again made the right decision, for by early
1888 it was clear that Mampon, Kokofu, and Nsuta
withheld their recognition from Agyeman Prempe
after all and undertook renewed hostilities. In
June 1888 Kokofu was defeated and the dissidents
driven into the Gold Coast Colony for refuge.
Asante under Agyeman Prempe now turned to deal with
the rebellious states of the north. The Mamponhene
Owusu Sekyere and Nsutahene Kwaku Dente were both
militarily defeated in late 1888 and took refuge
near Atebubu within the Bron Confederation.

The Dente Bosomfo was now prepared "to help these two Kings to fight against the Kumasis" and to give the refugees land on which to settle. However, the British Governor in Accra, with whom the Dente Bosomfo consulted, encouraged him to give the refugees land but discouraged him from escalating the fighting. Mamponhene and Nsutahene were also offered protection in the Colony, but they were determined to fight "the Kumasi people" again, and so refused.[44] Thus in September 1889 Mamponhene and Nsutahene launched a renewed attack from Atebubu against Prempe forces, but this offensive was badly defeated.

The supporters of Mamponhene and Nsutahene soon began to slip back to Asante and make their own peace with Agyeman Prempe, who was rapidly rejuvenating that state. Once again, with the restoration of peaceful conditions within Asante, the benefits of protection from the Bron Confederation diminished (though presumably the Confederation's need for prepared defense increased). By early 1890, relations between the Nsutahene Adu Agyei II (Adu Tre), enstooled in exile (his predecessor, Kwaku Dente, had died near Atebubu), and Dente Bosomfo Gyantrubi became strained. Although making use of the Dente oath for litigation, the Nsutas were not sending the requisite fees and fines to the Atebubuhene to be forwarded to Krachi:

> To pay himself the fetish priest seized at Kraki, under various pretences about sixty of the subjects of the Nsutas and he threatened to take similar steps towards the Nsutas residing at Atebubu.[45]

Adu Agyei "preferred to treat for peace with Prempe" and returned to Asante, leaving only a few die-hard dissidents under an Nsuta chief, Yaw Effrim, living near Atebubu.

The Bron Confederation still remained independent and secure from attack, even if the hesitant Asante members were drifting back to allegiance with Kumase. About 1891, then, a new crisis developed which would test the strength of the Confederation to its utmost: Nkoransa, a Bron province to the northwest of Atebubu, had remained aloof from the Bron Confederation for fifteen years (see Figures 5 and 15). Under the leadership of Nkoransahene Kwasi Poku, that region had been loyal

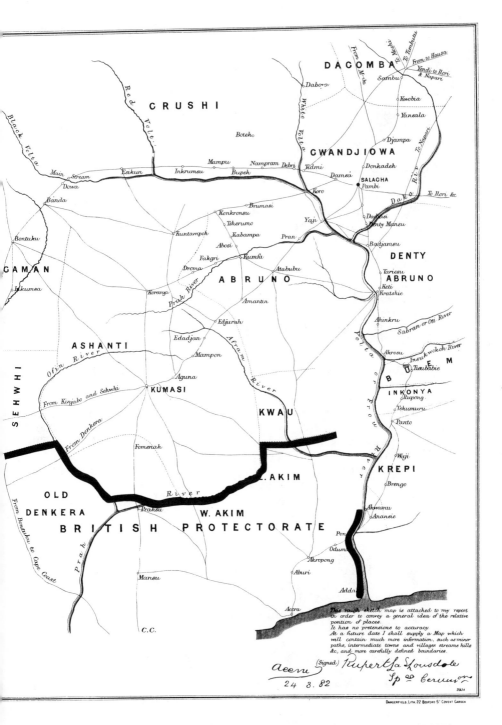

Figure 15: Asante and Bron Regions as seen by Lonsdale (1882)

to Agyeman Prempe and had even provided troops for
the battles against Mampon. However, in September
1888, Kwasi Poku committed suicide to avoid
imminent destoolment by secessionist groups in
Nkoransa.[46] His successor, Kofi Fa, refused to
take the oath of allegiance to Agyeman Prempe and
to surrender Asante refugees in his territory.
Although initially attempting diplomatic reconciliation, Asantehene Agyeman Prempe felt compelled
by early 1892 to plan a military expedition against
Nkoransa. In May Ferguson reported that were
Asante to be successful in this endeavour, they
planned to "proceed with their conquest to the
subjection of the Bron tribes, including Atebubu".[47] Amankwatia Kwame was placed in command of
the Asante army and swore to the Asantehene:

> I will proceed to Nkoranza or wherever the
> King of Nkoranza may be and bring him to
> you. I will visit Brumasi, I will take my
> breastplates from the King of Prang, Yegi
> and Gwan. I will encamp at Atabubu where
> the shady trees will give shelter to my
> troops and on my return I will bring
> Atabubu, Nkoranza and all the Brong nation
> with me to you as part of your kingdom by
> conquest.[48]

In anticipation of the war the Nkoransas sent
twelve slaves and some gold to the Dente Bosomfo
and received charms and gunpowder in return. The
Atebubus also had "great concern about the expected
conflict" and sent to Dente "for a charm to protect
them."[49] Dente Bosomfo now once again consulted
the British Governor Branford Griffith, requesting
advice regarding the impending attack. Griffith
replied:

> You state the Attabubus are your friends
> and allies and if you wish to assist them
> in defending their country, I do not see
> why you should not do so, but that is your
> palaver and I cannot undertake any respon-
> sibility with regard to it.[50]

Indeed, British policy was still unclear at
this point. In 1889 the British altered their
policy of abstinence from direct involvement and
responsibility in hinterland affairs by signing

treaties of protection with Sefwi (west of central
Asante) and Kwawu (east of central Asante) and
Gyaman (northwest), though the latter treaty was
immediately repudiated by the Gyamans. The instigation of this new policy was largely in response
to the activities of the French and Germans in the
northwest and northeast, respectively, of the
Asante hinterland. Consideration had even been
given to negotiating with Buem and Krachi in the
northeast to prevent German claims, but diplomacy
in Europe declared otherwise and Governor Griffith
in 1888 had quickly to order his representative in
the area to cancel negotiations.[51]   In November
1890 Atebubu was made a British Protectorate, once
again to ensure that at least the west bank of the
Volta and the approach to Salaga would not pass to
the control of another European nation. The net
result, however, was to assure dissidents from
Asante not only a nearby place of refuge and the
protection of the Dente shrine, but also at least
nominal British protection.
     In 1892, however, although Atebubu was in
theory a British protectorate, and though it was
being threatened by Asante attack, the British
refused to send any armed support there. The
British did have a "system of spies on the Ashanti
army" circulating in the area, but seemed to feel
either that the attack would not come about, or
that the chaos of the situation would serve to
weaken Asante as the civil wars had earlier.[52]
Only when, in late 1893, the intelligence sources
confirmed that the attack would most certainly be
successful did the British choose to act.
     Meanwhile Dente Bosomfo Gyantrubi began prepar-
ations for war in mid-1892. He called a war
council of the major Confederation chiefs, and
ordered mobilization. Owusu Sekyere, the Mamponhene in exile, counselled Gyantrubi not to come to
the aid of Nkoransa and Atebubu, saying that,

> the priest should represent to the Nkoranza
> monarch the fate not only of Senkere
> himself, but the fates of Asafu Ajei of
> Juabin, Asibe of Kokofu, and Edu Tre of
> Nsuta and that the Nkoranzas should be
> induced to yield to their sovereign.[53]

The Dente Bosomfo chose, however, to fight.
Perhaps he knew that Asante would attack the

Confederation as soon as they were finished with
Nkoransa. Perhaps, as Ferguson commented, this
"fetish priest and an excellent man of business
besides" did not want to "lose the slaves and gold
which accompanied the appeals of Nkoranza for help
against the common foe."[54] Dente Bosomfo Gyantrubi
sent word to the members of the mutual defense
alliance (Yeji, Pran, Kwawu and Buem, among others)
requesting their participation in the war effort by
supplying men and arms.

A few signs of weakness in the Confederation
revealed themselves at this point. The Buem did
not respond to the call to arms immediately.[55]
Governor Griffith, perhaps alarmed at the vigorous
response of the Dente Bosomfo to his tacit approval
of the Bron taking up arms against Agyeman Prempe,
now, only one month later, ordered the Kwawu "not
to join with the Krachi as in all probability he
[Kwawuhene] would get himself in trouble by the
connection."[56]   Overall,   however,   the   Bron
Confederation mobilized with some enthusiasm.
Kwabena Kru of Abease and Kwabena Asante of Atebubu
sent armed contingents to the aid of Nkoransa. The
Prasihene and Kofi Do, principal advisors to the
Atebubuhene, "swore that they [would] assist the
King of Nkoranza and the fetish priest to the last"
and, during the war councils, "opposed every
measure except what was in consonance with the
dictates of the fetish priest." Dente Bosomfo
Gyantrubi ordered that all the roads leading from
Asante to Atebubu, Krachi, and Kwawu be closed, to
prevent surprise attack and to intercept any secret
negotiations that some pro-Asante factions might
want to undertake.[57]

In August 1892 the Nkoransa forces defeated
some Kumase forces, although Nkoransa itself was
badly burned and pillaged in the process. Additional slaves and gold were sent to Gyantrubi in
appreciation for the success thus far, which was
ascribed to the powers of Dente.[58] At least two
more engagements had occurred by August 1893,
however, in which the Asante were victorious.
Intelligence sources once again claimed that the
Asante army would next attack Atebubu and the Bron
Confederation, to which many Nkoransa had
retreated.

Dente Bosomfo now called a major council to
coordinate strategy. The fugitive Nkoransahene
together with the chiefs of Yeji, Pran, Abease,

Dwan, and Basa gathered at Wiase, east of Atebubu, where they were joined by the Dente Bosomfo Gyantrubi in October 1893. Gyantrubi had collected between 1200 and 1500 Krachis armed with flintlocks as well as another 500 Brons to come to the aid of Atebubu and Nkoransa.[59] Other chiefs also contributed men, and the Nkoransahene still had some of his own army in tact. The opposing Asante forces were reported to number at least 8,000 and were probably better armed.[60] The men under Gyantrubi were given special water to drink to protect them from bullets, and the women and children wept as they left for war.[61] Ferguson described Gyantrubi as "federate head of the Confederation composed of Atabubu, Gwan and Basa and the Bron tribes." As such, Gyantrubi swore to the Nkoransas that he would "restore them to their country and would make Atebubu his base of operations against the Ashantis."[62]

This was the first overt military action against Asante which the Dente Bosomfo and Confederation had undertaken, and Asantehene Agyeman Prempe could no longer ignore them. Intelligence sources for the British reported now that the Asantehene was preparing to "march against Krake" and was soliciting the aid of Salaga for this purpose (the regime in Salaga by this time was quite anti-Krachi because the losers of the 1892 Salaga civil war had been given asylum in Kete-Krachi).[63] The Asantehene sacrificed a fat sheep at the Dente branch shrine in Kumase and asked that justice be done.

Though the likelihood of their forces succeeding was questionable, the members of the Bron Confederation had by and large responded to the Dente Bosomfo's orders for mobilization. A military encounter would surely have taken place with the Asante had the British not now decided to interfere. The latter chose to make an example of their protectorate over Atebubu and sent a Hausa force of 300 men equipped with a maxim gun and rifles under the command of Inspector-General Scott. Asantehene Agyeman Prempe immediately wrote the Governor claiming that he had no intention of attacking Atebubu and that he had only gone to punish Nkoransa. Agyeman Prempe then withdrew his army.[64] Dente Bosomfo Gyantrubi, despite Griffith's earlier approval of Krachi assistance to Atebubu, was ordered by the British to take his

army back to Krachi. As in 1888, when Gyantrubi
cancelled his plans to aid Nsuta and Mampon militarily because the Governor advised him to do so,
Gyantrubi now withdrew. Krachi and most of the
peoples east of the Volta had been placed under a
German sphere of influence several years previously, and the British now wrote the German
Governor of Togoland to act on his authority and
curtail the authority of the priest, which Herr
Boeder did,[65] thus effectively breaking up the
Confederation.

                              IV

    The Bron Confederation was never really co-
hesive -- confederacies rarely are. As a mutual
defense pact, though, it was reasonably successful.
From 1875 onward, Asante never attacked Krachi or
Atebubu or any of the northeastern secessionist
provinces, despite the fact that they harbored
refugees of all types, many of great importance,
and disrupted the old authorized trade routes
between Kumase and Salaga. Asante did take certain
measures to counteract and circumvent the effect of
Krachi secession, many of the measures being at
least temporarily successful. Examples are the
establishment of an alternative authorized Asante
market at Kintampo and the use of amnesty and
negotiation to bring wavering groups of Nsutas and
Mampons back into the Asante state. But certainly
there were other more pressing matters (such as
internal strife over Asantehene elections) with
which central Asante had to deal before turning to
re-conquer the troublesome northeastern provinces.
Nevertheless, the Bron defense alliance was an act
of preparation on the part of these provinces for
what they viewed as an inevitable Asante attack.
    The central role of leadership which Krachi and
particularly Dente Bosomfo Gyantrubi played in this
alliance is indisputable. Secure refuge was to be
found in Krachi. The formal oath of alliance was
taken at Krachi, and the oath of the Dente shrine
was used. The Dente Bosomfo bought arms and raised
an army. He was able to place an arms embargo on
Asante and had the power of capital punishment over
peoples throughout the Confederation who disobeyed
his federal policy. He was able to close the roads
from Asante to Confederation states even to

travellers and messengers when he chose. He could
provide land for refugees and a base for political
conspiracy. He could collect dues and tribute from
the use of the Dente oath in litigation and securing contracts. He even capitalized on a form of
indirect, but significant, taxation by selling the
oracular advice, charms, and medicine the shrine
provided. Thus the prestige, religious legitimacy,
and economic foundation of the traditional shrine
of Dente provided Dente Bosomfo with the basis for
expanding his political authority. He manipulated
this to his utmost advantage and enhanced his power
tremendously. Under his leadership the northeastern provinces were able to present a cohesive
front in the face of external threat from Asante.
The Dente Bosomfo was almost successful in mobilizing traditional power toward a rapidly increasing political matrix. Such power and prosperity
did not occur, however, without the appearance of
severe internal conflicts and contradictions, as
the following chapter demonstrates.

7

Islam, Traditional Religion, and Politics in Kete-Krachi

Competition for Control

The economic and political effects on Krachi of expanded commercial opportunities in the late nineteenth century were dramatic and straining. Although the basic mode of production in the area remained virtually unaltered during the period, there were significant changes in the social relations of groups to the productive process and a rapid increase in the level of exchange value realized within the community. These economic changes correlated with a dynamic political restructuring of the community. Strain on the support services in the town of Kete-Krachi as well as competition among the elites for privileges of appropriation led to factional and ethnic strife and, finally, broadly based violence.

I

Krachikrom was originally a religious center and, as with many pre-colonial African towns, this was a sufficient basis for a limited existence. With the arrival of Muslim traders in the 1870s, however, it also became a commercial center of increasing profitability, a change paralleled by Krachi development of a strong agricultural system producing for the market, and Krachi leaders experimenting in expansive politics via the Bron Confederation. By the late nineteenth century Kete-Krachi had become an example of the twin-town phenomenon so common in West Africa: generally twin towns were two towns located immediately adjacent to each other in symbiotic relationship. One partner of the twin settlements consisted of a traditional, older nucleus with its indigenous chiefs, religion, and strong ties of kinship. The other twin, a stranger's quarter or zongo, centered around a major market, was inhabited by Muslim traders and their relatives, provided commercial and transit facilities for the traders, and usually possessed some political autonomy, though it was ultimately subservient to the traditional authority. Twin towns could be located contiguously or several kilometers away from each other, and they often took on dual names. The example of Kumbi-Saleh, capital of the ancient Ghana, is well known. Nineteenth and twentieth century towns such as Salaga-Kpembe and Djougou-Kilir instance the same feature. In the case of Kete-Krachi, Kete was the name of the zongo and Krachikrom that of the original village.

The foundations of Kete town can be accurately placed in the year 1877. Prior to that date there is no reference in European records to a Muslim trading zongo near Krachikrom and oral traditions also maintain that Kete was not in existence until the late nineteenth century. Nevertheless, the preceding chapters demonstrated that a degree of trade, exchange and transit took place at Krachikrom increasingly as the nineteenth century progressed. Muslim traders -- Hausas and Wangaras (Dyulas) -- had always been the mainstay of trade at Salaga, into which the Krachi/Volta trade was feeding. Likewise, in consideration of the fact that Bowdich and Dupuis' informants were Muslim traders, there is little reason to doubt that even in the early nineteenth century individual Muslims travelled through Krachikrom, spending one or two nights there, conducting some trade.

In 1876, however, because items other than salt could finally be brought up the Volta -- a result of Asante's weakened control -- Bonnat observed that "the people of Salaga" wanted very much to come to Krachikrom to trade but were prevented from doing so by order of the Dente Bosomfo.[1] Yet in 1877, with the route more open as a result of Gouldsbury's treaty, Opoku recorded visiting the "slave-market village" of Kete, about forty-five minutes walking distance from Krachikrom. Here and

in the village of Kantankofore (fifteen minutes
further), he met "many Nta-men, Housas and Angwas
(Dagombas) who have exported many slaves, ivory,
shea-butter, etc., from Salaga and are selling
them."[2]

An undefined relationship between Kantankofore
and Kete is hinted at frequently in the sources,
particularly the oral ones. Kantankofore for
example is often asserted to be the first site of
the Hausa settlement in Krachi:

> When Hausas came, they came first to
> Kantankofore. They first settled under
> teak trees beside the road here in Kantan-
> kofore. Kete was not there then. Hausas
> came and met the Kantankofore chief, Nana
> Kwadwo Donkor, to see Krachiwura Nana
> Besemuna who was also from Kantankofore.
> Later they moved to go to a place called
> Kete because they were disturbing the
> Kantankofores every evening with their
> drums.[3]

A Muslim version of this maintains that one of the
earliest Muslim settlers at Kete-Krachi, by the
name of Sofo, befriended the Krachis and "let them
[the Krachis!] build at Kantankofore."[4]   More
accurately it is stated that "Kete town grew up as
the zongo for Kantankofore."[5]   The relationship
between the Muslim community and Kantankofore
continued, gaining strength as the twentieth
century progressed, and will be analyzed in greater
detail in Chapter 9.

Almost all sources agree, even as to detail,
that the Muslims were initially drawn to Krachikrom
to participate in the salt trade there.   The
following account is given with regard to Sofo:

> He [Sofo] was from the other side of the
> river [the west side] and the Adas used to
> bring salt from the south. When the Adas
> brought salt, Dagombas came to buy salt and
> Sofo and his people carried the salt to the
> north for the Dagombas. They had a con-
> tract and this went on for a long time.
> Later Sofo and his people decided to settle
> at this bank of the river so that when the
> Dagombas came they went together to buy
> salt . . . So they made huts with zana mats

. . . When this went on, people from the
north came and this place became bigger and
bigger.[6]

In addition to salt, slaves constituted an important element in the trade, as Opoku observed:

When I came to Kete I was saluted with many
cries by several voices: Come buy a fine
young woman! a fine lad! a fine girl,
etc., thinking that I came there to buy
slaves.[7]

One Muslim also recalls:

My father came here when Sofo was then
Sarkin Zongo . . . My father said that when
he came he began trading with Asantes in
slaves. He even went to Samori and places
far in the north and then came and sold the
slaves to Asantes.[8]

Since neither Gouldsbury nor Bonnat made
mention in 1876 of a Muslim town or market at or
near Krachikrom (and indeed they were both looking
for indications of trade wherever they travelled),
and since Opoku described Kete in detail in 1877,
it is reasonable to assume that Gouldsbury's formal
request that the Krachis open the Volta route to
all traders was successful; and the British military officer Glover was proven correct when he
predicted in 1874 that as soon as "the power of
King Coffee Calcalli [Asantehene] [has] been
broken, these enterprising men [Hausas] will press
down to the Coast."[9] The implication of this,
however, is that there was an extremely rapid
expansion of population (see Figure 16) and consequent demand for goods and services in and around
Krachikrom within the period of one year. Severe
competition and factional struggles were the
predictable result as the expansion continued.
    The first evidence of conflict is to be found
in the report of Lonsdale who travelled to Kete-
Krachi in early 1882, five years after Opoku's
visit. Governor Rowe had sent Lonsdale to Salaga
to encourage use of the Salaga-Accra route circumventing Kumase. Asante traders at this time were
reportedly being prevented from travelling to
Salaga, but had established the large kola market

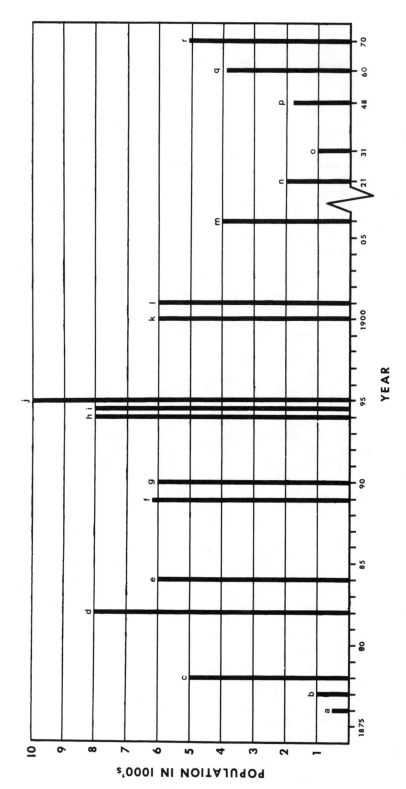

Figure 16: Recorded estimates of Kete-Krachi's Population, 1876–1970[10]

at Kintampo, thereby detracting from the Salaga
market and trade to Accra.[11] Lonsdale was instructed

> . . . to make a special point of visiting
> Crackey Dentey and of conciliating the
> authorities of that place. They are
> reported to still have more power than any
> of the other chiefs on the way to facili-
> tate the free passage of travellers along
> the route from Salagha to Accra. [12]

Lonsdale travelled to Kumase first and there the
Asantehene confirmed that the Dente Bosomfo did
indeed have sufficient power to prevent or permit
passage on roads in the interior, complaining that
"the King of Salagha and the Fetish Priest of Denty
were the two principle persons," blocking Kumase
traders. [13]
    Lonsdale found Kete "a young Salaga" when he
arrived there, and wrote a vivid description:

> [In] the trading town of Keti . . . one
> notices the circular or Mahomedan hut, the
> Ashanti building, the coast house having
> windows and several non-descript styles.
> Keti stands on a high ground half an hour
> north-by-east of Kratshie, and is its place
> of trade. Here may be seen men and women
> from every one of the surrounding countries
> except Ashantis, and even they are repre-
> sented by the refugee Insutahs. The
> principle portion of the population is
> Mahomedan, and of this the larger number
> are Houssas. Between 7000 and 8000 I
> estimate as the population of this thriving
> market town. [14]

Lonsdale remained in Kete-Krachi four days and
during that time "daily had interviews with the
Chief Priest of Denty, Chief of Kratshie, and the
traders of Keti. Trade formed the principle
subject of discussion." He was quickly informed
that there was

> . . . difficulty existing between the
> strangers at Keti and the authorities at
> Kratshie as to their relative positions.
> They each explained to me their side of the

question, and I had no difficulty in
putting matters straight between them.
They requested I would leave a memorandum
relative to the subject with them. [15]

Exactly what the nature of the "difficulty" was
Lonsdale did not explain in detail, but the Memoranda he left, quoted below in full, suggest that
insults, possibly pillage and extortion, and
unequal "opportunities of trading" were the errors
of which the Krachis were accused. The Muslims on
the other hand were allegedly uncooperative with
"the established laws or customs of the country."

Memorandum for the King and Chiefs of
Kratshie, and the Chief Priest of Denty.
                 Kratshie January 31, 1882
The following are points to which I, on
behalf of the Governor of the Gold Coast
direct your attention:
1. You must afford your protection to all
traders of whatever tribe, residing in your
country, giving to them equal opportunities
of trading as enjoyed by your own people.
2. A number of Houssa and other Mahomedans
have taken up their residence at Keti for
the purpose of trade; they have complained
to me that they received ill treatment at
the hands of the natives of this country,
and that they fail to obtain that protection from you to which they are entitled. That because they are strangers
they are called slaves and otherwise
insulted. I must make you distinctly
understand that these men are by no means
considered as slaves by the British Government, many of them having served in Her
Majesty's Gold Coast Constabulary, and that
they are in every way your equals. By the
treaty entered into by you with Dr. Gouldsbury, on the day of March 1876, you are
bound by your oath to give them and their
merchandize your protection.

To those Mahomedans of Keti whom it may
concern.
                 Kratshie, January 26, 1882

> This memorandum does not entitle you to
> presume upon your position and act in any
> way contrary to the established laws or
> custom of the country, and if you have
> occasion to appeal to the King of Kratshie,
> or the Chief Priest of Denty, to settle any
> difference between yourselves and others,
> you must be prepared to abide by their
> decision.
>
> Rupert La T. Lonsdale
> Special Political Agent [16]

The matter was not settled quite so readily as
Lonsdale had anticipated, however. Indeed, there
quite likely was some misunderstanding as to the
precise import of his Memoranda, the Muslims and
Krachis perhaps thinking that such afforded them
both official British recognition. For example, in
June 1883, a Hausa named Alli travelled to Accra to
solicit official recognition of himself as "Headman" of Kete. He made the following statement:

> I am a trader and reside at Keti. I am the
> Headman for all the Houssa people in that
> part of the country. The paper I now
> produce was first given to me by Captain
> Lonsdale but he has not put my name down.
> As I am headman and the people obey me I
> have come to ask the Governor to give me a
> written authority to settle any matter that
> may arise between Houssas. The reason I do
> this is because I find that the paper given
> me by Captain Lonsdale gives me not power .
> . . I ask the Governor to give me power to
> settle cases at Keti. Captain Lonsdale
> took me to Kratshie and put my hand into
> that of the King of Kratshie and handed me
> the paper he gave me. The chief Priest of
> the Fetish was present. The King said that
> he made me Headman of all the Houssas and
> no one else. [17]

Perhaps Alli was a predecessor of Malam Mayaki, or
perhaps "Alli" was another name of Mayaki, but it
is Mayaki who is recalled today as the first Sarkin
Zongo (Chief of the Zongo) of Kete. His murder is
one of the earliest remembered clashes within the
Hausa community and between the Krachi and Muslim

communities. Apparently Sofo desired to be Sarkin
Zongo and therefore conspired with several Krachis
to kill Mayaki. [18] This presumably was accomplished
with the aid of a Krachi woman with whom Mayaki was
having a liason:

> It was through this woman that one day when
> he [Mayaki] was taking his bath they
> surrounded and killed him. She was a
> Krachi woman and she betrayed him. This
> story was told to my father and the people
> from Salaga. Then they asked who became
> Sarkin Zongo and the people here said that
> Sofo was installed as Sarkin Zongo. [19]

This murder is corroborated and dated as March
1887 by correspondence from Inspector R.E. Firminger, [20] who was sent on an expedition in April 1887
to Salaga to recruit for the Hausa Constabulary
Force of the Gold Coast Colony. He passed through
Kpandu and Kete en route to Salaga and in Kpandu
gave audience to a case brought before him which he
entitled "The Murder of Mayaki, Chief of Keti by
two Accras named Abdulai." Firminger sent the case
down to Accra where, much to his displeasure, it
was dismissed because "the men stated they were
born in Dutch town Accra," and thus apparently
enjoyed immunity from Gold Coast Colony laws. It
is curious that two Accra men were arrested for the
murder, because the oral account that Mayaki was
killed by Krachis is confirmed by the missionary
Muller who was in Kpandu at the same time as
Firminger. Muller reasoned that the "notable
Muslim" (he does not refer to him by name) may have
been murdered for his quarrelsomeness or perhaps
because of Krachis' "greed for gold."[21] Although
Firminger singled out two Muslim Accra men as
guilty of the actual murder, he was certainly aware
of the broader factions and forces that underlay
the violence. Unable to have the two men found
guilty in a Colony court, he made efforts, like
Lonsdale, to settle the palaver in Kete-Krachi and
to establish a recognized leader at Kete. He
wrote:

> Kete, the second Salaga, in which half a
> dozen factions were quarrelling for suprem-
> acy, has now elected a chief in the place

Figure 17:   One of the First Mosques in Kete-Krachi, 1898

of the murdered Mayaki and is again rapidly
becoming the large market it formerly was.

In fact, it was Sofo whom Firminger confirmed as
the new Sarkin Zongo of Kete in August 1887. [22]
    Firminger additionally found that the Dente
Bosomfo's interference with free trade was a point
at issue between the Muslims and Krachis:

> The Great Fetish Priest of Dente was made
> to sue humbly for forgiveness for molesting
> and imposing heavy dues on the traders, and
> for refusing to allow the special messen-
> gers sent to your Excellency [the Governor]
> to proceed by canoe from Kratchie. [23]

Yet, although Firminger reprimanded Dente Bosomfo
Gyantrubi for imposing "heavy dues," he still
recognized the Dente Bosomfo as being generally
responsible for the trade route (as did Lonsdale),
and this was to be a constant source of friction
between the Krachi and Muslim communities.
    About one year after Firminger's visit, another
appeal was made to the British regarding this
conflict. The outcome was much more ambiguous. In
November 1888, the Dente Bosomfo Gyantrubi and
Krachiwura Kwaku Badumegya sent a delegation with
various gifts including a tusk of ivory to the
Governor of the Gold Coast. The embassy registered
a complaint against two Muslims named "Abuduba"
(Abdullah Badi, referred to at times as Audu Badi
or Abudu Badi) and Sofo, who were causing the
Krachis "troubles." Demonstrating an astonishing
ignorance of Firminger's activities of the preceding year, the Colonial Secretary Hodgson replied
that Governor Griffith "knows nothing about these
men who are not in any way connected with this
Government. You [Dente Bosomfo and Krachiwura] are
therefore at liberty to deal with them in such a
manner as will ensure respect for your authority."
However, the Governor also refused to give the
Krachis an official message stick. [24]
    The Krachis up to this point had perceived
themselves and were perceived by others as having a
certain, albeit undefined, relationship with the
British, and the Dente Bosomfo as having the
support of the colonial government. Their belief
that there was an alliance between Dente and Queen
Victoria, and that this influenced the outcome of

the 1873-1874 war to Asante's disadvantage, has already been discussed. Gouldsbury's treaty in 1876 assuredly implied that some sort of formal arrangement was confirmed. In the following year, 1877, Krachi messengers were sent to Cape Coast to establish specific channels for communication with the Government and to determine exactly what the Government's policy was towards the exiled Dwaben-hene Asafo Agyei, Krachi's former ally. A "Houssa" who had falsely represented himself in Krachi as a messenger of the Governor was given thirty-six lashes in the presence of the Krachi messengers. In 1881 Lonsdale was told that the Atebubus, having determined that they no longer wished to serve Asante, "went over to 'serve' Denty and the white man," Krachi and the British being so linked in their minds. [25] Again, at least Alli and probably the Krachi leaders as well had perceived Lonsdale's Memoranda as official British recognition of their respective positions of authority. Lonsdale repeatedly reported that the Krachi leaders had "a strong inclination to do whatever the Government wished." [26] All the discussions between British representatives and Krachis concerning trade -- in conjunction with official British expeditions passing through Krachi leaving treaties and notes behind -- doubtless convinced Dente Bosomfo Gyan-trubi that he had British support and consent for his policies of regulating and taxing trade. [27]

Now however, in response to the Krachi delega-tion of 1888, the British government denied knowing who Sofo was (even though one of their own offi-cers, Firminger, had confirmed him as Sarkin Zongo) and rebuffed the embassy by refusing them a message stick. [28] One reason for this was that London and Berlin resolved at this time that Krachi would fall under the German sphere of influence, though Krachi was not informed of this by the British. In 1890 Krachiwura Kwaku Badumegya received a notice from German Lieutenant Herold informing him, among other things, that traders from the English coast (i.e., Accra and Ada) would have to pay duty which he, Badumegya was to collect:

All traders coming up the Volta River from the English coast must pay duty at Kratschi on the following articles: guns, powder, spirit, salt and tobacco . . . Having now

not time enough to come up to you myself at
Kratschi I authorize you, the true and old
friend of the masters of the Adeli station
"Bismarckburg" of Captain von Francois and
Dr. Henrici [early German travellers
through the area] to receive yourself the
above customs till I come to you myself or
send you up a receiver of tolls or some
German soldiers. Concerning the taking of
customs it will be divided into two, one
part to yourself and the other to the
German Government. [29]

If the Krachis had not been given official
responsibility by the British to tax trade, they
certainly were given it by the Germans. Unfortunately the Germans had authorized the Krachiwura,
not the Dente Bosomfo, to collect tolls. Despite
all the confusing signals from various European
officials, however, the Dente Bosomfo's long-
standing claims to tax trade persisted and the
quantity of the tax continued to exacerbate the
factionalism forming in Kete-Krachi over privileges
of appropriating the spoils of the new wealth.
  The German Kling, travelling through Kete-
Krachi in 1891 encountered a nearly exact repeti-
tion of Firminger's experiences four years previous. Kling reputedly "averted a veritable
bloodbath" between the opposing camps of the two
Muslim rivals Sofo and Abdullah Badi, and confirmed
Sofo once again as first Sarkin Zongo of Kete and
Abdullah Badi as second, charging them both to
swear on the Koran to uphold the arrangement. [30]
Kling also found transit tolls being levied by the
Dente Bosomfo on caravans coming from Salaga and
attempted to forbid this. Once again, however, the
results of these efforts to settle affairs in Kete
were not enduring and the Dente Bosomfo continued
to tax the trade. In May 1894 Lieutenant Doering
wrote:

The trade conditions in Kratji are very
unfavorable. The Houssas are assaulted by
the natives in every way. Robbed, thieved,
swindled, and in addition to these crimes
there are daily cases of abuse. The Kratji
people plunder the rich daily market, often
taking away the property of the Houssas
without any apparent justification and

without taking the trouble to give any
excuse. Mossomfo the fetish man of Kratji
is the source of all the trouble.[31]

This taxation, the Germans believed, was the
point of irritation between the Krachis and Muslims, and later in 1894 Lieutenant Herold commented:

The enmity between the Muslim Haussas in
Kete and the heathen inhabitants of Krachi
is as old as Kete itself . . . Already in
the past years he [Dente Bosomfo] had made
trouble by annoying the Haussas of Kete
through all kinds of harassment and often
robbery and making road blocks north
towards Salaga.[32]

It is evident that the Krachis, under the leadership of the Dente Bosomfo, Gyantrubi, were attempting to exact, perhaps excessively, tolls and
controls on the lucrative north-south trade. This
in effect thwarted the private accumulation of
capital in the hands of individual Muslims.

                              II

The Kete zongo underwent steady growth regardless of the Dente Bosomfo's tax policies. The
Zongo acquired additional vigor in 1893 when many
refugees and traders who were displaced by a civil
war in Salaga chose to settle there.[33] The Salaga
civil war concerned rival claimants to the position
of Kpembewura, paramount chief of Eastern Gonja,
which included Salaga. The Kete Hausas, especially
Abdullah Badi's faction, rather strenuously supported the losing side in this conflict. When the
battles were over and lost, the defeated Kpembewura
took refuge at Bagyemso in Krachi territory.[34] It
appeared for a while that the Krachis might take
the side of the ousted Kpembewura as the Kete
Muslims had already. A great battle was feared
that would surely have been, as one observer noted,
"an awful butchering and there would be not peace
for 20 years."[35]
In the end, Krachis did not enter battle in
support of Kpembewura Napa, the defeated chief, but
the Salaga supporters of the latter were given the

protection of the Dente shrine at Bagyemso in Krachi:

> The Kabachewura [Kpembewura's rival] declined to attack the enemy in Bajemso as the town was under the jurisdiction of the Krachiwura. If he had fought there he would have caused damage to the personal property of its citizens and thus provoked the anger of Krachi Dente. [36]

Some refugees surrendered but they were so severely abused by the victors that most of them elected to remain in Bagyemso or move on to Kete-Krachi where their new leader Lempo, the eldest son of Kpembewura Napa, "called himself Kpembewura. He was the Kpembewura of the Gonja in exile."[37]

A large number of Muslims and traders flooded into Kete-Krachi now. Krause, a German trader who had been in Salaga at the outbreak of the civil war and moved about from Yeji to Kete-Krachi, wrote in 1894 that Salaga was "a heap of ruins" with only a few huts inhabited. Most of the population had fled to Kete and "all the efforts of the chief of Kabache, who is now the unjustly elected King of Kpembe, to persuade the refugees to return have been in vain."[38] Klose visited both Salaga and Kete-Krachi in late 1894 and wrote that upon entering Salaga his "visions of this big commercial city, this proud negro metropolis, were shattered. Seeing the miserable remnants of the town one could say Salaga had ceased to exist." On the other hand, "through the downfall of Salaga, Krachi has inherited the largest part of its commerce and has increased its population through a steady flow of immigration."[39]

The precise extent to which Kete's population increased as a result of this civil war is difficult to determine. As shown in Figure 16, in the early 1880s, when there was a boom in trade resulting from the newly opened route down the Volta, the population of Kete grew to approximately 8000; but Asante's alternate market at Kintampo which developed in the mid-1880s, probably drew away a portion of Kete's trade, thereby reducing its population slightly to about 6000. Yet, owing to internal strife in Asante, the market of Kintampo collapsed in 1892. Thus the majority of the displaced traders from Salaga viewed Kete-Krachi as the most

attractive market place. Probably the permanent
population of Kete increased following the Salaga
civil war by only about 2000 -- sufficiently
burdensome in itself -- but the "floating population" as the influx in caravan season was called,
would now soar in excess of 10,000. Certainly
Doering's qualitative account of Kete constitutes
fairly convincing evidence that at least in 1894 it
was a major market, no longer a mere "second
Salaga":

> All the produce of the Sudan is brought to
> the market at Kete. I saw there not only
> people from Salaga and Yendi, the latter
> with products from Mossi land -- ivory and
> cloth -- but also from the west from
> Gyaman, from Bontuku, Ateobu and Kintampo,
> from the east from Yoruba and above all
> naturally Houssas. The Houssas carry on
> regular communication with the mother land.
> From Ngaundere and Yola, from Kano and the
> farthest Sudan state Bornu and even Bagirmi
> the people arrive here. I spoke with many
> Houssas, two from Timbuktu who thus knew
> Tripoli, an example of the inherent wander-
> ing and trading instinct of these people.
> On the return march to Dutukpene I met a
> Houssa caravan of 300 people who were
> bringing fresh products from Sokoto; they
> travelled with a heard of loaded horses,
> hump backed cattle and 60 or more donkeys.
> In Kete naturally there live a large group
> of coastal traders also. They buy here in
> mass the products of the interior, espe-
> cially rubber, shea butter, ivory and palm
> oil. Land roads and the Volta serve as
> routes to the coast. Whoever wants to move
> his wares down the Volta must buy a log
> canoe. At the time of high water, one of
> the firms, Chevalier, comes up the Volta
> with their steam boat. [40]

Most of this trade meant new opportunities for
wealth for Krachis and Salagas as the level of
exchange value in the community rose. [41] But social
relations of production were changing too as new
elites found new power bases and old elites strug-
gled to maintain control over production.

The increase in Kete's population, both permanent and seasonal, escalated Muslim demands on the
resources and services of the Krachi district and
its leaders. The Dente Bosomfo was expected to
provide protection for the trade routes leading
through the district.[42] Increased quantities of
food were required, and indeed Klose stated that
fifteen cows were slaughtered each day in Kete.
The missionary Rosler, visiting Kete-Krachi in the
rainy season, noted that even then, three to four
cows were slaughtered daily and all prices, especially of provisions, were very high.[43] Part of
the Krachi response to these mounting needs was to
expand agricultural cultivation (as thoroughly
discussed in Chapter 2). This policy was facili-
tated by the large numbers of Asante and Bron
refugees arriving who wanted to farm. Slaves were
made available as well to the Krachi authorities in
the form of taxes and duty. At times this tax was
probably collected by force by the Dente Bosomfo
and/or his aides:

> Often small caravans, walking on lonely
> paths are said to have been seized by Okla
> [Dente Bosomfo's aide] and his helpers.
> Their goods were taken away and anyone
> trying to defend himself was killed while
> women and children were taken as slaves to
> one of the fetish villages.[44]

Even on the west bank of the Volta, where there
were only small farms and a few hunters, the
British reported that "much extortion has been
practiced [there] by the Fetish priests of Dente,
whose headquarters are at Kraki on the left bank of
the Volta."[45] In effect the Dente Bosomfo was
somewhat crudely taxing profits of the entrepeneurs
and diverting them into benefits for his expanding
state, specifically into state agriculture via
slaves and settlements attached to the shrine.
Some of the taxes must also have been used for
purchasing arms for the Bron Confederation (see
Chapter 6).
    In addition to the increasing demand for
food-stuffs and protection, similarly escalating
demands must have been made on the judicial system,
the town's sanitary system, the building supplies
for houses and warehouses, laborers for transporting goods and repairing roads, and even the

drinking water. The German Klose, for example, described Kete's water supply, the Volta, as being used for washing clothes and bathing by indigenes and travellers -- by men and women, Mossi, Yoruba, Grussi, Hausa and Krachi, as well as horses, sheep and donkeys. [46] Such water was unsatisfactory for drinking, in other words, and wells were needed desperately.

The Salaga civil war resulted in such a rapid acceleration of ecological, cultural, judicial, economic, and production demands on Kete-Krachi that the institutional framework for the management of Krachi's resources proved inadequate. Moreover, the town's growth may have caused previously satisfactory services to break down or regress. In many ways Kete-Krachi must have seemed a rough frontier settlement to the cosmopolitan Salaga traders arriving from the century-old, smoothly functioning market place of the Asante Empire. In the same sense Krachis may have felt their rural, ethnically isolated way of life threatened.

The Krachi elite also began to perceive that what control of trade, services and production they did possess was being undermined after the Salaga civil war. Prior to that event their relationship to the Muslim traders had been strained but was still based on accepted patterns of patronage and obedience for strangers settling in West African towns. Following the civil war, however, the permanent presence of wealthy, respected, and politically significant Salaga families and the arrival of major caravans from Hausaland, whose contacts and patronage had always lain with these Salaga people, increased the capacity of the Muslims and traders to assume the regulation of their own economic, judicial, and political affairs. The Dente Bosomfo must have felt simultaneously powerful because of and threatened by the increasing numbers of peoples and goods under his authority.

                              III

Violence is not an uncommon phenomenon in situations of this type involving rapid growth, changing power relations, and keen competition for scarce resources, services, and privileges of control. The entire process of competition,

response, conflict and benefit within and between
the Muslim and Krachi elites had occurred
throughout the 1880s, as Lonsdale's and Firminger's
experiences demonstrate, and this had already
resulted in some violence. However, the breakdown
of authority in Salaga that resulted in insecurity
throughout the entire region, a striking population
increase in Kete, and excessive demands on Krachi
finally precipitated the broader civil violence
which did indeed erupt in Kete-Krachi. At some
point Dente Bosomfo Gyantrubi began to menace
Sarkin Zongo Sofo and Abdullah Badi. Sofo's son
provides an account:

> When my father was Sarkin Zongo, the chief
> fetish priest used to come to his place
> with African drumming. His name was
> Okyrikoko [Gyantrubi, known as Daade Kotoko
> -- Iron Porcupine]. He came with chains to
> threaten my father and would say that
> within a week he would have my father
> hanged with those chains. Then the priest
> would go around and threaten all of the
> Muslims. He did the same thing to another
> man called Badi. Then the priest would go
> back to the house. He continued this
> weekly. When he continued like that my
> father thought if something were not done
> one day there will be big trouble. [47]

As noted earlier, the Muslims had since 1882
made appeals to the British Government to aid in
the settlement of some of the issues under dispute,
but without much success. It will be recalled that
Lonsdale had instructed in his Memorandum that the
Muslims must not "act in any way contrary to the
established laws or custom of the country" and that
they must abide by any decision of the Dente
Bosomfo regarding a case brought before the priest;
moreover, in 1888 the Colonial Secretary had
encouraged the Krachis to deal with the Muslims "in
such a manner as will ensure respect for your
authority." Consequently, in 1894 the Muslims
turned to the Germans for support. Sofo, with
sixty men, made a personal visit to German Lieutenant Herold in July of that year at Misahohe:

> He [Sofo] appeared in gala clothing on a
> horse beautifully saddled and bridled in

the Haussa manner, with numerous Koran
verses sewn on his Haussa over- and under-
garments. The rider as well as the horse
was covered all over with heathen amu-
lettes, and he wore colorfully sewn riding
boots and baggy trousers; the head was
covered with a turban and a broad-brimmed
leather Haussa hat placed on top; on the
side hung a broad tassled Haussa sword; in
his hand he carried a good smooth spear
inlaid with brass. . . . Shortly after his
arrival Sofo pledged an oath to me on his
sword to be my friend forever.[48]

Herold reaffirmed Firminger's recognition of Sofo
as "Headman" of the Hausas at Kete." Sofo's action
actually influenced German policy, for shortly
after Doering's visit to Kete-Krachi in May 1894
and Sofo's visit to Herold in July of that year,
the Germans made a decision to establish a
government station at Kete-Krachi in order to
control the trade there and protect the Muslims.
Doering for example felt that the station was
"urgently necessary for the security of trade in
Kratji," and that if the Germans did not act
quickly the Muslims would abandon Kete.[49] Herold
summarized this new policy for the doubtful German
Colonial Society at home:

All along it has been a fundamental principle of the Administration of Togo to view
favorably the trustworthy and obsequious
Haussas who eagerly desire and justly
deserve our German friendship . . . The
primary purpose of the Kete station should
consist of securing and protecting the
Houssas' trade to the coast.[50]

The crisis in the Krachi-Muslim conflict
climaxed shortly thereafter in November 1894 during
the annual Dente Festival, Akwammoa Naneba, when
the path to the Dente shrine is cleaned by Krachis
and representatives of all those peoples who
recognize Dente as a protector or ally. The Dente
Bosomfo Gyantrubi ordered that the market be closed
in honor of the festival and that the Muslims
participate in the cleaning of the path. The
Muslims defied the Dente Bosomfo, carried on
trading, and refused to participate in the

festival. A riot in the market ensued resulting in
looting, beatings and several deaths.[51] A Krachi
informant described the incident as follows:

> A day came for the performance of Krachi
> Dente when the Dente Bosomfo should be at
> Ope [Krachikrom] . . . Now when it is the
> day for the Dente celebration the people
> are not allowed to sell but the Hausas went
> and sold. About 8 AM the Dente Bosomfo
> came to Kete and asked why they are market-
> ing. He became annoyed and said didn't
> they know that day was time for Dente
> festival? And yet they have come to
> market. So he ordered his followers to
> loot the Hausas' selling articles. Then
> they looted the things and beat the Hausas
> up severely. Some were wounded.[52]

Muslim accounts do not differ greatly from the
contemporary or Krachi oral accounts quoted above,
except to make one group look more to blame, and
the following Muslim description is included to
demonstrate the similarities:

> The Krachis then celebrated their festival
> called Naneba. Dentemanso, Kantankofore and
> all Krachis go to Krachikrom to wait on
> Dente. On the way back they passed Kete
> town, broke into the market to collect
> goods from the people. When this happened
> the people of Kete said they would retali-
> ate. There came the next years' celebra-
> tion when Krachis came to break the market
> and steal goods. This time the whole men
> in Kete surrounded them and beat them
> brutally. Then the fetish priest at
> Krachikrom said they should call their men
> from the bush on the other bank of the
> Volta and everywhere to come and fight.
> Some said that they should wait until all
> the Muslims had gone to the Friday mosque.
> They would attack them all.[53]

The missionary Clerk, stationed in Worawora at this
time and having visited Kete-Krachi in September
1894, confirmed in his written account of the
crisis that following the riot the Dente Bosomfo
proceded to "declare war on all Muslims in Kete."[54]

The Muslims' response was to seek external support and assistance from the German expedition under Gruner which was already en route towards Krachi to establish the station there. The German accounts of what transpired include not only references to violence in the market but also to threats against themselves, thus justifying in the Germans' view their own rather violent behavior that was to follow. Hausa messengers, the Germans claimed, warned them a day's march from Kete of the violence and that the Dente Bosomfo had "forbidden the Kete people to provide porters or sell provisions to the Germans."[55] This antagonism towards the Germans, and the Muslim communication of it, is corroborated by Krachi accounts, albeit with a sense of humour:

> Then the Hausas went to report that the market was being looted to Dente Bosomfo who was under a mango tree. He replied, why should they report such a thing to him? His people have a right to take anything they can get in the market. Then the Hausas became annoyed and said that when the white people came they had brought peace and that it was only in the old days that people used force. Then the Dente Bosomfo replied that if the white men have got power over the Hausas fine, but no white men have got power over him. And they can tell the Germans that he has said that. Then Dente Bosomfo told the Hausas that the Germans use them. They should go and tell the Germans that the German's mouth is like the mouth of a certain fish called Obori.

The Hausas, it is said, then went to the river and caught an Obori fish, which has a very long, ugly mouth, and conveyed it along with the Dente Bosomfo's insult to the Germans in the approaching expedition. [56]
Gruner's own account of what followed suggests that he was more severely threatened than just with the insult of a dead fish:

> As leader of the German Togo Expedition, I arrived before Kratschi in November 1894. The Natives of that place immediately on my

arrival addressed a petition to me that I
should protect them against the oppression
of the fetish priest Mossumfu. This
occurred before I had marched into Kratschi. The Natives informed me at the same
time that Mossumfu was preparing to attack
me, and to oppose my entrance into Kratschi. I marched, notwithstanding, on
Kratschi, taking military precautions
against attack, and by means of a night
march was able to surprise the town and lay
hands at once on an adviser and accomplice
of Mossumfu, whose name was Okra. Mossumfu
himself escaped me.[57]

Oral accounts add that when the Germans arrived
late that night, Gruner went to Sarkin Zongo Sofo
and demanded to be taken forthwith to the house of
Dente Bosomfo Gyantrubi. Although Sofo had sent
for the Germans, he apparently had not expected
such violent and immediate measures and pleaded
that the Germans wait at least until morning.[58]
After some delay, Gruner prevailed upon Sofo to
take him to the Dente Bosomfo's house anyway, which
was then attacked -- but too late, for both Gyantrubi and Okra had fled. By morning however Okra
had been arrested, betrayed, it is said, by his
"best friend," a Muslim named Seidu May Baba.[59]
     Dente Bosomfo Gyantrubi escaped to the British
side of the Volta River, and Gruner permitted his
soldiers to cross the river to retrieve the priest.
This latter action sparked considerable protest
from the Great Britain Foreign Office when it came
to their attention.[60] The protest of course came a
good year after the Dente Bosomfo's execution, but
it at least stimulated the submission of some
detailed German accounts of what the Germans did
and what they thought they were accomplishing at
Kete-Krachi.
     According to many non-German accounts, Dente
Bosomfo Gyantrubi was captured on the British side
of the Volta and conveyed back to Kete bound, with
his achilles tendons pierced, and "all agreed that
he was most cruelly treated."[61] He and Okra were
shot by a firing squad in the presence of the
entire Kete-Krachi population on November 25,
1894.[62] Gruner's own account, he having ordered
the execution, is as follows:

> Mossumfu was convicted of having committed
> the crimes laid down to his charge, of
> murder and theft, and was accordingly
> punished with death. The sentence was
> received by the whole population with
> satisfaction, as they were thereby relieved
> from a dreaded robber and source of dis-
> orders. The population of the English
> territory near to Kratschi also showed me
> their delight at Mossumfu's depredations
> being put a stop to by sending me presents.
> . . . If I have been able to put an end to
> Mossumfu's proceedings, I have, in my
> opinion, not only acted in the interest of
> humanity, but also done a service to German
> as well as English authorities in the
> neighbourhood.[63]

The part of Gyantrubi's property which the Germans
were able to confiscate, including six tusks of
ivory and twenty-three boxes of effects, were
distributed to the Muslims.[64] The only Krachi
resistance to the execution seems to have been the
refusal by some "freed" slaves of the Dente Bosomfo
to carry loads for the Germans afterward; and "when
a squad of soldiers went to the farm to fetch them,
they were fired upon by the slaves."[65] Some
Krachis also emigrated "with energy" to British
territory across the river.[66]

The German flag was now raised and work begun
on building the German headquarters on a hill
overlooking Krachikrom in one direction and Kete in
the other. The Krachiwura placed pictures of
Kaiser Wilhelm I and Kaiser Frederick (III) over
the doorway to his house.[67] On 31 December Lempo,
the son of the ousted Kpembewura, was crowned
"Chief of Salaga" in Kete by the Germans, and there
was a grand celebration. Although Lempo did not
possess the military strength to return to Salaga
in order to defeat the Kabachewura (who was by now
Kpembewura), the Germans were hopeful that Lempo's
presence would draw more Salagas to Kete-Krachi, or
at least encourage those Salagas already present in
Kete to remain. On 2 January 1895 Okra's premises
-- a tolling station of some sort in the market --
were blasted away with dynamite to make room for
enlargement of the market.[68] The Krachiwura,
apparently thoroughly convinced that the Germans

were now his masters, went to them requesting that
they help bring rain. [69]

IV

The competition described here between the
Muslim and traditional elite over privileges of
appropriation and control of the economy in this
period of rapidly shifting relations of production
was more than either group was able to dominate
completely. Slave labor for agricultural production was the major economic resource that the
Krachi elite expanded successfully as the Muslims
were expanding the caravan trade. The supply of
foodstuffs to the urban population of Kete does not
seem to have been one of the services that threatened to collapse, and in this sense, the hinterland
of Krachi became more economically integrated with
the urban centers and the trade routes than had
been the case before the 1870s and than would be
the case during Kete's decline in the early 1900s.
Had the Dente Bosomfo been as successful at managing and protecting trade and its taxation as he was
at mobilizing farm production, as successful at
integrating the urban center itself as he was at
integrating the center with the hinterland, there
may have been less strife in Kete-Krachi.

As it was, the excessive demands for slaves and
tolls made by the Dente Bosomfo on the traders were
a response to the excessive demands being made on
the goods, services, and cultural adaptability of
Krachi by the much too rapid influx of trade and
population to Kete. He tried to divert the wealth
accruing from the trade away from individual Muslim
pockets and into state expansion. Over-taking the
caravans for slaves, for example, was an attempt by
the Dente Bosomfo to increase food production in
order to satisfy the urban populations' demand, and
thus assure his expanding authority. But without
Muslim trade there could be no wealth to tax, and
the Muslims and strangers controlled the market-
place. The power struggles, violence, and civil
strife that resulted were means by which these
conflicting yet mutually dependent demands were
gradually being brought into equilibrium.

The forceful imposition of a settlement by a
third party, the Germans, might seem to have
smothered the power struggle: both Krachi and

Muslim headmen were acknowledged, while the real power lay with the Germans. As soon as they built their Kete-Krachi station, Germans claimed rights of taxation, judicial fees, and communal labor. The rewards of power struggles ceased to be so tangible and civil war was averted. Muslims continued however to maintain control of the actual caravan trade and the labor involved in it, while the Krachi continued control of agricultural production and its labor. Thus competition for power and wealth did persist. The Krachiwura stepped into the vacuum left by the execution of Dente Bosomfo Gyantrubi and took a leading role in the soon-to-follow destoolment of Sarkin Zongo Sofo, who was replaced by Krachiwura's ally Abdullah Badi in 1895. Indeed, as the following chapters will show, factional conflict between Muslims and Krachis never ceased entirely, and continues to this day.

8

Early German Colonial Rule
Survival and Realignment

The major units vying for access to and command
of the Krachi community and its resources in the
late nineteenth century continued to be the Krachis, Muslims, British and Germans.[1] Descriptions
of the Kete market in the 1890s leave little doubt
that the trade and its revenue were well worth
competing for. Doering's description of the Kete
market in 1894 has been given above (see p. 135)
and one year later the missionary Hall, who had
been in Kete prior to the execution of the Dente
Bosomfo, observed that Kete was still growing:

> The town Kete is extending rapidly. Large
> gardens full of corn and atoko are in and
> around the town. Different tribes espe-
> cially the Mohammedan refugees from Salagha
> have come to settle here. They have built
> a large Mosque which is not yet completed.
> Kete is a real Moslem town, drunkenness,
> boisterous play, and dances are heard on
> all sides. The market [is] larger than
> formerly . . . The town is kept clean every
> day by order of the [German] Government.[2]

British Inspector Parmeter gave an equally impressive description of Kete in 1897, despite the fact
that there had been a severe fire which burned much
of the town in the preceding month. He listed,
like all observers, the vast variety of West
African groups and cities represented by traders at

the market, the myriad of goods coming from all parts of Africa and Europe, and again acknowledged that Kete had inherited the trade from Kintampo and Salaga, these latter two having been destroyed by wars.[3]

In the years following the establishment of an official German presence, the Germans did diminish some of the stress of Kete-Krachi as an expanding urban entrepot, and this was accomplished in two ways: First, the Germans helped develop services. They provided police to make the roads secure, standardized caravan and market taxes, dug wells, built excellent roads, created a German administrative center which provided ultimate judicial and legal decisions, encouraged Muslim scholarship, developed cattle trade to southern Togoland, and prevented the re-emergence of civil violence. Second, they inadvertently decreased the demand on services and goods, hence the level of exchange value, in the community. Their ruthless methods which included forced labor, beatings, and the burning of small villages and markets which showed the slightest suspicion of resistance and their merciless competition with the British in the Gold Coast (which resulted in rigid trade barriers and in merchants being lured back to British territory) killed off much trade and petty capitalist incentive. It induced a large population drop in Kete from 1899 to 1900.[4]

Kete's population stabilized at 6000 by 1901, however, by which time the services provided by German rule had become obvious and sufficient and had come into balance with reduced demand. This was not entirely due to German input. The religious basis of Kete-Krachi continued as an attraction for traditional sectors, and to a certain degree Kete-Krachi became a center for Muslim learning as well. Despite the decrease in trade, then, Kete-Krachi did not disappear, nor did its conflicts. The combination of religious, administrative, and commercial functions were enough for it to persist as a central place through the colonial period. It is worthwhile to examine some of the specific actions taken by the Germans (and the British) and the realignment of Kete-Krachi elites during the early years of colonial domination in order to determine how much of traditional values, local solutions, and local dynamism persisted through that era. Such analysis surely

makes possible a more accurate evaluation of the
success of the Dente Bosomfo's power and policies
and the strength of the Muslim commercial class,
though it can not provide predictions as to what
might have happened had the Germans not interfered.

I

     In early 1895, diversion of the hinterland
trade to German territory and to Lome from British
territory became the prime aim of the German
administrators in Kete-Krachi. They exacted heavy
duty on goods originating in British territory, and
traders not possessing a receipt showing that duty
had been paid had their goods confiscated. South
of Krachi, at Nkami, the houses of "English"
traders (i.e. African traders carrying British
goods) were burned and their merchandise appropri-
ated. 5 German expeditions were sent from Kete-
Krachi to Yendi, Sansanne Mangu, Gurma and even to
Say on the Niger River, with the intent of pre-
empting British and French claims to these areas.
Caravans were encouraged to follow the routes to
Kete and Lome -- not to the British trade centers
of Atebubu, Kumase (the British finally occupied
Asante militarily in 1896) and Accra. 6
     Salaga was a particularly heated focus of
competition. In 1888 it had been declared part of
a Neutral Zone which was to be equally accessible
to Germans and British. However, competition
between the two nations for more "influence" in
this by now highly over-rated trade center occasioned numerous quarrels and protests: for
example, the British were angered at Klose's
forceful purloining of the treaty document given
the Kpembewura by Ferguson; Klose countered that
the treaty was a violation of the Zone's neutrality
by the British; and the British charged that the
Germans were arresting "English" traders in Salaga,
escorting them to Kete-Krachi, and confiscating
their wares. 7 The Germans attempted to force their
own protege Lempo back to Salaga from Kete-Krachi
in 1896 so as to guarantee that the Salaga trade
would be directed to Kete and Lome. They met
resistance from Kpembewura Issafa, and Salaga was
burned by von Zech in retaliation. 8 Another
expedition was sent in 1896 to Yendi to force it to
cooperate with the Germans and to keep the trade

routes safe. The Dagbanes of Yendi, who had been merely uncooperative with the Germans up to that time, presented armed resistance. A battle was fought in which many notable Yendi chiefs were killed. The Germans dispersed the Dagbanes, and Bimbila and Yendi were burned as punishment.[9]

In Kete-Krachi German trade policy seemed to be a little more pacific and less self-defeating, though more intent than ever on skimming profits off the indigenous trade. The Germans quickly assumed control over the Volta ferry, previously operated by and for the income of the Krachiwura. Ferry duties for goods crossing either way were established and amounted to 6d. or 1000 cowries per unit of goods.[10] (For comparative purposes, the Germans at this time paid their laborers 6d. per day[11].) The tolls established were roughly comparable to what had been charged in the past. In 1884 Ramseyer was informed that a duty of 100 nuts per load of kola was levied at Krachi, 100 nuts being worth on the average 1000 cowries.[12] Ferguson also observed in 1890 that a transit fee of 6d. on each horse, bull and sheep was common.[13] The Krachiwura protested to the Germans about his lost income, but "it was pointed out to him that he is amply compensated through peace and order prevailing now in the country and through the protection of the trade routes."[14]

In addition to these ferry tolls, customs duties were collected by the Germans at Krachi on British merchandise coming from Accra, such as cloth and guns, because many of these goods entered German territory for the first time at Krachi. The duty on guns, for example, was two Marks or two shillings each.[15] In order to encourage trade in salt, however, that commodity was allowed to be sold without duty, and this apparently continued throughout the period of German control.[16] Figures on the quantity of goods passing through Kete-Krachi and the resultant revenue accruing to the German station there first become available for the years 1899/1900 and 1900/1901, as they were given in the German annual reports for Kete-Krachi. In these two periods the total incomes were roughly equivalent to £325 and £465, respectively.[17] The figures do not, however, take account of duties on salt (which the Germans did not collect) and on slaves (which the Germans did not report) which the Dente Bosomfo certainly had been taxing and which

were in effect the mainstays of the Kete market.
Therefore these figures are not a totally accurate
representation of the wealth of the Kete market.

The Germans initially ignored the slave trade,
for although they officially forbade the trade,
they sanctioned slavery itself by, for example,
accepting responsibility for the settlement of
slave palavers. [18]   The Germans informed the Krachiwura that slaves could be owned

> . . . to make farms and to supply the
> market with labourers it requires, and as
> they are slaves, it is not feasible to give
> them freedom all at once; it was therefore
> agreed that the labourers must be well
> treated and not sold or bought in public. [19]

The slave trade of course continued, much to the
righteous indignation and perhaps jealousy of the
British who protested that "slave trade [is] said
to be actively carried on at Kraki notwithstanding
the Brussels Convention," and that "if it were not
for the slave market, trade would cease to exist"
at Kete. [20]   It is conceivable that the Germans even
encouraged the slave trade, for Samori was reportedly granted permission by them to bring slaves to
Kete-Krachi. [21]   The German merchant-adventurer G.A.
Krause, who had lived several years in Salaga and
Kete-Krachi and had been instrumental in encouraging the German acquisition of northern Togoland,
returned to Germany in 1895, displeased with German
activities in the hinterland, and wrote inflamma-
tory protests against the German tolerance of the
slave trade.   The German government quietly attempted to suppress him and finally persuaded him
to go to Nigeria on a "scientific expedition." [22]

The salt trade constituted an additional focal
point of dispute between the Germans and British at
Kete-Krachi.   The Anglo-German boundary from Kpandu
to Tinkranku followed not the thalweg of the Volta
(as in the case with most international boundries),
but the east bank of the river (i.e. placing the
entire Volta River within British territory).
Therefore the British in 1898 were able to retali-
ate against German customs duties on their goods by
forbidding salt or kola to be carried across the
river at Kete-Krachi. [23]   But the salt market at
Kete was too established to be starved out, and an
average of 660 tons of salt and 260 tons of kola

were smuggled through and recorded by the Germans
each year at Kete-Krachi (see Tables 4 and 5).
Kling in 1890 had observed "unbelievable amounts"
and "hundredweights" of salt being measured, sacked
and bartered there, and Klose in 1894 described the
warehouses for salt by the river at Krachikrom
"filled with sacks right up to their conical
roofs." [24] The following gives some indication as
to how lucrative the salt trade could be for the
Europeans in the early twentieth century and
probably was for the Dente Bosomfo in the late
nineteenth century.

In 1898 the British built a Volta River Preventative Service Station across the river from
Kete - Krachi (see Figure 9) for the expressed
purpose of halting the movement of salt and kola to
German territory and of guns and powder from German
territory. [25] In 1903 however, in response to the
Ada salt traders' entreaties, the British altered
their policy to permit salt to be ferried to the
German bank. [26] It was sold on the British side at
6s. per bag, with the British setting a ferry
charge of 5s. per bag, and it was then sold by Kete
traders at roughly 14s. per bag in the Kete market.
Yet there was such a demand for the salt in German
Kete-Krachi (where the British embargo had been
quite effective for about three years, see Table 4)
that within ten days of the ban's being lifted,
£293.5.0 had been collected in ferry tolls by the
British, 1173 bags having been transported. By the
end of 1903, although the ferrying of salt had been
allowed only on certain days for only seven months,
3762 bags (roughly 170 tons, assuming that one bag
weighed 90 lbs.) had been sold to Kete-Krachi.
Approximately three times that quantity was being
shipped north from British Krachi by canoe to Yeji.
At 6s. per bag, £1,128 had been collected by the
Ada traders at British Krachi, with the British
exacting £940 in tolls. [27] Although the salt's
value assuredly varied across time, these figures
do not seem to be too unusual, for Cardinall
estimated in 1925, when the British controlled
Kete-Krachi once again and the trade was flowing
normally, that the salt arriving there averaged
£12,000 per year in value. [28] It will be recalled
that income to the Germans accruing from
trade-related taxation was already substantial, and

Table 4

Volta Salt Trade (in Bags) Through Kete-Krachi*

Year	Arriving British Krachi	Unloaded at Kete-Krachi	Shipped on to Yeji
1898/1899		21,767	
1899/1900		10,752	
1900/1901		7,528	
June-Dec.			
1903		3,762	
1906	16,163	2,445	13,718
1914	20,234	2,509	16,467
1915	31,662	6,258	22,844
1916	27,017	6,988	19,373
1917	25,522	6,205	16,997
1918	23,560	5,536	16,289
1919	25,524	6,321	13,740
1920	11,799	5,269	16,360
1921	13,317	3,953	14,314
1921/1922	15,049	4,206	8,047
1922/1923	23,198	5,389	15,059
1923/1924	18,755	6,429	15,217
1924/1925	25,255	6,027	16,018
1925/1926	18,748	5,755	14,622
1926/1927	16,551	4,451	12,273
1927/1928	15,064	5,761	9,303
1935		2,305	
1936		8,023	
1937		10,990	
Mean	18,944	6,626	15,040

*Based on Jahresbericht, Station Kete-Kratschi, dd. 1 July 1900 and 10 July 1901, Bibliotheque Nationale, Lome, G6; Hood to Colonial Secretary, dd. 22 June 1904, NAG Accra, ADM 56/1/39; Rodger to Secretary of State, dd. Accra 30 July 1907, NAG Accra, ADM 39/1/174; Kete-Krachi District Record Book.

Table 5

Quantities of Various Merchandise Passing Through Kete-Krachi*

Year	Yams (number)	Kola (lbs.)	Cattle, Sheep, Goats (number)	Shea Butter (lbs.)	Smoked Fish (lbs.)
1898/1899		559,486			
1900/1900		74,034	4,966	31,238	
1900/1901			1,629	23,157	
1915			c.7,200		
1916			c.6,000		
1922/1923		19,450			
1923/1924		36,900			
1924/1925		62,100			
1925/1926		92,900			
1926/1927		104,350			
1935/1936	85,250		915		
1936/1937	952,500	17,700	1,459	2,462	900
1937/1938	214,860	252,635	8,982	55,109	10,251

*Based on Jahresbericht, Station Kete-Kratschi, dd. 1 July 1900 and 10 July 1901, Bibliotheque Nationale, Lome, G6; Furley, Diary, entry dd. Kete-Krachi 27 Jan. 1915, NAG Accra, ADM 11/603; Lewis, "Report for November 1916," dd. Kete-Krachi 2 Dec. 1916, NAG Accra, ADM 39/1/10; Cardinall, Annual Reports, dd. Kete-Krachi 31 March 1925, 1926, 1927, and 1928, NAG Accra, ADM 56/1/507; Kete-Krachi District Record Book.

averaged £400 per year without considering salt and slaves.

Using these data to estimate what the Dente Bosomfo's income from direct taxation in the late nineteenth century might have been is still deceptive, however, for the Dente Bosomfo and his elders collected their taxes in kind and thus, by selling these products retail, were able to profit far more than the Europeans did. A conception of the profit to be made by retailing salt, for example, can be acquired by noting a price equivalency given by the missionary Rosler in 1895. He observed that in the lesser developed areas to the east of Krachi, shillings were not highly valued -- 1s. bought only two yams -- but that a handful of salt bought four to five yams. [29] This is reminiscent of Bosman's observation of two centuries previous that in the interior (north of Ada) "one, nay sometimes two slaves are sold for a handful of salt," and of the widely believed axiom of the Sahara trade that salt could be exchanged for its weight in gold. Indeed, in Adele not far from Krachi, salt was often used as a medium of exchange. [30]

Other important items passed through the Kete-Krachi market (see Table 5). Transit to the south of cattle and sheep was perhaps as important as the kola trade, for the Germans recorded that large numbers of sheep were ferried across the river and then driven to Atebubu to be traded for kola, and Furley estimated that roughly 600 head of cattle passed through Kete-Krachi per month. Even more enlightening of the amount of wealth generated at the Kete-Krachi market are the figures in Table 6 which are the amounts of treasury drafts sold to Kete-Krachi local traders in the 1920s (when trade was reportedly depressed). As the District Commissioner observed, these figures "represent most of the turnover in the local trade" except again for that in salt because the salt traders preferred to handle their own credit. The salt trade through Kete-Krachi was valued at £11,000 to £12,000 at this time; and hence at least £10,000 should be added to each yearly figure in Table 6 to provide a clearer indication of the value of trade exchange occurring annually in Kete-Krachi.

Table 6

Amounts Received for the Purchase of Treasury Drafts, Kete-Krachi*

Year	Amount (£)	Annotations
1922	5100	none for salt traders
1923	3250	none for salt traders
1924	5500	none for salt traders
1925	4800	none for salt traders
1926	7600	£1000 for salt traders
1927	8800	none for salt traders
1928	8800	none remitted in March owing to smallpox

*Based on Cardinall, Annual reports, dd. 31 March 1925, 1926, 1927, and 1928, NAG Accra, ADM 56/1/507.

The above trade data come from the colonial period, but on the average they cannot be overly discrepant from those which would be valid for the 1890s. The point is to demonstrate that Kete-Krachi in the 1890s was a wealthy market which, if one could tax it properly and efficiently, would bring its government considerable income. Of course this was what the Dente Bosomfo tried to do, though not successfully in all spheres, and ultimately he lost his position of power to, for all appearances, the Germans.

II

Much of the German success at mastering and taxing Kete, however, was due to an alliance they forged with the Muslim community there. This alliance dated back to some of the German's earliest contacts with Kete-Krachi and all of their actions leading up to and including the execution of the Dente Bosomfo were carried out with the intent of securing the Hausa trade from the north and northeast and routing it to Lome for the

financial benefit of their colony Togoland. In
Kete-Krachi their efforts met with relative success. The power of the Dente Bosomfo was broken
and the Germans now ruled Kete and its trade via
the authority of the Krachiwura and the Sarkin
Zongo, it being assumed by the Germans that these
two officials would be more cooperative than had
been the Dente Bosomfo. This doubtless took
account of the fact that Sarkin Zongo Sofo had
requested the Germans' assistance in settling the
civil strife that had broken out between the Muslim
and Krachi communities in Kete.

However, as indicated earlier, Sofo had been
reluctant to cooperate fully with the Germans and
had to be persuaded to lead them to the Dente
Bosomfo. The Germans soon became suspicious of
Sofo's loyalty, and believed that he was intriguing
with the Kabachewura (Kpembewura Isaffa of Salaga)
and the Ya Na of Yendi. Sofo clearly was associated with the "Yendi princess" who was the Ya Na's
representative in Kete and presumably head of the
Dagbane quarter of Kete.[31] The Germans thus began
to seek the counsel of Sofo's traditional rival,
Abdullah Badi, with respect to dealings with the
Salaga refugees,[32] and in March 1895 a case
entitled "Palaver of King Lempo against Chief Sofo"
was brought to court.

The Krachiwura was deeply involved in this
case, siding with Lempo. Indeed, the exiled Salaga
Hausas and Gonjas were especially friendly with and
even dependant upon the Krachiwura. In October
1894, when Klose first arrived in Kete-Krachi,
Krachiwura Kwaku Badumegya paid him an official
visit, introducing him to the exiled Lempo and his
followers, who came forward when the Krachiwura
raised his hand and were introduced as "Princes" of
Salaga.[33] There is little doubt that they were
under the protection of the Krachiwura, partly
evidenced by the fact that the Krachiwura -- not
the Sarkin Zongo -- presented them to the Germans.
On one occasion Klose informed the Krachiwura, when
the latter faltered in his commitment to Lempo in
the face of a threatened attack from the Kabachewura, that he (the Krachiwura) was answerable with
"his head" for Lempo's safety.[34] Further, Lempo
seems to have been viewed with some displeasure by
Sofo. The Germans learned that when Lempo had
originally fled from Salaga to Kete, Sofo had

wanted to kill him or hand him back to Salaga "for
money" but the Krachiwura prevented it. 35
     The net result of the "Palaver of King Lempo
against Chief Sofo," was the destoolment of the
latter with the full consent of the Krachiwura.
The German administrator in Kete-Krachi distilled
the German point of view:

> Sofo shall on the whole play a double game
> against the Government. He behaves as best
> friend while he is inciting King Issafa of
> Salaga and [the] King of Yendi against
> me. 36

Initially Sofo was allowed to retain the privilege
of hearing certain cases, 37 but there shortly
arose a demand for his total disbarment:

> Odukru [Krachiwura] sends a messenger
> saying: Yesterday another great meeting
> took place. They have got vexed about that
> blackguard Sofo and they were on the point
> of going to Kete to drive him [out] with
> his baggage. Odukru begs that I [the
> Station Administrator] may take proceedings
> once more but I refused because he [Krachi-
> wura] had enough time . . . to say all his
> complaints when the big palaver was held. 38

Abdullah Badi was made Sarkin Zongo, to be consulted by the Germans on "Government Affairs" in place
of Sofo. This hardly marked a conclusion to the
conflict within the Muslim community, however.
     The great Muslim scholar al-Hajj 'Umar b. Abu
Bakr moved to Kete-Krachi from Salaga at about this
time, after he had resided in Bagyemso for several
years following the Salaga civil war. 39 He soon
quarrelled with Sarkin Zongo Abdullah Badi, whom
Krause had once described as "always acting the
upstart." Al-Hajj 'Umar was so exercised by this
quarrel that he even wrote a poem concerning it. 40
Abdullah Badi protested that 'Umar had come to
"take his kingdom away" and over time tension
mounted. 41 A Muslim informant recalls:

> Audu Badi was jealous of Imoru ['Umar]
> because he was a learned man, and Audu Badi
> was only a trader. He didn't want Imoru to
> stay in Kete-Krachi. People were coming to

Figure 18: The Kete-Krachi Market, 1909

Figure 19: Hausa Traders at the Kete-Krachi Market, 1910

study under Imoru and Audu Badi wouldn't
talk to him. The community split into
supporters of Imoru and supporters of Audu
Badi.[42]

To keep the peace, Al-Hajj 'Umar departed from
Kete-Krachi, teaching in Gambaga and Wale Wale for
a short time, but remaining in contact with Kete-
Krachi.[43] Then in about 1907 Abdullah Badi was
destooled by the Germans (perhaps for embezzlement)
and imprisoned for six months, dying shortly
thereafter.[44] The new Sarkin Zongo, Issa Lawla, was
a former student of 'Umar, and the people of
Kete-Krachi prevailed upon 'Umar to return and
settle in their town permanently as their teacher.
The Imam at that time, Gadu, purportedly stepped
down voluntarily in favor of 'Umar, the latter
being acknowledged by Gadu to be far more educated.
However, some informants maintain that Gadu surrendered his office grudgingly and only after
pressure had been exerted by the German Bezirksleiter Adam Mischlisch, who recognized 'Umar's
superior knowledge.
    As Imam, 'Umar became closely associated with
Mischlisch (stationed at Kete-Krachi from 1900-
1909), and the latter became a minor Hausa scholar
in his own right, acquiring most of his knowledge
from 'Umar.[45] Mischlisch encouraged 'Umar to write
a history of Hausaland and an account of his
experiences on the Kano-Salaga trade route in the
latter half of the nineteenth century, and this
constitutes a most informative historical document
today.[46] 'Umar's other works and poems constitute
some of the most outstanding examples of West
African Islamic literature, and his presence in
Kete-Krachi inspired considerable Muslim scholarship and fame there. In the 1920s Cardinall wrote
of him:

He is probably the one Mohammedan in the
whole country who really has influence. He
was called in by his Excellency Governor
Clifford to settle the disputes in Accra;
he has been in correspondence with the
Emirs of Katsina, Kano, and Sokoto with
resulting enquiries from the Nigerian
authorities; he has been to Mecca (twice I

think); his influence reaches throughout
the whole of the Western Sudan; his correspondence does not come through the Post
Office.[47]

The Germans thus attempted to attract trade to
Kete-Krachi and Lome in part by encouraging Hausa
trade, Muslim authority and even Islamic scholarship. In 1899 the Basel missionaries had noted
that the Muslim Gonjas had become the real
"Princes" of Kete-Krachi and under later German
rule even Krachi court cases came under Muslim
jurisdiction (see below). The Muslim/German
alignment was neither fully successful nor unsuccessful. A strong core of Muslims and traders
remained in Kete town to teach and trade, taking
advantage of the security and excellent condition
of the German roads there, profiting from German
trade goods and from smuggling salt, gun powder and
slaves. They developed a vigorous cattle trade to
the new markets in southern Togoland. However, the
German burning of Yendi and Salaga served only to
worsen trade conditions for all parties involved.
Many Kete Hausas moved back to Salaga later when it
was rebuilt by the British, or moved to Nsunua
across from Kete-Krachi where a large zongo grew
up, or to Atebubu or to Kumase to take advantage of
British trade.[48]
     In fact, the importance of Kete's trade and
position, at least for those on the spot, stimulated a ruthless British policy which endeavored to
attract trade from the northern hinterland to Accra
at the expense of the Germans. The actions taken
by the British -- the forbidding of salt to be
taken across the river and landed at Kete, the
building of a road from Tinkranku down the west
bank of the Volta, the opening of Kumase to Hausa
traders, and the re-building of Salaga -- all had
the effect of luring traders back to British
territory, and the Germans could offer little to
counterbalance this.

                           III

     Early Krachi-British relations have been
discussed in detail in Chapter 6, and the utility
of the alliance between these two parties became

less obvious towards the end of the nineteenth
century. In 1885 at the Berlin Conference, Germany
claimed territory north from Lome, i.e. the area
which was to become Togoland, as a colony. Although the specific boundaries were not established, and despite earlier British activity in this
area, the Krachi and Yendi districts were included
in this German sphere of influence. International
diplomacy rather than local reality had determined
their fate. Thus from 1890 onward, as the boundary
between the Gold Coast and Togoland acquired
definition, the British voluntarily withdrew across
the Volta River, thereby removing themselves as
candidates for control of Krachi resources.

The Krachis were somewhat confused by this
behavior. Their alliance with the British had
dated as far back as Gouldsbury's treaty of 1876
and Krachiwura Besemuna's tribute of ivory to the
Gold Coast Governor in 1877. It was not a thoroughly reliable alliance as, for example, in 1892
when the Krachis assumed that they had the tacit
approval of Governor Griffith to offer military aid
to the Nkoransas; as noted earlier the Governor
rescinded this approval, and the Krachis were
harshly rebuffed upon their arrival near Atebubu,
ready for battle.

Although the British were not viewed by the
Krachis as the most consistent allies, they were
nevertheless apparently much preferred to the
Germans. Clerk observed in early 1894 that people
in Krachi were seriously concerned about the German
take-over, for the Krachis' official reply to his
request to establish a mission station there was:

> If you have nothing to do with the Germans,
> you can come (and settle) -- who drives
> strangers away? As for us we serve the
> English. And when you come, don't plague
> us and don't create disturbances.

"It makes one sad," Clerk wrote, "when after
preaching in a village the first question is 'are
you German or English?'"[49] Krachi disappointment
and confusion with regard to their being "handed
over to the Germans" was intense. Missionary Hall
was told in 1895 by the Krachiwura:

> Our country had formerly been under the
> Ashantees and the English had freed us from

their yoke by conquering Kumase. We
therefore concluded this benefactor is our
Master and we never knew any change had
taken place, till lately when the Germans
came and said we belong to them. And I
have now accepted the German flag. [50]

In 1920 Krachiwura Okuju Dente still recalled
bitterly:

. . . an English man passed by the Volta to
the North. We do not know his name. On
his return we collected many things as a
present to him. He refused to accept the
presents as he said we had been handed over
to the Germans. This discouraged Badumeja.
He said my elder brother put himself under
the British. I have done the same. If I
have done any wrong they did not tell me
but simply put me under the Germans. [51]

By 1894 however the rather violent and threat-
ening German activities in the "Neutral Zone" and
in Kete-Krachi had aroused British competition.
George Ferguson, an English-educated Gold Coast
mulatto, was sent to the region to encourage
British trade there without crossing boundaries,
and he was active for several years. [52] By 1898
the British had established their British Krachi
Preventative Station. Thus British Krachi, also
known as Nsunua, controlled the ferry across the
Volta in the 1900s and a sizeable Muslim zongo
developed there. The British secured the trans-
shipment of salt around the rapids by building a
monorail or tram at Nsunua which consisted of
hand-pushed carts and roughly two miles of track.
The traders paid 1d. per bag of salt and 1s. for
each canoe portaged on it. They could then take
their wares on up the Volta to Yeji and on to
Salaga without ever entering German territory.
Thus although the British had withdrawn from
Kete-Krachi itself, they continued attempts to
influence and control the people and resources of
Kete-Krachi. [53]
British Krachi then remained for the Krachis,
until 1914, the major alternative to German domination. As already noted, in 1894 Dente Bosomfo
Gyantrubi escaped to the British side of the Volta,
anticipating a certain amount of safety or

protection. Although he was pursued and captured
regardless, the notion that security from the
Germans was afforded by British territory persisted
in Kete-Krachi, no doubt encouraged by Ferguson and
other British officials posted there. In 1895
Ferguson noted that many Krachis including the
Asasewura chose to move to the British side of the
river following the execution of Gyantrubi. As
will be seen, this pattern continued until 1914
when the British invaded German Togoland and
occupied   Kete-Krachi.   Aside   from   the
above-mentioned   Asasewura,   at   least   two
Krachiwuras, the Firao Bosomfo, the entire village
of Kadentwe, and certainly many less prominent
people -- farmers and hunters -- migrated in the
early 1900s to British territory, building villages
along the west bank.[54]

IV

German efforts to manage and profit from the
trade in Kete and the rest of Togoland by use of a
certain amount of brutality and ruthlessness
influenced the migration out. The revenue from
trade and locally produced exports and the duty on
liquor and other imports developed Togoland into a
Muster Kolonie, or Model Colony (i.e. it paid for
itself as a colony); but the roads and railroads
that increased the quantity and efficiency of trade
were built and maintained through the application
of a head tax and the use of forced labor.

From the late 1890s onward all adult males were
required to provide the Government a certain number
of days of labor -- later it was set at 12 days
annually and from 1909 onward the alternative of
paying 6s. annually was instituted.[55] This direct
taxation was resented and is well remembered today:

> The Germans forced us all to work so
> sometimes we hid from them. They made us
> plant teak trees and mango trees and we had
> to fetch water. I would hide in the bush
> for the whole day, and then would come out
> at night. Sometimes I would come out to
> eat once they had got their quota for the
> day. In the early morning they would come
> and grab you. If you slept late they came
> and took you.[56]

Unfortunately, often more than twelve days of labor
were demanded, and there was certainly a lack of
understanding on the part of the Krachis as to how
much was really required of them. On the other
hand German administrators probably abused the
system as the following statement taken in 1918
demonstrates:

> During the period we served the German
> these are some of the troubles we had at
> their hands. They are as follows . . . If
> we worked for them what they paid you was
> little, or more often, nothing at all. On
> top of all this we were flogged . . . They
> caught our sheep and fowls and did not pay
> for them. Every six moons they collected a
> tax of 6s. each. They used to summons us a
> six days journey to come and work and it
> sometimes happened we had to remain about
> six moons (and work) without pay or even
> subsistence. On top of all this we were
> flogged.[57]

The labor was legislated to be used only for
the betterment of the district, i.e. for activities
such as building and repairing roads, working
plantations of the many cash crops which the
Germans attempted to introduce such as teak,
cotton, and novel types of kola and coffee, and for
beautifying the towns. To some extent the German
policies are justified by the wells, buildings,
roads, and teak and mango trees still bringing
benefit and profit to Krachi inhabitants in the
1980s, and many informants can be found today who
still remember the Germans with respect for their
"efficiency." They point to the remaining infra-
structure and note that "the German period was one
of planning and foresight for the future."[58] Some
Krachis remember even German discipline with
nostalgia because the Germans "gave powers to
chiefs to beat faulty people," and consequently a
child today "has not respect for you as they did
when the Germans were here. In those days children
do obey orders."[59] Adults clearly obeyed orders
too and suppression of crime, which did encourage
trade some, was also a German accomplishment. Thus
one Krachi who traded to Salaga and Bimbila under
German rule recalls:

> The trade ran down when the Germans left.
> The Germans had made trade good. When the
> Germans were here there was fear among the
> people, so there were not thieves. There
> were never robbers in those days, so this
> made trade good. When you leave something
> by mistake they will send it after you any
> place you go, for they might hang anybody
> who took it and did not return it. But
> when the English came, then there were
> thieves.[60]

Nevertheless, as the informant above comments, the
excessive law and order policy of the Germans
induced "fear among the people," and all German
accomplishments seem to have been achieved because
they "forced us and beat us brutally . . . they
maltreated us."[61]

Thus the overall result of the German presence
in Krachi was actually a general depopulation of
the district, at least of large villages along the
roads. Whole villages moved into British territory
in the 1900s, and the British political officer
sent to report on the Krachi district following the
surrender of the Germans in World War I found the
Krachi people a "miserable lot" and "completely
cowed." He continued:

> I was informed that, not only in this
> region but throughout the District whenever
> the German Resident travelled through with
> his escort, who looted everywhere, the
> people collected their belongings and fled
> into the bush until he had passed, leaving
> the chief and one or two old men to face
> the dreaded "white man."[62]

During German rule many Krachis even continued to
hold their farms on the east (and more fertile)
side of the Volta while living in British territory
on the west side and "regularly with the full
knowledge and permission and assistance of their
Togo brothers farmed and reaped their harvests" on
their farms on the German side.[63]

At one point an attempt was made to transfer
the political paramountcy of the Krachis to the
British side of the river by taking the Krachiwura's stool there. In 1901 Krachiwura Kwabena
Obridgya died (see Table 7) and Kwaku Tokuri from

Table 7

KRACHIWURA OFFICE LIST

Krachiwura	Dates of Office	Village	Annotations
Otebrebre	1825-1850	Kantankofore	
Kosokpene	1850-1865	Genge	
Kwasi Besemuna	1865-1880	Kantankofore	
Kwaku Bedumegya	1880-1897	Genge	
Kwaku Bendor	1897-1899	Monkra	
Kwabena Obridgya (Tokuri)	1899-1901	Kwaku	destooled; from British Kratchi
	1901	Abokono	died
Kofi Genge	1901-1910	Kwaku	fled to British Krachi
Kwasi Neda	1910-1912	Kantankofore	destooled
Kwabena Tawia	1912-1913	Genge	died
Kwasi Okuju Dente	1913-1935	Kantankofore	destooled
Yaw Kpebu	1935-1945	Genge	destooled; anti-CPP
Kwadwo Mprah Besemuna II	1944-1959	Kantankofore	destooled after coup; pro-CPP
Kofi Badumegya II	1959-1966	Genge	destooled during PNP; anti-CPP advisors
Kwabena Obridgyo II	1966-1979	Kwaku	
Kwame Bendor II	1979-	Monkra	

Abokono in British territory (a farming village of
Kantankofore) was the candidate to succeed him The
Basel missionary in Kete-Krachi at the time,
Reverend Awere, reported that at first the German
officer did not want Tokuri to be Krachiwura
because he was living in British territory, but
Tokuri promised he would induce all his subjects to
move back to German territory. Thus he won the
German's "love and confidence and was made King."
Soon however Tokuri saw that

> . . . the fruits of his hope turned to
> ashes in the months and as a proof of this
> he saw that his few followings or atten-
> dants with whom he came here, with some
> young men he gave to serve the government
> in the constabulary department, gradually
> deserted him or ran away to British Krakye,
> etc. Thus being the case he became deject-
> ed and depressed in spirit becoming unfit
> to govern and finally he was dethroned and
> another rightful heir [Kofi Genge] from
> this [German] side is now King . . . [64]

Several months following this, in April 1902,
"members of the royal family remaining naturalized
at British Krakye," i.e. Tokuri sympathizers, came
at night to Krachikrom and "stole" the Krachiwura
stool. "There was dancing one morning after which
the stool was missing," and it was taken to British
territory, hidden perhaps in Kwawu.[65] Hobbs, who
was District Commissioner of British Krachi at the
time, noted as the crisis intensified:

> The German Commissioner at Kete-Krachi
> stated that unless the stool was returned
> there would be fighting between the British
> and German Kratchis. I took every possible
> precaution to prevent this. A crowd of men
> assembled on the German side of the Volta
> and their attitude was so threatening that
> I feared a serious disturbance. [66]

Awere also recorded that "the German Krakyes on
hearing of it became enraged [and] mustered all
their forces to wage war with them."[67] At first
the British Krachis refused to hand over the stool,
but a column of troops under Chief Commissioner
Donald Stewart was sent there, followed later by

Governor Nathan to hear the palaver, and eventually the stool was returned by Tokuri in 1903. Tokuri's reign as Krachiwura however was so brief and inconsequential, or perhaps so controversial, that he is rarely listed as a Krachiwura except by a few Kantankofore people. [68]

The new Krachiwura, Kofi Genje from Kwaku, died on the stool in about 1909 and was succeeded by Kwasi Neda from Kantankofore. [69] The latter was in power in 1912 when Dente Bosomfo Abrekpa was executed by the Germans. Mass numbers of Krachis fled across the Volta River then, Krachiwura Kwasi Neda among them. In a fairly surrealistic account of what transpired, [70] von Rentzell, the Acting Administrator at the time and the person responsible for the execution, acknowledged that he (von Rentzell) was young, inexperienced, somewhat frightened, and sick from fever. He was however convinced that the Dente Bosomfo was causing the death of certain individuals in the district through misuse of the shrine (see p. 50). Von Rentzell therefore arrested Abrekpa and his three linguists without warning. The Dente Bosomfo Abrekpa and his successor-elect Kofi Donkor were hanged in the market from a tree by having boxes knocked out from under them. [71] Two of the linguists, Asetena and Yaw Gyankrubi, committed suicide in their cells to avoid the same end, and the remaining linguist Yaw Sakyi was sent away to prison (to Lome) where he remained until freed by the British in 1914. [72] Von Rentzell then dynamited the shrine. A contemporary newspaper account stated, exaggerating somewhat:

> Has [the Governor of Togoland] punished the officer of German Kratchies for his whole-sale murders of six fetish priests and the emigration of 8,000 people to British Kratchie? The awful catastrophy that has fallen on them has thrown into consternation the whole Northern Territories into one inconceivable ruin and woe; and British colony is the one place of refuge . . . The people of German Kratchie have set a noble example, would not my people [Ewes] follow suit, that sad, yea, that blood curdling event which occurred was a blessing in disguise. The immigrators are thriving in British Kratchie, they are building a town,

where they will move their legs freely.
Killing poor innocent people on account of
their own religious frenzy is downright
barbarity. [73]

Eyewitness accounts corroborate the reference to
mass emigration:

On the day the shrine was blown up I was
crossing the River Sene to Nkomi over the
bank. As soon as I reached the middle of
the river I heard the noise in the forest,
thinking that it was a gun, not knowing it
was a dynamite. When I reached Nkomi the
chief sounded the gong-gong that all the
men should take boats and canoes and go to
the other bank to carry the Krachis across
to secure protection from the Germans. So
I turned myself back to Abokono. There
they crossed many people to the other bank,
to Nsunua; they used canoes to take Krachis
to the other bank to hide. [74]

In this "Krachi Dunkirk," Krachiwura Kwasi Neda
also fled, settling at British Krachi, and numerous
oral accounts claim that he took the Krachiwura
stool with him. [75] Although this was probably the
case, candidates were nevertheless enstooled or at
least elected to the Krachiwura office in German
Krachi for the remainder of the German regime. In
1915 however Krachiwura Kwasi Okuju Dente on the
east bank of the river stated to the occupying
British that Kwasi Neda was still the rightful
holder of the position of Krachiwura and expressed
a willingness to step down in the latter's favor. [76]
Although the British would not permit Neda to
return to German Krachi until the war was over,
many Krachis apparently continued to take cases to
him for arbitration until his death in 1917. [77]
    Subsequent to Kwasi Neda's flight in 1912 the
Germans enstooled a new Krachiwura, Kwabena Tawia
from Genje. By this time the elders' town of
Krachikrom was virtually deserted, and the rapid
turnover of Krachiwuras from 1897-1912 had weakened
the continuity and authority of the Krachiwura
office. Simultaneously, and perhaps out of neces-
sity, ties between the Kantankofore Krachis and
certain factions of the Muslims at Kete gained
strength. The Muslims had been given so much

support and authority by the Germans, and the
Krachis had been so weakened, that as early as 1899
Awere had recorded: "these Ntas [Gonja Muslims]
are seemingly becoming the Princes of Krakye."[78]
The focus of Krachi government shifted to
Kantankofore, which was more spatially removed from
the German headquarters than Krachikrom and did not
possess the trappings of a political capital and
residences for sub-chiefs and representatives. The
Kantankofore elders in conjunction with the Muslims
at Kete brought pressure for Kwabena Tawia (from
Genje) to be destooled. Charges, possibly invented
ones, were levied against him -- he was accused of
impotency and said to have "a weak heart."
Kwabena Tawia was thus ousted, and a younger
"brother" of Kwasi Neda, Kwasi Okuju Dente from
Kantankofore, was elected in 1913 with strong
support from the Muslim community (see Chapter 9).
Krachikrom was now completely abandoned and only
rebuilt by special order of the British after the
Germans had left.[79] Krachi political control was
administered from Kete or Kantankofore, and Krachi
court cases began to be taken to the Sarkin Zongo's
tribunal.

Despite the insecurity and trauma which Krachis
suffered under German rule, there were certain
advantages associated with it for traders -- both
Muslim and Krachi -- and, as indicated earlier, a
stabilized population of c.5000 remained in
Kete-Krachi from 1900 on. There is no doubt that
the area was still sufficiently desirable to the
British that they were eager to repossess it in
1914, and indeed they did so on the first day of
World War I. Within a few years the station of
British Krachi was abandoned, and the German
premises at Kete-Krachi became official British
district headquarters.

Krachis as well were most anxious to move back
to the eastern side, and the elders continually
petitioned the British for permission to do so (the
British tried to prevent it until the end of the
war).[80] If the salt statistics are any guide,
trade never lapsed even through the war (though
annual passage of salt dropped about 35 per cent
during the world depression of 1920-1925).
Krachikrom was rebuilt even before World War I
ended, and in 1921 the Dente shrine was allowed to
be re-instituted. This too was a calculated effort

to secure trade and revenues, as the District
Commissioner's comments at that time reveal:

> I have the honour to inform you that the
> Fetish "Dente" returned to its former
> habitat, the cave on the left bank of the
> River Volta at Kete on the 30th [Septem-
> ber]. The cult is once again in full swing
> and already a number of people have been
> down to consult the oracle. It is to be
> hoped that the ferry receipts will now
> appreciably increase and that the many
> devotees from distant parts who are expect-
> ed, will give a stimulus to local trade.[81]

Krachis gradually moved back to their original
dwelling sties on the east bank of the river and by
the 1930s the western villages were greatly depopu-
lated. [82]

The Germans had done their best to halt the
trend of African solutions to characteristic
problems of development. They were solutions
pioneered by the Dente Bosomfo and stimulated by
the equally African but antithetical Muslim political hold on the market place. The Germans imposed
their own solutions. By improving services (as
begun by the Dente Bosomfo) and reducing demands
(accomplished by the depopulation of Kete both
because of brutality and more desirable trade
conditions in the British Gold Coast) the Germans
helped cause the economic and power struggles of
Kete-Krachi to diminish to lower levels of ordinary
factionalism. But the raw materials were still
fundamentally African -- the Dente shrine, the Ada
salt, the ethnic and religious antagonisms.
Further, while the Germans bolstered the Muslim
elite at the expense of the Krachis, the British
were to pursue the reverse policy and thus it is
not surprising that Krachi relationships with
Muslims soon, or perhaps always, superseded in
importance and duration their relations with the
Germans and the British.

9

Factionalism Past and Present
The Persistence of Fundamentals

The two preceding chapters have demonstrated
that the town of Kete-Krachi was divided in a
Muslim-Krachi dichotomy along religious, ethnic,
and spatial lines, reinforced by external (European) alliances. However, visualization of Kete-
Krachi's late nineteenth century conflict in terms
of purely Muslim vs. Krachi (or German vs. British)
antagonism is at best only one level of analysis.
Evidence suggests that from the beginnings of the
Muslim settlement at Kete in the 1870s factions
emerged within the Krachi and Muslim communities
which forged alliances across communities to
influence local politics and secure management of
resources and services. Indeed, in the 1950s and
1960s, as will be seen, these inter-community
factional alliances became quite clearly defined as
they identified with competing political parties,
and thus constituted an important facet of independence and post-independence politics.

Anthropologists have seen factions as groups
which "structure conflict differently from formal
traditional organizations such as clans and lineages."[1] In the case of Kete-Krachi, the factions
definitely were and are more complex in composition
and more representative of socioeconomic affinites
than clans and lineages. Kete-Krachi factions have
elements of patron/client relationships, which some
social science literature emphasizes.[2] If however
the Kete-Krachi factions were strict patron/client
relationships, they would focus more around

personalities and would not have endured as long as
they have -- and persistence over time seems to be
their most challenging characteristic. On the
other hand, the control of political and economic
benefits which the factions apparently strive for
does indicate a strong clientage support system.

Kete-Krachi factions cannot be classified as
political parties or even pre-parties because they
do not seem to have articulated philosophies,
ideologies, or policies. (Except perhaps for the
days of Dente Bosomfo Gyantrubi's domination of the
Krachis: He attempted to limit private capital
accumulation by the Muslims and apply the profits
to the support and expansion of his state.) The
factions do seek to secure political office for
themselves -- usually the Krachiwura or Sarkin
Zongo office -- and hence they must be defined as
units which were and are organized for political
competition. As such, self-serving goals and
strategies are shared within factions and sometimes
strategies might be shared with other factions.
Thus cross-cutting alliances might be constituted.
Political competition, cross-factional alliances,
and historical continuity are the most obvious
characteristics of the Kete-Krachi factions.

                               I

Hints of a Krachi-Muslim alliance among some
members of the community emerge early in the
sources. As indicated earlier (see p. 122), Kantankofore, a Krachiwura royal village, is frequently mentioned as the first settling place of
the Muslim traders in the 1870s. At that time the
Krachiwura was Kwasi Besemuna from Kantankofore,
and it is he who is remembered as having provided
the Muslims with a place to build their houses,
both at Kantankofore and later at Kete a short
distance away. Northern traders were seen in large
numbers at both places by Opoku in 1877. Perhaps
the Dente Bosomfo opposed Muslims locating at
Krachikrom proper, or perhaps they chose themselves
not to lodge there, even though it was closer to
the rapids and salt landing than Kantankofore (or
Kete).[3] Probably the Krachiwura already had
experience as a political go-between for Asante as
suggested in Chapter 4, and had already been
dealing with strangers in the sense that he seems

always to have been in charge of the Krachi ferry.
So, it was the Krachiwura who assumed the
responsibility of being the Muslim's adamfo or
patron, and Kantankofore's role in establishing the
traders indicates that the Kantankofore members of
the Krachi community were willing, even eager, to
cooperate with and encourage the Muslim community.

Additional evidence suggestive of Krachi-Muslim
collaboration in the earlier years of Kete's growth
is the murder of Mayaki in 1887 (see p. 128). The
murder was committed, according to Firminger, by a
group of Muslims. According to oral sources it was
committed by Krachis at the instigation of the
Muslim Sofo who coveted the position of Sarkin
Zongo which Mayaki held. Thus, factionalism in the
early Muslim community is verified by Firminger's
account, with the oral sources indicating that
Krachi support and aid was sought by at least one
Muslim faction. In regard to this incident, it is
also stated that Mayaki was having a liaison with a
Krachi woman -- more evidence that the lines
between the Krachis and Muslim communities were
hardly inflexible.

Again, when the Germans entered Kete-Krachi in
November 1894, they found Sofo somewhat uncooperative about leading them to the Dente Bosomfo.
Okra, it will also be recalled, was said to have
been betrayed by "his best friend" Seidu May Baba,
which suggests that prior to the German's arrival
the latter had viewed cordial relations with
influential members of the Krachi community as
worthy of cultivation. The reverse must also be
true, i.e. Okra must have valued Muslim relationships in order to have perpetuated this friendship.
Okra's appearance -- he was described as dressing
"according to Hausa tradition [in] a precious
embroidered blue robe" -- and for that matter the
Dente Bosomfo's silk trousers (see p. 60) imply
that even cultural differences between the two
communities could be bridged.

Following the execution of Dente Bosomfo
Gyantrubi, Krachiwura Kwaku Bedumegya persisted in
and apparently intensified his alliance with the
son of the ousted Kpembewura, Lempo. This relationship dated back at least to 1892 when the
Krachiwura contemplated coming to the aid of
Kpembewura Napo (Lempo's father) in the Salaga
civil war (see p. 133). In March 1895 the combined
political influence of the Krachiwura, Abdullah

Badi, and Lempo was marshalled against Sarkin Zongo
Sofo, resulting in the latter's deposition just
five months after the execution of Dente Bosomfo
Gyantrubi. The case against Sofo was clearly a
manifestation of a long-standing division in the
Kete Muslim community between Sofo and Abdullah
Badi (and perhaps Mayaki before his murder). This
is the same antagonism which, according to Kling in
1890, had nearly led to "a bloodbath" within the
Muslim community and which Firminger, Kling, and
Herold all attempted, unsuccessfully, to reconcile.

None of these three European observers provided
details regarding the Muslim split. Nevertheless,
the two Muslim factions were most obviously
characterized by their respective leaders, Sofo and
Abdullah Badi, and it seems reasonable to attempt
to infer more general attributes of the factions by
examining the identities of these two individuals.
Both leaders had been in Kete for some time -- Sofo
since before 1887, Abdullah Badi since at least
1890 -- but whereas Sofo was a Wangara from Kano in
Hausaland,[4] Abdullah Badi's mother was a Gonja[5]
and he definitely associated himself with the
Salaga refugees in Kete, many of whom, despite
their calling themselves "Hausa," were of Gonja
extraction and had either very distant or no
ancestry in Northern Nigeria.

One might therefore characterize the
bifurcation in the Kete Muslim community as being
based on place of origin, or even ethnic identity
-- Gonja Muslim vs. true Hausa -- not an uncommon
division in Ghanaian stranger quarters. The
Atebubu Muslim community, for example, is also
divided along lines of ethnic origin, between Mossi
Muslims (northern Ghana to Upper Volta) and
Hausa/Nigerians (there are very few Gonja Muslims
in this case). The Sarkin Zongo in Atebubu is
almost invariably Hausa, the one Gonja Sarkin Zongo
having been a most controversial election.[6] In
Kete-Krachi most Muslims are either Gonjas from
Salaga or Hausas. The latter are perhaps a
generation or two removed from Nigeria, and often
return to Nigeria for wives and husbands. There
are a few Mossis in Kete-Krachi, and some Kotokoli
peoples, with their own sub-group leaders, but they
obey the Sarkin Zongo's authority in major matters.

On a very general level these ethnic affilia-
tions harbor economic overtones. The people of
Gonja-Salaga origin had a tendency to be less

wealthy than the true Hausas, to be petty traders,
lorry drivers (later on), blacksmiths, even
farmers. They also apparently participated in the
slave trade, while the Hausas were more involved in
the kola trade,[7] although the two commercial
networks were not mutually exclusive. The families
directly from Northern Nigeria or who maintained
strong ties with their relations there (through
marriage for example, avoiding marriage into
indigenous Gonja families when they could) generally earned their livelihood by loaning and investing
money, financing business undertakings (caravans,
etc.) and overseeing prestigious occupations such
as butchering. For example, the Hausa chief
butcher in Kete-Krachi is, as Levtzion found in
other West African communities, "one of the richest
and most influential Muslims,"[8] and this is
probably to be accounted for both by the occupation's ritual significance (e.g. religious sacrifices) and its association with (and profits from)
the north-to-south medium-distance cattle trade.
Factional cleavage in the Kete Muslim community
seems to have been prone to follow these lines of
division. The alignment may not have been widely
perceived by the general populous, but it was
certainly an important element in leadership
fluctuation and decision-making processes.

Consider, for example, the antagonism between
Al-Hajj 'Umar and Abdullah Badi (see p. 157). The
former, a Hausa, had been born in Kano, Nigeria,
was extensively educated, and maintained his ties
with Northern Nigeria until his death. His dispute
with Abdullah Badi split the community into supporters of each. Upon the latter's deposition in
about 1907 (see Table 8), Issa Lawala, of Nigerian
extraction, head butcher in Kete, and a student of
Al-Hajj 'Umar,[9] was made Sarkin Zongo, and 'Umar
became Imam (see Table 9). However Issa Lawala
died within a few years and was succeeded by Malam
Binta, a Gonja, who "did not see eye to eye" with
'Umar.[10] Nevertheless, with both the Hausa and
Gonja factions thus represented in high office a
truce of some sort must have developed, for no
notable disruption of peace occurred and there were
no depositions in the Kete Muslim community until
the death of both leaders in 1934. By 1940,
however, Sarkin Zongo al-Hassan Biosama (a Gonja)
had been deposed and replaced by Ibrahim Baba
Galadima (a Nigerian Hausa) of the opposing faction

Table 8

SARKIN ZONGO OFFICE LIST

Sarkin Zongo	Dates of Office	Annotations
Malam Mayaki	-1887	killed
Sofo	1887-1895	deposed
Abdullah Badi	1895-1907	deposed
Issa Lawala	1907-1910	died
Malam Binta	1910-1934	died
Ali Dansachi	1934-1938	died
al-Hassan Biosama	1938-1940	deposed
Ibrahim Baba Galadima	1940-1945	died
Malam Bako Mijimata	1945-1960	deposed; anti-CPP
Malam Ladan	1960-1966	deposed after coup; pro-CPP
al-Hassan Biosama	1966-1971	restored after 2nd coup; died
Malam Ladan	1971-	restored

Table 9

IMAM OFFICE LIST

Imam	Dates of Office	Annotations
Mikaratu	1890-1900	
Gadu	1900-1907	stepped down
al-Hajj 'Umar	1907-1934	died
Tahiru	1934-1935	died
Muhammed Baba	1935-1936	died
al-Hajj Muhammed Thani	1936-1960	deposed; anti-CPP
Abu Bakr Titibrika	1960-1962	deposed; anti-CPP
Malam Shaibu	1962-1966	deposed; after coup; pro-CPP
al-Hajj Muhammed Thani	1966-1969	restored after 2nd coup; died
Abu Bakr Titibrika	1969-	restored

and he in turn was replaced upon his death by Malam Bako Mijimata, a brother of Biosama. [11]

Thus, as Table 8 shows, a precedent developed of alternating leadership between one faction and the other, a practice not uncommon in West Africa and which often gives rise to the assumption within the community that alternation must take place. Stool, skin, and other office disputes then result when one group tries to break with "tradition" and change the rotation order to keep the office two turns in a row. Notable examples of this kind of dispute are the Salaga civil war of 1892, and the Yendi skin dispute of the 1960s and 1970s, though disagreements among Krachis for the Krachiwura stool also conformed to these lines at one point (see below). Following the introduction of political parties in Ghana and Kete-Krachi in the 1950s, depositions of the Sarkin Zongo began occurring with a regularity which corresponded to national political changes, with alternate candidates taken from Hausa and Gonja groups as national governments were overthrown and installed.

II

Another trend emerging in the late nineteenth century was the forging of a coalition between the Krachiwura and Gonja Muslims. For the Muslim community this was an essential relationship during and following the Salaga civil war when settlement and protection of the Salaga refugees in Kete-Krachi was necessary. During the German regime the coalition remained useful because the Germans had eliminated the authority of the Dente Bosomfo and chose to rule through the Krachiwura on some matters (e.g. Krachi slaves, and forced labor) which directly affected the Muslims. The Krachiwura and his followers also needed the Muslim alliance more than ever because for many trade, financial, and judicial matters the Germans worked through the Sarkin Zongo.

The power of the Krachiwura office of course had been greatly enhanced by the execution of Dente Bosmofo Gyantrubi and by recognition and support from the German regime. Simultaneously, however, the office was weakened by the rapid turnover of its holders beginning in 1897 (see Table 7), irregular elections, and German manipulation and

Muslim ascendancy. Further, whether or not Krachi-wura Kwasi Neda removed the stool and official paraphernalia to Nsunua in British territory in 1912 (see p. 170), his presence across the river made it difficult for his successor in German Krachi to maintain authority. After the second German attack on the Dente shrine in 1912, there was not even a Dente Bosomfo, Krachikrom was abandoned, and the Krachiwura's court ceased to be convened. Some matters were still settled at Kantankofore, but in general Krachis were commanded by the Germans to take (or perhaps they voluntarily took) their disputes to the Sarkin Zongo's court. A coalition of Muslims under Sarkin Zongo Malam Binta and Krachis led by Kantankofore elders effected the destoolment of Krachiwura Kwabena Tawia from Genge, and the enstoolment of Krachiwura Okuju Dente from Kantankofore in 1913. Okuju Dente had been trained in legal matters by Malam Binta, as some Muslims recall:

> Now when any quarrel happened Malam Binta judged it, even if it was between Krachis. Then Malam Binta went to the fetish priest and said he should give him one of his clever children who would be with Malam Binta in the court so as to interpret proceedings in the court in order to educate Krachis. Then the fetish priest gave him one Okuju Dente. He was the first one with Malam Binta in the court. Later Okuju Dente told Binta it was better for them to have separate courts for Krachis and Muslims. So he Okuju Dente could judge cases with Krachis and give a final report to Malam Binta. This was agree upon. Now Muslims do not take drinks so the Krachis brought Malam Binta £5 for making Okuju Dente official judge. [12]

The Krachi's version of Okuju Dente's Muslim contacts is similar:

> It was through Malam Binta that Okuju Dente became the Krachiwura. He was helped by the Zongo chief before he was installed, that is how he got the chance. Now Okuju Dente had not enough money to give to Binta so through arbitration cases the money was

collected. Okuju Dente and Binta sit down
to share it to themselves. So when we had
any arbitration Kwasi Okuju Dente will go
to Binta, the Sarkin Zongo, to settle the
case. That is how Krachi people came to
settle cases before Binta at that time. [13]

In certain aspects, a full reversal of power
had taken place since 1895. In that year Krachiwura Bedumegya had been highly instrumental in
Sofo's deposition and replacement by Abdullah Badi.
From 1912 to 1918 Sarkin Zongo Malam Binta was
equally influential in the destoolment of Kwabena
Tawia and enstoolment and subsequent support of
Okuju Dente. From 1895 onward, "mutual dependency"
probably best describes the relationship between
the Gonja Muslims and what came to be the Kantankofore faction of Krachis. Neither acted in total
isolation from the other, and collaboration between
the two factions proved highly effective against
opposition to either's interests -- whether the
opposition was German, British, Muslim or Krachi.
The Krachi community became increasingly
polarized during the British colonial period.
Opposition to Krachiwura Okuju Dente by non-Kan-
tankofores -- specifically those Krachis from Genge
and Kwaku, but also other Twoboaes and some Dentewiae and Kononae people -- was so strong that only
resistance by the District Commissioner prevented
Okuju Dente from being destooled in 1932. [14] In
1935, when Okuju Dente died, the Kantankofores
attempted to elect another candidate from their
town, but the Genge and Kwaku people objected,
"claimed it their turn for the stool and alleged
that Kantankofore was trying to keep the stool and
exclude all other sections of the royal family."
The District Commissioner exerted strong pressure
on the Kantankofores this time, and a candidate
from Genge, Yaw Kpebu (the son of Kwabena Tawia[15])
was selected. [16]
In October 1937 the Kantankofores attempted to
destool Yaw Kpebu, and an assault "resulting in the
removal of the Krachiwura's stool, stick and
clothes" led to a riot in which 54 persons were
arrested and imprisoned by the authorities. [17] Here
again there is evidence of the Gonja-Kantankofore
alignment for some Muslims were strongly opposed to
Yaw Kpebu and during his reign "part of the Muslims
went to Kwame Danso," refusing to return until his

death. Krachiwura Yaw Kpebu, it is said, "almost
became mad," owing in part to Kantankofore and
Muslim resistance to his rule and he "died in the
bush," possibly committing suicide. [18] His successor, Kwadwo Mprah Besemuna II, from Kantankofore, was a "good friend" of one Salifu Sarkinbude,
a Gonja, who had moved to Kwame Danso earlier and
returned with many Muslims after Kwadwo Mprah's
enstoolment. [19]

There are other economic overtones to the
Krachi factions -- Kantankofore Krachis vs. "Other
Krachis". The division seems best viewed as a rich
vs. poor, town vs. rural dichotomy, where Kantankofore's proximity to the goods and services of
Kete [20] and the consequent financial benefits
accruing from the former are contrasted with the
rural isolation and dependency on farming for a
livelihood of the other Krachi villages such as
Genge and Kwaku. The possible importance of other
factors such as long-standing family, marital
and/or inheritance quarrels requires further
research. However it is clear that the Krachi
factional division can be traced back to conflict
of powers between the Dente Bosomfo and the Krachiwura. The Other Krachis faction, if not identical
in constituency to the Dente Bosomfo power base of
the past, certainly quickly filled the vacuum left
by the decimation of the Dente Bosomfo office,
1894-1912. Although not an obvious leader of the
faction, the Dente Bosomfo in the 1930s does appear
in the sources, often protesting against or testi-
fying against Krachiwura Okuju Dente (Kantankofore)
and is even cited by the Kantankofores as a major
opponent to their objections over the installation
of Krachwura Yaw Kpebu of Genge. [21] The Dente
Bosomfo elected in 1950, seems to have presented a
fairly apolitical profile into the 1980s however.

III

To summarize thus far, it is quite evident that
by the early twentieth century both the Muslim and
Krachi communities in Kete-Krachi were divided
within themselves (Gonja Muslims vs. Hausa Muslims
and Kantankofore Krachis vs. Other Krachis) and
that an alliance was operating at least between the
Gonja Muslims and the Kantankofores. It is proposed here that all four factions existed almost

from the founding of Kete town, that factionalism
was fairly intense in the 1890s and, was dampened
but not eliminated by colonial rule. In fact when
the Germans favored rule and administration through
Muslim office-holders, the Muslim factions became
more clearly active; and when the British favored
rule through Krachi elites, the Krachi factions
became more clearly active. Finally, during the
years of independence-winning and competition for
political office the intensity of factions again
reached the levels of the 1890s.

The polarization over time of the Krachi
community is represented schematically, with some
simplification, in Figures 20-23. The Muslim/
Krachi dichotomy is represented by the line dividing the Krachi factions -- and although some strong
cross alliances were made, a cultural division was
and is always present, hence the dividing line
remains through all the diagrams.

Figure 20: In the latter part of the years
1880-1894 represented in this figure the Dente
Bosomfo Gyantrubi behaved most threateningly toward
Sofo and Abdullah Badi and probably permitted the
abuse and extortion of Muslims in Kete. The
Twoboae Krachis (not merely Kantankofore Krachis,
for Bedumegya was from Genge) constituted the
adamfo for all the stranger Muslims. There is
evidence that the Dente Bosomfo and Krachiwura
Bedumegya however were not wholly in accord on all
matters. The latter is said to have been annoyed
with Gyantrubi in 1894 for failing to inform him
and the Kete Muslims in advance of the date of the
riot in the market that Akwammoa Naneba was to be
celebrated that day.[22] Moreover, Herold claimed
that although the Krachiwura was in favor of the
Muslims settling in Kete, and making them feel
welcome, he acquiesced to the Dente Bosomfo's
harassment of the Muslims out of weakness; and
Krause noted in 1894 that Gyantrubi and Bedumegya
lived "in enmity" with each other.[23] Sofo and
Abdullah Badi and their respective constituencies
were competing with one another at this time too,
and murders and "averted bloodbaths" between them
are recorded. Gyantrubi had some alliance with the
Muslims through Okra and Seidu May Baba's friendship, but fuller understanding of the nature of
this alliance requires future research.

Figure 21: From 1895 to 1912 the Muslim
community was strongly polarized, owing in part to

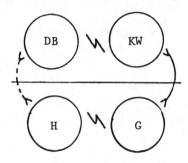

Figure 20: 1880–1894
Traditional Factions

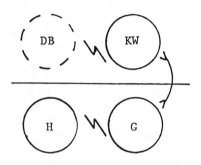

Figure 21:   1895–1912
German Rule, Favors
Muslims

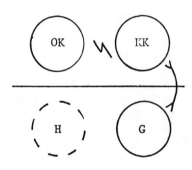

Figure 22: 1912–1945
British Rule, Favors
Krachiwura

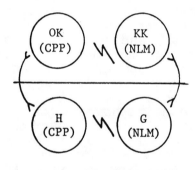

Figure 23: 1945–1979
Independence; Political
Parties Clarify

KEY:

◯   Faction

〈   Alliance

⋀   Conflict

———   Separation

H: Hausa

G: Gonja

DB: Dente Bosomfo

KW: Krachiwura

OK: Other Krachis

KK: Kantankofore Krachis

the dispute between al-Hajj 'Umar and Abdullah Badi, with the Krachiwura's patronage definitely residing with the Gonja Muslims, even contributing to the deposition of Sofo. The execution of the Dente Bosomfo in 1894 may have caused the Dente Bosomfo faction initially to move closer to the Kantankofore group, perhaps out of sheer survival tactics. The two groups seem to have been cooperating when members of both were arrested in 1912 and accused of taking land for themselves from an inheritance "gift" to the shrine. Nevertheless there must have been some antagonism lingering for the shrine now had to share its proceeds with the Krachiwura, probably for the first time. Thus the two groups are not shown schematically to be totally unified.

Figure 22: The second execution of a priest in 1912, the banning of the shrine's operation, and the partial physical desecration of the Dente grotto created a vacuum which occasioned the splitting-off of a faction, or perhaps just the re-formation of the old Dente Bosomfo faction. It took the form of a Kantankofore opposition, referred to as Other Krachis here for want of a better label. The Dente Bosomfo may have participated in the Other Krachis faction, but domination of the Krachiwura office was the group's ultimate goal. Thus from 1912-1945 the Krachi schism intensified and surfaced in destoolment movements led by the respective Krachi factions. The Krachiwuras from Kantankofore consolidated their control over land, court cases, and even the Dente shrine. In 1930 the Dente Bosomfo Bawiya went so far as to complain to the British District Commissioner that Krachiwura was withholding "his [Dente Bosomfo's] share of the tribute" which derived from the Dente shrine and the Dente Kwasida oath.[24] The factionalism was exacerbated by British introduction of taxes to be paid to a Native Treasury which in turn was to be controlled by the Krachiwura and his elders (with British supervision of course). A long spell of peace in the Muslim community was broken only once by the deposition of Sarkin Zongo al-Hassan Biosama in 1940. The draining series of depositions and reinstatements that have yet to cease did not really begin until 1945. The alliance between the Kantankofore Krachis and Gonja Muslims continued throughout this period, particularly through the

mutual support of Krachiwura Okuju Dente (1913-
1935) and Malam Binta (1911-1934).

There were probably splinter groups and re-ad-
justments of the factions' membership in the course
of the first half of the twentieth century but the
general trends of polarization and alliance described schematically here represent the essential
character of faction dynamics in Kete-Krachi. This
waxing and waning of faction visibility and antagonism correlates fairly well with what much of the
social science literature on the subject suggests,
that is, that factioning occurs in societies
experiencing stress and rapid social change. Some
authors argue further that while factionalism may
be disruptive, it is a natural response which is
more functional and less corrosive than no political system whatsoever.[25] Stated another way,
however, the linkage of _sturm_ _und_ _drang_ to factionalism contains an underlying assumption that
factionalism results from the breakdown of social
order and legitimacy.[26] Thus when conditions of
pressure and societal change increase, so does
factionalism.

In contrast, it is proposed here that while
factionalism did appear in Kete-Krachi whenever
conditions of stress and change increased (beginning even before overt European impact), the
phenomenon was related, not to weakened societal
patterns and breakdown of legitimacy, but to higher
political returns and societal development.
Factionalism increased whenever the rewards of
political competition appeared greater and decreased whenever the opportunities looked less
tantilizing. Thus German support of Muslim rule in
the early 1900s increased the desirability of
political office regardless of whether such support
increased or decreased political legitimacy (and
about which we can not be certain anyway). Hence
Muslim factionalism increased for a while under
German rule. German execution of priests made
competition for the Dente Bosomfo office seem a
poor idea and Krachi factionalism diminished some
(though did not disappear). Similarly British
favoritism towards the Krachiwura office and
introduction of the Native Authority, which gave
the Krachiwura control of a tax-based treasury,
made his office well worth fighting for. Thus
under British rule Krachi factionalism became more

visible and Muslim conflict diminished some (though not entirely).

Finally, the introduction of independence politics in the 1950s, while increasing stress and social change did nothing to weaken the political legitimacy of the Krachiwura or Sarkin Zongo office, or to cause societal breakdown, or to cause even fundamental social re-structuring, but it certainly increased the political profitability of the offices. Thus the historical patterns of Kete-Krachi antagonisms persisted into the 1950s and 1960s and intensified with the mounting political activity and the high stakes of the independence movement.

In 1957 Kwame Nkrumah's mass-based pro-independence Convention People's Party (CPP), having overwhelmingly won countrywide elections, swept into power and began ruling the newly independent country of Ghana. Krachiwura Kwadwo Mprah Besemuna II (from Kantankofore), Sarkin Zongo Malam Bako Mijimata (a Gonja) and Imam al-Hajj Muhammed Thani (of a Gonja mother) all opposed the CPP. [27] In 1960 when Nkrumah consolidated his own power by declaring Ghana a republic (instead of a dominion) with himself as President (instead of prime minister), and simultaneously began to rule more and more through the CPP rather than the regular government structure, repercussions were felt throughout the country. The above mentioned three office holders in Kete-Krachi were all deposed and pro-CPP candidates took office. The new ones were coincidently members of the local level factions opposing their predecessors. Malam Ladan, a Hausa, became Sarkin Zongo and Bedumegya II from Genge became Krachiwura. The new Imam was chosen by the Sarkin Zongo.

This did not quell anti-CPP agitation, and in 1964 the previous Imam (Thani) and two prominent leaders from Kantankofore (one of whom later became a Member of Parliament in the Busia government) were arrested and exiled from Kete-Krachi to Kumase by the CPP. In 1966, at the time of Nkrumah's overthrow, all of the pro-CPP office holders were deposed, and anti-CPP candidates were reinstated (see Tables 7, 8, and 9). [28] People arrested returned from exile. In the case of the Krachiwura stool, Kwadwo Mprah in the interim having died, a young candidate was selected who appears to have had anti-CPP advisors. There were no depositions in 1972 when the military overthrew the Busia (NLM become Progress Party) government, as there had been in 1966, though there were arrests of various elders (including once again those who had been exiled to Kumase in Nkrumah times) who were held in jail for as much as one year. Through the normal channels of election and a long Krachiwura destool-ment case, the former CPP leaders appeared to re-assume control during the Acheampong/ Akuffo government which was neutral-to-CPP-rehabilitative in its leanings. Under the new PNP which won the 1979 elections and was a fairly obvious descendant of the old CPP, the trend continued.

For purposes of reading Figure 23 it is evident that the factionalism of Kete-Krachi intensified in the years of independence politics and that the Kantankofore Krachis and Gonja Muslims were allied against the pro-CPP Other Krachis and Hausa Muslim factions. It is not entirely clear, however, why the factions aligned with the political parties that they did. The Gonja Muslims in fact worked through the Muslim Association Party (MAP) which later combined with the National Liberation Move-ment (NLM) to form the United Party (UP). They may have perceived MAP and later UP as serving their special interest needs. Similarly, the Kantanko-fore Krachis, being committed to chieftaincy through their domination of the Krachiwura office, conceivably felt threatened by Nkrumah's effort to control chieftaincy. Hausa Muslims and Other Krachis, however, chose to support the CPP at least in part because it promised offices and rewards which they were not receiving at the time and hence the party was viewed as a new ally in their local opposition struggle.

Rathbone (1968) has suggested that "the most local of local politics" were perceived by Ghana-ians as more relevant to their needs and wants than "the rituals" of national party ideologies and slogans in the competition for power which emerged with independence in the 1950s. [29] The situation in Kete-Krachi would bear this out. It could also be argued on a broader level of analysis, however, that particularly the Other Krachis who had been most brutalized and disenfranchised by colonialism, and the Hausa Muslims whose trans-national trade was limited by colonialism, saw in Nkrumah an opportunity to benefit from state investment and limitations on private capital development. In contrast, the Gonjas and Kantankofore Krachis had benefitted from colonialism: they had come to control not only political office, but land rentals and wage labor. Indeed yam farms developed in Krachi in the 1930s and 1940s much like cocoa farms did in Asante at that time, that is, through ruling class investment in land and labor and political manipulation of land tenure. (The cocoa farmers of Asante were likewise strong supporters of the anti-CPP party, the NLM.) Certainly the Kete-Krachi factions read the situation correctly if this actually were their evaluation, because private capital investment and chieftaincy were limited to some extent under Nkrumah, and when Busia, an old NLM candidate, finally became president in 1969, his policies encouraged for a brief while private capital investment and the expansion of cocoa (and yam) farms. At the same time he enacted legislation which forcibly expelled from Ghana Nigerian Hausas lacking work permits or Ghanaian relatives, and many were forced to leave Kete-Krachi.

IV

It is not surprising that national party allegiances in Kete-Krachi from the 1950s onward have followed local factional divisions there. It is however interesting and noteworthy for comparative purposes that these allegiances confirm consistent and enduring historical patterns, and careful examination of their roots is fundamental to understanding them. It seems clear that the modern political alliances in Kete-Krachi exemplify the pattern, dating possibly from 1877, that local factions have not necessarily been religiously or entirely ethnically aligned, despite the fact that religious and ethnic differences were sometimes played upon for political demogoguery. Throughout the late nineteenth and early twentieth centuries, Muslim-Krachi alliances played at least as influential a role in the control of and competition for resources as Muslim-Krachi conflict did. Thus the cohesion afforded by Islam or traditional religious authority was and is insufficient in Kete-Krachi, particularly when resources were scarce and stakes were high, to preclude the development of polarization along other, more potentially rewarding lines of division.

The stakes of course were highest under Dente
Bosomfo Gyantrubi's rule and it was probably then
that factions came closest to resembling political
parties representing or pursuing policies of
development. Gyantrubi tried to limit the accumulation of capital and profits among Muslim entrepeneurs, and divert the money into state management
-- providing agricultural production under state
auspices (slaves tied to the Dente shrine), and
providing defense against Asante attack through an
aggressive foreign policy. He was surprisingly
successful in managing agricultural production,
marginally successful in foreign policy, and
unsuccessful in combatting the Muslim political
threat and hold on the market place. He certainly
did not have the force or power base or flexibility
to survive violent colonial assault. His were
attempts at indigenous African solutions to Kete-
Krachi's problems of development and it is difficult to judge whether they might have been more
successful in the end if German colonialism had not
dropped upon the region with such ferocity.
Nevertheless the most intriguing part of this
historical power matrix in Kete-Krachi -- the
religious or myth power of the Dente Bosomfo -- was
largely destroyed and so one cannot follow through
what its role might have been in managing the
contemporary factional struggles. The office has
remained until today untouched by destoolment
vagaries and in this sense might have some role in
managing political mobilization in the future, but
the present Dente Bosomfo is not particularly
political.
    The divisions and factionalism continued in
Kete-Krachi despite the execution of Gyantrubi.
Throughout the colonial era the factions were muted
or activated at different times, depending on the
rewards to be won from conflict, but the fundamental divisions remained. In the 1950s and 1960s the
rewards of politics were once again high and
factions became quite visible. By allying with a
political party, members could secure for themselves money, contracts, loans and clientage. Thus
the correlation of national parties to local
factions was real, though local affinity to national ideologies was more vague. Today, however,
after 25 years under one party or another, military
or civilian rule, nothing has altered on the
national level. Ghanaian society in general still

reflects many traditional divisions because the
national parties (including the military) pursued
no real policies of development and change after-
all.
     Further, the incentive for allying one's
faction with a national political party has actually diminished because the chances of being finan-
cially depredated, publically humiliated, destooled, imprisoned, or even executed when your party
goes out and theirs comes in have increased dramat-
ically. The rewards are low once again for political competition in Kete-Krachi. The factions
persist but the visible issues are petty, the
tactics those of gossip. Only a complete re-
orientation of goals in Kete-Krachi (and places
like it throughout Ghana) will achieve fundamental
changes. As one recent author has perspicaciously
suggested, all of Ghana is presently limited to
such a conclusion:

> It would in principle be possible for the
> state either to devote greater energy to
> fostering domestic capital investment or
> alternatively to collectivize and socialize
> the economy, each of which moves would
> break down traditional relationships
> relatively rapidly. The gyrations at the
> center of national political life in Ghana
> do not mirror these structural relationship
> with any clarity. . . . But essentially it
> remains true that Ghana has exhibited a
> degree of stability in such relationships
> over time. The toils at the centre have
> represented little more than political
> manoeuvres within an urban 'middle class'
> and have made for little if any significant
> structural change in Ghana. [30]

I would like to say more than just that Kete-Krachi
demonstrates consisting and enduring historical
patterns, but only when Krachi factions cease being
like national factions -- pursuing only parasitic
benefits in political office -- can real social, if
not economic development take place in the country.

Notes

Abbreviations

ADM   Administrative File
BMA   Basel Mission Archives
C.   By Command of Her Majesty presented to
          Parliament of Great Britain
CO   Colonial Office
FN   Field Note
FO   Foreign Office
GBPP   Great Britain, Parliamentary Papers
IAS   Institute of African Studies, University of
          Ghana
NAG   National Archives of Ghana
PRO   Public Record Office, Great Britain

Introduction

1   Bonnat (1876) II: 665 and IV: 5.
2   GBPP, C. 1402 (1876) encl. in no. 77:   Bonnat
    to Strahan, 30 September 1875.
3   Bonnat (1876) IV: 5.
4   Bowdich (1821) map facing xxvi; Bowdich (1819)
    176 and 483; Dupuis (1824) Part II xxviii, xl,
    and map facing i.
5   Bowdich (1819) 176.
6   Dupuis (1824) xxxiv and xl.
7   NAG Accra, ADM 39/1/32:   German District Diary,
    Kete-Krachi, entry for 4 January 1895.
8   IAS JEK/2:   Ntwumuru-Gbede Traditions, recorded

by J.E.K. Kumah (1964) 3.

9   See D. Maier, "Kete-Krachi in the Nineteenth Century," Phd Dissertation (Northwestern University (1975) II: FN 104, Interview with Horrocks Gyiniso, Kete-Krachi 8 August 1973; also NAG Accra, ADM 56/1/368: Cardinall, diary entry for Kete-Krachi 11 October 1926, observing a Krachi chief being carried in a Dahomeyan palanquin. There is little evidence for Krachi political contracts with Dahomey, but some for the Dukoman (people living just south of Krachi) who had antagonistic relations with people in Dahomey (IAS AM/20: Dukoman Traditions, recorded by Ameyaw, 1964). Kumase definitely had political interaction with Abomey, some communications perhaps passing through Krachi: see GBPP, C. 3326 (1862) encl. 2 in no. 42: R. Lonsdale, "Report of his Mission to Coomassie, Salagha, Yendi, &c.," October 1881 to February 1882 [hereafter Lonsdale (1882)], 74-75; PRO FO 84/816: Beecroft's Journal of a Mission to Dahomey in 1850, entry of 1 June 1850; Duncan, (1847) I: 237-238 and 255; and, McCaskie, (1974) 161.

10 Bowdich (1819) 176.
11 Bowdich (1821) 17 and 60.
12 Ibid., 17-18.
13 Lee (1835) 153.
14 See for example NAG Accra, ADM 56/1/242: Norris, "Memo on the Salt Trade," Krachi 4 March 1922.
15 Bowdich (1819) 173.
16 Field (1960) 87-90
17 See NAG Tamale, ADM 1/632: Duncan-Johnstone, diary, 24 July 1930, reporting a discussion with the Krachiwura about the management of the ferry.
18 Lonsdale (1882) 78.

Chapter 2: Salt, Yams, and Slaves

1   Deutsche Kolonialzeitung, VII, 12 (10 November 1894) 153-154: Herold, "Kratchi und Bismarckburg."
2   Opoku (1885) 269, and Maier (1975) II: Field Note 37, interview with Amankrado Kwasi Osagyei, Kete-Krachi, 22 March 1973. The figure of 3% is a compromise estimate based on

Bonnat's contribution of 450 pounds of salt to the Dente Bosomfo from about 10,000 pounds of salt which he was transporting, and the fact that canoes carried 25 to 60 bags of salt each. The percentage could be quite difference under different circumstances and for different persons. The point it, however, that the quantity of salt required by the trade tax was far more than the Krachi elders' immediate households could consume and was therefore sold or traded.

3   Just recently an article by I.B. Sutton, "The Volta River Salt Trade: Survival of an indigenous industry," Journal of African History 22, 1 (1981) 43-61 was published. It is based on many of the same sources used here though directed toward a different purpose. Both Sutton and I however must be greatly indebted to the pioneer work on this subject by Ray Kea (1966).

4   Dapper (1668) 459.
5   Villault (1670) 263-264; Bosman (1705) 308.
6   Atkins (1735) 96 and 107.
7   See Bosman (1705) 308.
8   Bowdich (1819) 334 and 336.
9   Isert (1797) 67.
10 Barbot (1732) 320.
11 Isert (1797) 36.
12 See Multhauf (1978) Chapter 2 on the secrecy always involved in lagoon evaporation processes throughout the world.
13 NAG Accra, ADM 56/1/242: Le Lievre to Chief Commissioner of Eastern Province, 5 August 1922.
14 Wakkad (1961) 18.
15 NAG Accra, ADM 56/1/242: Hutter to District Commissioner Kete-Krachi, 10 June 1922.
16 Ibid, Le Lievre to Chief Commissioner of Eastern Province, 5 August 1922.
17 Ellis (1883) 194.
18 Der Evangelische Heidenbote, XLIII, 10 (October 1870): "Die Gefangen und der Krieg," quoting Ramseyer to David Asante, Kumase 8 July 1870; and Ramseyer and Kuhne (1875) 63, 222, and 226.
19 Kea (1966) quoting "Lind's Report on the Volta River, April 1828," in Extracts from Guineisk Journaller, 37-41, Furley Collection, Balme Library, University of Ghana, Legon.
20 Bowdich (1819) 176.

21 NAG Accra, ADM 56/1/242: Norris, "Memo on the Salt Trade," Krachi 24 March 1922.
22 Bonnat (1876) III: 664 and IV: 3-4.
23 Based on Ghana Surveys Map, Sheet 220, 1:50,000, 1953, and von Francois (1972) 78.
24 Proceedings of the Royal Geographic Society, nsVIII, 4 (April 1886): "Recent Explorations in the Basin of the Volta (Gold Coast)" 253.
25 Deutsche Kolonialzeitung, XIV, 5 (10 May 1911): Seidel, "Bilder aus Kete Kratschi."
26 Bonnat (1876) IV, 37.
27 See, for example, PRO CO 879/52, African (West) 549, Encl. in No. 27: Kenny-Herbert to Colonial Secretary, Yegi 9 February 1898 comparing the cost of canoe-borne loads with that of carrier transport. The weight carried by a canoe is estimated from the following figures: By 1890 salt was shipped in bags (Kling, 1890) which weighed according to Norris (1922) 100 lbs., to Hutter (1922) 90 lbs., and to Kenny-Herbert (1898) 60 lbs. Crabb (1902) maintained that the average canoe carried 25 to 60 bags. Thus a canoe could carry 1500 to 6000 lbs. This would accord with Bonnat for his barrels weighted at most 450 lbs. (1876, IV:5), his average canoe apparently carried only five barrels (III: 665) and he was delighted and surprised to find a canoe for sale large enough to carry 3000 lbs. of salt.
28 See Lonsdale (1882) 79-82; Wilks (1975) 30-31; and Maier (1975) II: Field Note 10, Interview with Gilbert Kpeglo, Kete-Krachi 16 February 1973. The informant reports that two or three days were required to reach Anum by canoe, going downstream.
29 Bosman (1705) 308.
30 BMA D-1, 41 (1884) No. 21: Muller to Basel, Aburi 5 May 1884.
31 Maier (1975) II: Field Note 13, Interview with Malam Momuni, Kete-Krachi, 22 February 1973.
32 Bowdich (1819) 341-342.
33 Kea (1966) quoting "Lind's Report on the Volta River, April 1828," in Extracts from Guineisk Journaller, 37-41, Furley Collection, Balme Library, University of Ghana, Legon; and Lonsdale (1882) 79.
34 The African Times, X, 110 (23 August 1870): 17; and Reade (1873) II: 170-173; and GBPP, C. 670

(1872): Salmon to Kennedy, 19 October 1871,
Encl. 1 in No. 13.

35 Wills (1962) 377.

36 Idem., and Allan (1965) 236.

37 Wills (1962) 377. See also Food and Agriculture Organization (FAO) of the United Nations,
Land and Water Survey in Ghana (1968) I: 9.
Yields as high as 15,967 1b./acre in Bimbila,
the region most resembling Krachi ecologically
of those surveyed by the FAO, are shown in IV,
27, Table 4.

38 Allan (1965) 238-239. Allan is giving statistics for Dagomba, but both he and the FAO
(1968) IV, 27, Table 4, maintain that yields
increase as one moved from Dagomba towards
Krachi, so the statistics are assumed to be
conservatively applicable for Krachi.

39 NAG Accra, ADM 11/1773: "Palaver Book,"
Kratschi 28 April 1903, 354; Krachi District
Office: "Comparative Statistics of Traffic in
Merchandise Passing through Krachi," Kete-
Krachi District Record Book; NAG Tamale, ADM
1/305: Commissioner to Colonial Secretary, 10
March 1938; NAG Accra, ADM 39/1/64: Page,
"Diary," Kete-Krachi 28 December 1932. See
also IAS AM/8: Traditions of North Afram,
recorded by Ameyaw, 1964, iii, where Krachis
opening a new yam village are described as
producing 100,000 yam per year.

40 Allan (1965) 231-232.

41 von Francois (1972) 24.

42 Klose (1899) 349.

43 Lonsdale (1882) 91, gives the largest population figure (2800) of any source. Most sources
average estimates of 300-400 huts. See BMA
D-1, 41 (1884) No. 21: Muller to Basel, Aburi
5 May 1884; Mittheilungen aus den Deutsche
Schutzgebiet, VI (1893) 67, Tafel 2; Klose
(1899) 340; and Bibliotheque Nationale, Lome,
G6: Jahresbericht Kete-Kratshi 1 July 1900.

44 Maier (1975) II: Field Note 19, Interview with
Malam Titibrika, Imam, Kete-Krachi 25 February
1973.

45 Ramseyer (1886) 82.

46 BMA D-1, 63, No. 128: Mischlisch to Basel, 4
May 1895.

47 GBPP, C. 1402 (1876): Bonnat to Strahan, 30
September 1875, Encl. in No. 77; and
Christaller (1886) 251, quoting Ramseyer.

48 NAG Accra, ADM 11/1770: Palaver Book, 26
    September 1887: The African Times, XVI (2
    October 1876) 39-40; Maier (1975) II: Field
    Note 16, Interview with Nana Krachiwura
    Obridgya II, Kete-Krachi 22 February 1973 and
    Field Note 38, Interview with Kwadwo Kumah,
    Genge 30 March 1973.
49 IAS JEK/5: Basa Traditions recorded by J.E.K.
    Kumah 1964.
50 PRO CO 96/191: Firminger to Griffith, 30 March
    1881.
51 PRO CO 879/39, African (West) 458, Encl. 1 in
    No. 45: G. Ferguson, "Memorandum," 24 November
    1893, para. 14.
52 Klose (1899) 342.
53 Dickson (1969) 121.
54 Isert (1797) 106.
55 Klose (1899) 342.
56 BMA, D-1, 61, No. 153: Clerk to Basel, Wora-
    wora, 28 September 1894.
57 PRO CO 96/195, Encl. 7 in confidential of 12
    November 1888: Evidence taken 27 March 1888.

Chapter 3: THE DENTE SHRINE

1   Dobson (1892) 24.
2   Westermann (1930) 228-231: quoting oral text,
    "The Story of the God Dente of Krachi."
3   PRO CO 879/9, African (West) 9: Gouldsbury,
    "Journey into the Interior," 27 March 1876.
4   Lonsdale (1882) 78.
5   Ramseyer (1886) 82.
6   PRO CO 879/39, African (West) 458, Encl. 1 in
    No. 45: Ferguson, "Memorandum" 24 Nov. 1893,
    para. 3.
7   IAS/203: Twomaduase Stool History, recorded by
    J. Agyeman-Dua (1964). See also IAS JEK/10:
    Basa Traditions, recorded by J.E.K. Kumah
    (1964) 5.
8   GBPP C. 892 (1874) Encl. 6 in No. 156: Glover,
    "Intelligence," 2 October 1873.
9   Lonsdale (1882) 100-101: Encl. of Graves,
    "History of Abruno Rebellion," n.d. Londale
    claimed (78) to have been told this personally
    by the Dente Bosomfo.
10 IAS JEK/5: Basa Traditions, recorded by Kumah
    (1964) 5.

11 IAS unaccessioned: Praman Traditions, recorded
    by Kumah (1963).
12 Lonsdale (1882) 78: IAS JEK/32: History of
    Krachi, recorded by Kumah, 1964, 43.
13 NAG Kumase, D 87: Nana Kofi Boaten Juabenehen
    to DC Juaso, Old Juaben 1 January 1925, and DC
    Juaso to Commissioner, 9 January 1925.
14 Cardinall (1931) 56.
15 NAG Accra, ADM 56/1/343: Cooper to Commis-
    sioner, Kete-Krachi 25 November 1930.
16 NAG Accra, ADM 11/1/603: Furley, Diary, 29
    January 1915.
17 See IAS JEK/32: "Traditional History of Krachi
    & Fetish Dente," recorded and edited Kumah
    (1969), a collapsing of several traditions.
    See also Maier (1975) II: Field Note 16,
    Interview with Nana Krachiwura Obridgya II,
    Kete-Krachi, 22 February 1973, Field Note 38,
    Interview with Nana Kwadwo Kumah, Genge 30
    March 1973, and Field Note 80, Interview with
    Nana Kwadwo Kumah, Genge, 16 July 1973; IAS
    AS/CR/42, 49-55: Kumawuhene vs. Dwanhene,
    Asantehene's "A" Court, 1951-1953; IAS AS/15:
    Juaben Stool History, recorded by Agyeman-Duah
    (1966); and NAG Tamale, ADM 1/180: Duncan
    Johnstone, "Memorandum," 26 August 1930, para.
    15.
18 Maier (1975) II: Field Note 16, Interview with
    Nana Krachiwura, Obridgya II, Kete-Krachi, 22
    February 1973, and Field Note 51, Interview
    with B.K. Mensah, Kete-Krachi 2 May 1973.
    Linguistically the Krachis and Lates are
    related, both speaking a dialect of Guan.
    However this hardly proves the case, for the
    Late and Krachi dialects are not mutually
    intelligible; moreover while Nchumuru is easily
    understood by Krachis, Nchumurus migrated from
    the north, not the south. See Chapter 4.
19 Kwamena-Poh (1972) 36-37.
20 Reindorf (1895) 91-92.
21 BMA Special File on Salaga Journeys: D.
    Asante, "Report on the Salaga Journey of 1877,"
    19 September 1878. Asante commented, in
    accordance with Reindorf, that the Krachis
    migrated from the 30 towns of Late, but he did
    not say that the Dente shrine also came from
    there. Rottman (1894) 367-369.
22 IAS JEK/10: Basa Traditions, recorded by Kumah
    (1964).

23 Klose (1902) 191.
24 Idem. Meyerowitz (1958) 140 comments that
    Dente abhorred the spilling of blood. This
    presumably accounts for the Late's burying
    their victims alive, as described by Rottman
    (1894). However, contrary to Meyerowitz's
    suggestion, this does not imply that Dente
    hated war, for as will be seen, the Dente
    Bosomfo led Krachis to several wars. Legge
    (NAG Accra, ADM 39/1/221: "Report on Dente
    Fetish," 9 February 1916) agrees with the
    latter point of view, although Cardinall (1931)
    64-65 is in accord with Meyerowitz, even
    suggesting that Dente's hatred of blood
    accounts for refugees settling there.
25 Hall (1965) 27-28.
26 Brokensha (1966) 89.
27 NAG Accra, ADM 11/1/782: "History of the
    Kratchis as Related by the Head Chief Kuji
    Dente to the District Political Officer,"
    Kete-Krachi, April 1920.
28 Cardinall (1931) 60 also doubted the
    authenticity of the Konkom story, commenting:
    ". . . when one considers that the Akwapim
    people were at one time interested in claiming
    rights over the Krachi the story is quite
    likely to have been mostly invented to support
    that claim. in any case the Krachi themselves
    refuse to admit that they have ever heard of
    such a romance . . ."
29 Maier (1975) II: Field Note 16, Interview with
    Nana Krachiwura Obridgya II, Kete-Krachi, 22
    February 1973.
30 Dobson (1892) 24.
31 Fisch (1911) 36-37.
32 Idem. The "countless bats" are a problem in
    Kete-Krachi even today as the author can
    testify. Almost every house there has a
    bat-infested roof, the odor being the most
    distressing aspect. Duncan-Johnstone (NAG
    Tamale, ADM 1/222: Diary, 17 December 1931)
    nick-named the District Commissioner's house in
    Kete-Krachi "Bat Villa."
33 von Rentzell (1922) 109.
34 NAG Tamale, ADM 1/132: Duncan-Johnstone,
    Diary, Kete-Krachi 5 March 1930. Rattray
    (1916) 52 also visited the shrine about 1915
    and gave a very similar description.

35 BMA Special File on Salaga Journeys: D. Asante, "Report on the Salaga Journey of 1877, 19 September 1878.

36 Maier (1975) II: Field Note 40, Interview with Horrocks Gyiniso, Kete-Krachi, 4 April 1973.

37 Idem.; see also Ramseyer (1886) 82.

38 Opoku (1885) 268.

39 Hall (1965) 55; Opoku (1885) 268; BMA Special File on Salaga Journeys: D. Asante, "Report on the Salaga Journey of 1877, 19 September 1878. However, Ramseyer (1886) 83 claimed that no one protested his use of lights, but the Dente Bosomfo was not in Krachikrom at the time.

40 Moxon (1969) 171.

41 Deutsche Kolonialzeitung, VII 12 (10 November 1894) 153-154: Herold, "Kratchi und Bismarckburg;" Bonnat for example (1876) III, 663, while travelling past monkey-infested Ajena Island on the middle Volta, had to refrain from the "desire to try my skill [at shooting] not wishing to expose myself to attracting an affair with the natives," for the monkeys there were considered sacred. Dobson (1892) 22 also mentioned dire penalties for killing the monkeys there.

42 Maier (1975) II: Filed Note 14, Interview with Horrocks Gyiniso, Kete-Krachi, 15 February 1973.

43 Klose (1899) 341 and Opoku (1885) 268. Goody (1971) 57-72 discusses several shrines that were "anti-horse" and views this as representing autochthone's symbolic resistance to the ruling estates whose dominance was based on cavalry and who were invaders and thus not linked to the land where the autochthone's superiority lay.

44 BMA Special File on Salaga Journeys: D. Asante, "Report on the Salaga Journey of 1877," 19 September 1878.

45 Opoku (1885) 267.

46 Warren (1971) II: "History of the God Dente at Techiman," by Nana Kwasi Minka, Akonnuasoani, collected 13 February 1971. Rattray (1923) 168 recorded a prayer from Tekyiman which included the statement "I went to Krakye Dente about snails that they might remain near the town," which indicates how much this branch shrine anyway was seen as an urban property shrine.

47 NAG Kumase, D 87: Kofi Boaten, Juabenhene to DC Juaso, Old Juaben, 1 January 1925.
48 Von Rentzell (1922) 76-78.
49 Maier (1975) II: Field Note 22, Interview with Yaw Atokra, Kete-Krachi 27 February 1973; Field Note 49, Interview with Nana Kwadwo Kumah, Genge, 13 April 1973; Field Note 51, Interview with B.K. Mensah, Kete-Krachi, 2 May 1973.
50 Debrunner (1961) passim discusses and analyses many of these "witchcraft" shrines and priests.
51 Deutsche Kolonialzeitung, VIII (19 October 1895) 329.
52 Klose (1899) 45 and 58.
53 Maier (1975) II: Field Note 49, Interview with Nana Kwadwo Kumah, Genge, 13 April 1973 and Field Note 93, Interview with Dente Bosomfo Kofi Tawia, Kete-Krachi 29 July 1973.
54 Ibid., Field Note 40, Interview with Horrocks Gyiniso, Kete-Krachi 4 April 1973.
55 Ibid., Field Note 75, interview with Nana Kwame Adotia, Kete-Krachi, 10 July 1973.
56 Klose (1899) 342.
57 NAG Tamale, ADM 1/135: Cooper, Diary, Kete-Krachi 28 October 1930.
58 Maier (1975) II: Field Note 24, Interview with Yaw Atokra, Kete-Krachi, 1 March 1973.
59 Krachi District Office: Burn, "Notes on Krachi History," 1932, Kete Krachi District Record Book.
60 NAG Accra, ADM 56/1/343: Cooper, Diary, Kete-Krachi 19 December 1930. See also NAG ADM 39/1/32: Burn, "Krachi Stool Conference, 24 October 1930; Kweku Kantankufureh to CCNT, Kete-Krachi 31 October 1932; and Krachiwura to DC Kete-Krachi, 16 November 1932.
61 BMA Special File on the Salaga Journeys: Opoku, "Annual Report," 12 April 1878, 11-12.
62 Klose (1899) 44.
63 GBPP, C. 892 (1874), Encl. 6 in No. 156: Glover, "Intelligence," 2 October 1873; and Bonnat (1876) IV, 5.
64 BMA D-1, 41, No. 4: Muller to Basel, 28 March 1884.
65 Deutsches Kolonialblatt, V, (15 August 1894): quoting letter from Doering 12 May 1894.
66 NAG Accra, ADM 39/1/64: Burn Diary, Kete-Krachi 20 October 1932.

67 Maier (1975) II: Field Note 74, Interview with
    Adontenhene Sreagyema, Kete-Krachi 10 July
    1973.
68 von Francois (1972) 23.
69 Bonnat (1876) IV, 5.
70 BMA, D-1, 69 (1898) No. 210: Awere "Yearly
    Report," Krakye-Kantankofore 28 December 1898.
71 Westermann (1930) 231:   "The Story of the God
    Dente of Krachi," oral text.
72 PRO CO 879/39 African (West) No. 458, Encl. 1
    in No. 45: Ferguson, "Memorandum," 24 November
    1893, para. 9.
73 Ramseyer (1886) 74.
74 PRO CO 879/30 African (West) No. 384:   Sunter
    to Colonial Office, Burnham, Somerset 25
    October 1890.
75 See Opoku (1878) 68; Ramseyer (1886) 82; and
    Proceedings of the Royal Geographic Society,
    nsVIII, 4 (April 1886) "Recent Explorations in
    the Basin of the Volta (Gold Coast)"   254,
    quoting Muller.
76 BMA Special File on the Salaga Journeys: D.
    Asante, "Report on the Salage Journey of 1877,"
    19 September 1878; Buss (1879) 34; and Muller
    (1884) 42.
77 Klose (1899) 358-359.

Chapter 4: Krachi Organization

1 Brokensha (1966) 80.
2 NAG Accra, ADM 39/1/32: Burn, "Notes on Krachi
   History," Kete-Krachi 4 September 1932.
   Several District Commissioners found Krachis
   "vague" about their early history, commenting
   that they "don't seem to know much about it;"
   they "muddle/it/up;" and they "lie" about it.
   Burn wrote, "I am . . . burning much midnight
   oil trying to piece it together but without
   much to show for it." See also NAG Tamale, ADM
   1/135: Cooper, Diary, 20 August, 23 and 24
   September 1930; and NAG Tamale, ADM 1/12:
   Luchan, 13 July 1931.
3 NAG Tamale, ADM 1/135: Cooper, Diary, Kete-
   Krachi 24 September 1930.
4 NAG Accra, ADM 56/1/343:   Court Evidence,
   Kete-Krachi 19 December 1930.
5 Maier (1975) II: Field Note 38, Interview with
   Nana Kwadwo Kumah, Genge, 30 March 1973.

6   See NAG Accra, ADM 56/1/343: Court Evidence,
    Kete-Krachi, December 1930; NAG Tamale, ADM
    1/132: Cockey, Diary, Kete-Krachi 26 June
    1931; NAG Tamale, ADM 1/123: Lochan, "Judgment
    in the Dispute between Asasewura and Krachi-
    wura," Tamale 13 July 1931; and NAG Accra, ADM
    39/1/32: Duncan-Johnstone, "Historical and
    Ethnological Notes on the People of the Krachi
    District to Supplement the Annual Report
    1931/32."
7   PRO CO 879/41 African (West No. 479) Encl. 1 in
    No. 80: Ferguson to Griffith, 22 February
    1895.
8   NAG Accra, ADM 56/1/330: Asasewura to Chief
    Commissioner, Kete-Krachi, 1 June 1931.
9   NAG Accra, ADM 56/1/343, Court Evidence,
    Kete-Krachi 18-19 December 1930; and NAG Accra,
    ADM 56/1/330: Asasewura to Chief Commissioner,
    Kete-Krachi, 1 June 1931.
10 IAS JEK/5: Basa Tradition, recorded by Kumah,
    1964.
11 Reindorf (1895) 88-89.
12 IAS JEK/7: Gyamboae Nkomi Traditions: re-
    corded by Kumah 1964; Maier (1975) II: Field
    Note 46, Interview with Kofi Kyikyade,
    Osramani, 10 April 1973; and NAG Accra, ADM
    56/1/343: Court Evidence, Kete-Krachi 19
    December 1930.
13 IAS JEK/2: Traditions of Ntwumuru-Gbede and
    Ajanae-Krachi, recorded by Kumah 1964.
14 Idem.
15 IAS JEK/7: Gyamboae Nkomi Traditions, recorded
    by Kumah 1964.
16 Idem., and NAG Accra, ADM 56/1/343: Court
    Evidence, Kete-Krachi 19 December 1930.
17 Maier (1975) II: Field Note 73, Interview with
    Akpawia Kusun Amoa, Kete-Krachi 6 July 1973.
18 Kete-Krachi District Office: Walker, "Notes on
    the Constitution of the Krachi Native
    Authority," Kete-Krachi 1940, Kete-Krachi
    District Record Book; IAS JEK/23: Traditions
    of Krachi, recorded by Kumah 1965; Maier (1975)
    II: Field Note 90, Interview with Kachipa
    Kwame, Kete-Krachi 28 July 1973.
19 NAG Accra, ADM 11/1/794: "History of the Pai
    Land by the Omanhene of Kwahu," 13 December
    1920. See also NAG Accra, ADM 11/1/694: Morris
    "Palaver at Kete-Krachi," 15-20 October 1920;

and IAS AM/26: "Apai Ahenkro Tradition," recorded by Ameyaw 1964.

20 NAG Accra, ADM 56/1/368: Cardinall, Diary, Nkanero 20 November 1924; and Cardinall (1931) 56.

21 Maier (1975) II: Field Note 33, Interview with Nana Kwasi Mensha, New Gyanekrom, 14 March 1973. See also IAS JEK/4: Atafie and Dadiase Traditions, recorded by Kumah 1964.

22 Maier (1975) II: Field Note 51, Interview with B.K. Mensah, Kete-Krachi, 3 May 1973.

23 Idem.

24 Klose (1896) 201-202; Kete-Krachi District Office: Cooper, "Notes on the Krachi people," 1930, Kete-Krachi District Record Book

25 See Maier (1975) II: Field Note 51, Interview with B.K. Mensah, Kete-Krachi 3 May 1973 and Field Note 60, Interview with Nana Kwame Ambonya, Dambae, 30 May 1973; and NAG Tamale, ADM 1/385: McKenzie-Ingles, "Report on the Nchumuru People," Salaga 26 March 1935.

26 NAG Accra, ADM 39/1/32: Burn, "Krachi Stool Conference, Kete-Krachi Stool Conference," Kete-Krachi 24 October 1932. See also the order of signatures in ibid.: Krachiwura to DC Kete-Krachi, 16 November 1932.

27 Maier (1975) II: Field Note 75, Interview with Nana Kwame Adotia, Kete-Krachi 10 July 1973.

28 Idem., and ibid., Field Note 61, Interview with B.K. Mensah, Kete-Krachi 5 June 1973.

29 Lonsdale (1882) 92: Graves, "History of Abruno Rebellion," n.d.; BMA, D-1 (1895) No. 131: Hall, "Travelling Report," Ntwumuru 17 September 1895.

30 BMA, D-1 (1894) 153: Clerk, "Report of a Visit to Krakye," 28 September 1894; and BMA, D-1 (1884) 21: Muller, 5 May 1884.

31 See for example BMA Special File on Salaga Journeys: Opoku, "Annual Report," 12 April 1878, 11-12.

32 Lonsdale (1882) 77-78.

33 Rattray (1932) 411.

34 Ramseyer (1886) 75.

Chapter 5: Asante-Krachi Relations

1 Reindorf (1895) 88-89.

2 IAS AS/16: Juaben Stool History: record by J.
   Agyeman-Duah (1963); IAS JEK/10:   Basa Traditions, recorded by Kumah (1964).
3 See Wilks (1975) 112-119.
4 Maier (1975) II: Field Note 52, Interview with
   Kwame Nsia, 3 May 1973, Kete-Krachi.
5 NAG Accra, ADM 11/1/794: "History of the
   Krachis as Related by Head Chief Kuji Dente to
   the District Political Officer," Kete-Krachi
   April 1920.
6 IAS JEK/5: Basa Traditions recorded by Kumah
   (1964); see also Maier (1975) II: Field Note
   74, Interview with Adontenhene Sreagyema 10
   July 1973, Kete Krachi, which relates the same
   incident.
7 IAS AS/16: Juaben Stool History, recorded by
   J. Agyeman-Duah (1963).
8 Reindorf (1895) 282-283.
9 Riis (1840) 229-230.
10 GBPP, C. 1402 (1876) No. 77: Strahan to
   Carnarvon Cape Coast 25 October 1875.
11 Riis (1840) 230-231.
12 Wilks (1975) 118.
13 Riis (1840) 230-231.
14 Maier (1975) II: Field Note 54, Interview with
   Nana Kwabena Kobi 10 May 1973, Kadentwe; see
   also Field Note 72, Interview with Dente
   Bosomfo Kofi Tawia, 5 July 1973, Kete-Krachi;
   see also Reindorf (1895) 293.
15 Maier (1975) II: Field Note 72, Interview with
   Dente Bosomfo Kofi Tawia, 5 July 1973, Kete-
   Krachi, and IAS AM/14:   History of Ajade
   recorded by Ameyaw 1964.
16 Maier (1975) II: Field Note 46, Interview with
   Kofi Kyikyade, 10 April 1973, Osramani; and
   Field Note 74, Interview with Adontenhene
   Sreagyema, 10 July 1973, Kete-Krachi. In all
   these cases -- Dente Bosmfo, Krachiwura, and
   Adontenhene office lists -- the founder of the
   group is sometimes mentioned, but either long
   gaps follow or the founders are ignored and the
   next earliest office holder is the person
   credited with fighting at Krupi.
17 See for example Maier (1975) II: Field Note
   57, Interview with Firao Bosomfo Kofi Brebe, 23
   May 1973, Dambae; Field Note 74, Interview with
   Adontenhene Sreagyema, 10 July 1973, Kete-
   Krachi; Field Note 37, Interview with Amankrado
   Kwasi Osagyei, 22 March 1973, Kete-Krachi; and

Field Note 31, Interview with Motodiahene Kofi
Fusu, 12 March 1973, Osramani.

18 NAG Accra, ADM 39/1/32: Burn, "Notes on Krachi
History" Kete-Krachi, 4 September 1932. See
also IAS, Comparative African Wordlists
(February 1966) No. 1.

19 Lander (1832) 373; see in contrast IAS JEK/5:
Basa Traditions, recorded by Kumah, 1964.

20 IAS JEK/5: Basa Traditions, recorded by Kumah,
1964.

21 Maier (1975) II: Field Note 39: Interview
with Kwame Nsia, 2 April 1973, Kantankofore.

22 National Archives, Copenhagen, Generaltold
Kammerets Arkiv. Guinea Journals (1832-1833):
Lind et al., Christiansborg 27 April 1833, from
Wilks (1975) 274.

23 Maier (1975) II: Field Note 34, Interview with
Nana Kwadwo Kumah, 16 March 1973, Genge.

24 Reindorf (1895) 293.

25 Maier (1975) II: Field Note 34, Interview with
Nana Kwadwo Kumah, 16 March 1973, Genge; and
Field Note 51, Interview with B.K. Mensah, 2
May 1973, Kete-Krachi.

26 Ibid., Field Note 51, Interview with B.K.
Mensah, 2 May 1973, Kete-Krachi.

27 Reindorf (1895) 293.

28 NAG ADM 39/1/32: Notes on Krachi History, by
Burn, Kete-Krachi, 4 September 1932.

29 Idem. See also NAG Tamale ADM 1/435: Cooper to
Manners, Kete-Krachi 10 November 1930; NAG
Accra, ADM 39/1/64: Spooner, "Diary," Salaga,
22 October 1934; IAS AM/14: History of Ajade,
recorded by Ameyaw (1964) 7; and IAS AM/15:
Akroso Tradition, recorded by Ameyaw (1964) 4.

30 Priestly and Wilks (1960) 91.

31 NAG Accra, ADM 39/1/64: Spooner, "Diary,"
Salaga 22 October 1934.

32 See Maier (1975) II: Field Note 33, Interview
with Nana Kwasi Mensah, 14 March 1973, New
Gyanekrom, in which some of the precursors of
the Dwabens at New Gyanekrom are said to have
fought with the Krachi Adontens at Pae.

33 Reindorf (1895) 293-294.

34 Ibid., 294.

35 NAG Accra, ADM 11/1/794: "History of the
Krachis as related by the Head Chief Kuji Dente
to the District Political Officer," Kete-
Krachi April 1920.

36 Idem.

37 GBPP (1874) C. 892, Encl. 6 in No. 156: Glover, "Crepee," 2 October 1873.
38 NAG Accra, ADM 11/1/794: "History of the Krachis as related by the Head Chief Kuji Dente to the District Political Officer," Kete-Krachi April 1920; see also Maier (1975) II: Field Note 21, Interview with Yaw Atokra, 27 February 1972, Kete-Krachi.
39 Henty (1874) 462, quoting "a gentleman;" also Croft (1874) 189.
40 Reade (1873) II, 170-173; see also Horton (1870) 75-89; and PRO CO 96/79: Simpson to Kennedy, Akwaum 2 March 1869.
41 GBPP (1875), C. 1140, No. 85: Strahan to Canarvon 13 July 1874.
42 BMA Special File on Salaga Journeys: Opoku, "Annual Report," 12 April 1878, 15.
43 Bonnat (1876) IV: 5, and III: 665 (diary entries dated 20 January 1876 and 15 December 1875, respectively.
44 PRO CO 879/9 African (West) 95: Gouldsbury, "Journey into the Interior," 27 March 1876.
45 BMA Special File on Salaga Journeys: Opoku, "Annual Report," 12 April 1878, 15.
46 Opoku (1885) 271.
47 BMA Special File on Salaga Journeys: Opoku, "Annual Report," 12 April 1878, 15.
48 Christaller (1886) 24, quoting David Asante.
49 Lonsdale (1882) 78.
50 GBPP C. 1402 (1876): Encl. in No. 77: Bonnat to Strahan, 30 September 1875; and L'Explorateur (1876) III: 238, which printed a complete version of Bonnat's treaty with the Asantehene and the Council.
51 GBPP C. 1402 (1876): Encl. in No. 77: Bonnat to Strahan, 30 September 1875.
52 Ibid., Encl. 2 in No. 74: Osei Mensah to Strahan, 2 September 1875.
53 Ibid., Encl. 1 in No. 87: Gouldsbury to Strahan, 8 November 1875.
54 Lonsdale (1882) 100-101: Graves, "History of Abruno Rebellion."
55 Bonnat (1876) III: 663, 665, and IV: 5.
56 Ibid., III: 665.
57 Ibid., III: 664.
58 Ibid., IV: 5.
59 Ibid., II: 665.
60 Ibid., IV: 5.
61 Idem.

62 PRO CO 879/9 African (West) 95: Gouldsbury, "Journey into the Interior, Accra 27 March 1876.
63 The African Times, XVII, No. 182 (2 October 1876) 39-40: quoting a letter from Owusa Ansa to Bonnat, Kumasi 17 February 1876.

Chapter 6: The Bron Confederation

1 PRO CO 879/9 African (West) 95: Gouldsbury, "Report on Journey into the Interior," 27 March 1876.
2 Idem.
3 Idem.
4 Idem.
5 Ibid., "Treaty between Gouldsbury and Kwasi Basamunah, King, and Kwasi Dentie, Fetish Priest," 8 March 1876.
6 BMA Special File on Salaga Journeys: Opoku, "Annual Report," 12 April 1878, 15-17.
7 Ibid., 3-4; and PRO CO 879/39 African (West) 458, Encl. 1 in No. 45: Ferguson, "Memorandum," 24 November 1893, paras. 5 and 12.
8 NAG Accra ADM 11/1/794: "History of the Kratchis as related by Head Chief Kuji Dente to the District Political Officer," Kete-Kratchi April 1920.
9 Croft (1874) 191. See also Bonnat (1876) III: 665 and IV: 4, 36, and 66.
10 Binger (1890) II: 587.
11 Bonnat (1876) II: 587; Bevin (1960) 1-12.
12 Dobson (1892) 23.
13 GBPP C. 3386 (1882) No. 18: Row to Kimberley, 16 January 1882, contains sample lists of the many items carried by various Accra-Salaga traders.
14 NAG Accra, ADM 1/467: Freeling to Secretary of State, 10 February 1877.
15 NAG Accra, ADM 1/470: Ussher to Secretary of State, 5 April 1880. See also Ellis (1883) 188-190 for a description of Asantehene Mensa Bonsu's successful plans for creating this force.
16 See Wilks (1975) and Lewin (1978) for more complete coverage.
17 Claridge (1915) II: 199.
18 The African Times (2 October 1876) XVII, No. 182: 39-40; and Rattray (1929) Fig. 83.

19   Rattray (1929) 262.
20   Maier (1975) II: Field Note 16, Interview with
     Nana Krachiwura Obridgya II, 22 February 1973,
     Kete-Krachi; and Field Note 38, Interview with
     Nana Kwadwo Kumah, 30 March 1973, Genge.
     "Kete" can be a dance; it can also refer to a
     particular type of band or orchestra which
     consists of drums, pipes and singers. It is a
     state orchestra attached to an important chief
     or queen mother. (Nketia, 1963, 128-133 and
     143). The Asantehene had his own Kete band,
     and Ramseyer and Kuhne associated it with
     unpleasant times: "The Kind seldom dances this
     Kete dance, but when he does many shudder who
     are usually indifferent" (1875, 120). However
     the Kete band also plays for state reception
     and funerals and in Kete-Krachi case had
     probably been brought with the Queen Mother of
     Nsuta who had settled at Krachi.
21   Ramseyer (1886) 252; PRO CO 879/28 African
     (West) 356, Encl. in No. 9: Firminger to
     Griffith 20 March 1888; and PRO 879/39 African
     (West) 458, Encl. 1 in No. 45: Ferguson,
     "Memorandum" 24 November 1893, para. 4.
22   GBPP C. 1402 (1876) Encl. in No. 77: Bonnat to
     Strahan, 30 September 1875; BMA Special File on
     Salaga Journeys: Opoku, "Annual Report," 12
     April 1878, 7; PRO 879/39 African (West) 458,
     Encl. 1 in No. 45: Ferguson, "Memorandum," 24
     November 1893, para. 4. See also PRO CO
     96/215: Ferguson, "Report on Mission to
     Atebubu," 1891.
23   Lonsdale (1882) 78-79.
24   Ramseyer (1886) 75.
25   See especially Rattray (1929) 103-104, where a
     sample oath of allegiance is given, and Rattray
     (1927) 205-215, which contains a long dis-
     cussion of oaths.
26   BMA D-1, 79 (1903) No. 64: Clerk, "Meine
     Missionsarbeit im Voltagebiet, 1888-1903," 36.
27   Maier (1975) II: Field Note 38, Interview with
     Nana Kwadwo Kumah, 30 March 1973, Genge; and
     PRO 879/39 African (West) 458, Encl. 1 in No.
     45: Ferguson, "Memorandum" 24 November 1893,
     para. 10.
28   Lonsdale (1882) 77-78.
29   Ibid., 70.
30   Ramseyer (1886) 74.

31 Lonsdale (1882) 100-101: Graves, "History of
    the Abruno Rebellion." Many of the inhabitants
    had still not returned in 1884, for which see
    Ramseyer (1886) 81.
32 The African Times (2 October 1876) XVII, No.
    182: 39-40; Lonsdale (1882) 75; and GBPP C.
    4052 (1884) Encl. 4 in No. 15: Quacoe Cuah, a
    Messenger, "Statement," Christiansborg 16
    August 1883.
33 PRO 879/39 African (West) 458, Encl. 1 in No.
    45: Ferguson, "Memorandum," 24 November 1893,
    para. 14.
34 Ramseyer (1886) 75.
35 BMA D-1, 61 (1894) No. 132: Perregaux to
    Basel, Abetifi, 10 Mai 1894.
36 Comparisons with the Gold Coats Colony are
    interesting in this aspect because the Colony
    was serving the same purpose of a secure site
    for subversion of Asante throughout the nine-
    teenth century, although the Colony was being
    used to a much greater degree than Bron.
37 Lonsdale (1882) 66.
38 See Wilks (1975) 527-543.
39 PRO CO 879/21 African (West) 277, Encl. in No.
    48: Kirby, "Report," Accra 15 April 1884.
40 NAG Accra, ADM 11/1/1170: "Palaver Book,"
    entry of 26 September 1887, 196.
41 Wilks (1875) 577-578.
42 GBPP C. 5615 (1888): Barnett to Governor,
    Eduabin, 24 February 1888, 31.
43 NAG Accra, ADM 11/1/1170: "Palaver Book,"
    entry of 26 September 1887, 196.
44 GBPP C. 7917 (1896) No. 5: Hodgson to Knuts-
    ford, 9 December 1889.
45 PRO 879/39 African (West) 458, Encl. 1 in No.
    45: Ferguson, "Memorandum," 24 November 1893,
    para. 10.
46 Wilks (1975) 297.
47 PRO CO 879/38 African (West) 448, Encl. 1 in
    No. 21: Ferguson to Griffith, Ateobu, 17 May
    1892.
48 PRO 879/39 African (West) 458, Encl. 1 in No.
    45: Ferguson, "Memorandum" 24 November 1893,
    para. 14.
49 Ibid., para. 12; PRO CO 879/38 African (West)
    448, Encl. 1 in No. 21: Ferguson to Griffith,
    Ateobu, 17 May 1892; and PRO CO 96/232:
    Williams and Hull to Griffith, 1 June 1892.

50   NAG Accra, ADM 12/5/184: Griffith to Ramseyer, 31 August 1892.

51   NAG Accra, ADM 1/9/4: Griffith to Williams, 29 March 1888, and Griffith to Ferguson 21 October 1890.

52   NAG Accra ADM 12/5/181: Hodgson to Inspector General, 29 September 1893; and NAG Accra ADM 12/5/184: Griffith to King Kwabina Asante of Atebubu, 1 September 1892.

53   PRO 879/39 African (West) 458, Encl. 1 in No. 45: Ferguson, "Memorandum," 24 November 1893, para. 13.

54   Idem.

55   BMA D-1, 58 (1893) No. 58: Muller to Basel, 13 October 1893, quoting Clerk to Muller, Wora-wora, 23 September 1893.

56   NAG Accra ADM 12/5/184: Griffith to Ramseyer, 31 August 1892.

57   PRO 879/39 African (West) 458, Encl. 1 in No. 45: Ferguson, "Memorandum," 24 November 1893, para. 14.

58   Ibid., para. 12.

59   PRO CO 879/39 African (West) 458, Encl. 2 in No. 24: Hull to Hodgson, 17 September 1893; Ibid., Encl. 2 in No. 39: Ferguson to Hodgson, Atabubu, 27 October 1893.

60   NAG Accra, ADM 12/5/181: Hodgson to Inspector General 29 September 1893.

61   Maier (1975) II: Field Note 74, Interview with Adontenhene Sreagyema, 10 July 1973, Kete-Krachi; and Field Note 53, Interview with Isaac Kwadwo Boame, 4 May 1973, Genge.

62   PRO CO 879/39 African (West) 458, Encl. 2 in No. 39: Ferguson to Hodgson, Atabubu, 27 October 1893; Ibid., Encl. 1 in No. 45: Ferguson, "Memorandum," 24 November 1893, para. 9.

63   GBPP C. 7917 (1896), Encl. 3 in No. 43: Scott to Colonial Secretary, 7 November 1893; and Ibid., Encl. 4 in No. 43: Ramseyer to Acting Governor, 5 November 1893.

64   Ibid., Encl. 1 in No. 42: Vroom to Colonial Secretary, 20 November 1893.

65   PRO CO 879/39 African (West) 458, Encl. 5 in No. 39: Hodgson to Herr Boeder, 14 November 1893.

Chapter 7:   Islam and Traditional Religion

1   Bonnat (1876) IV: 5.
2   BMA Special File on Salaga Journeys: Opoku, "Annual Report," 12 April 1878, 12.
3   Maier (1975) II: Field Note 39, Interview with Kwame Nsia, 2 April 1973, Kantankofore.
4   Ibid., Field Note 19, Interview with Imam Malam Titibrika, 25 February 1973, Kete-Krachi.
5   Ivor Wilks, FN/63:   Interview with al-Hajj Muhammed Limam Thani, Kete-Krachi, 16 June 1963.
6   Maier (1975) II: Field Note 19, Interview with Imam Malam Titibrika, 25 February 1973, Kete-Krachi.
7   BMA Special File on Salaga Journeys: Opoku, "Annual Report," 12 April 1878, 12-13.
8   Maier (1975) II: Field Note 17, Interview with al-Hajj Saidu, 24 February, 1973, Kete-Krachi.
9   Glover (1874) 290.
10 This population chart is based on the following sources:
   a   Bonnat (1876) IV, 5.
   b   Opoku (1977) 12.
   c   Buss (1879) 35.
   d   Lonsdale (1882) 91.
   e   Ramseyer (1886) 82.
   f   von Francois (1889) 34.
   g   Mitteilungen aus den Deutshe Schutzgebieten (1893) VI, Tafel 2.
   h   Deutsches Kolonialblatt (15 August 1894) 426.
   i   Klose (1899) 335.
   j   BMA, D-1, 63, No. 128:A: Mischlisch to Basel, 4 May 1895.
   k   NAG Accra, ADM 56/1/242:   Hutter to DC, 10 June 1922.
   l   Bibliotheque Nationale, Lome, G6:   Jahresbericht Kete Kratschi, 10 July 1901.
   m   Sprigade Map of Togo (1906).
   n   Gold Coast Census (1921).
   o   Gold Coast Census (1931).
   p   Gold Coast Census (1948).
   q   Ghana Census (1960).
   r   Ghana Census (1970).
11 See GBPP C. 3064, (1881) No. 130:   Rowe to Kimberly, Elmina 12 June 1881; and GBPP C. 3386

(1882), Encl. 1 in No. 7: Rowe to Lonsdale, 15 October 1881.

12 GBPP C. 3386 (1882), No. 7: Rowe to Kimberley, Accra 17 October 1881.

13 Lonsdale (1882) 61.

14 Ibid., 77.

15 Ibid., 78.

16 Ibid., 82.

17 NAG Accra, ADM 11/1/782: "Statement made by Alli . . . this 4th day of June 1883."

18 Maier (1975) II: Field Note 19, Interview with al-Hajj Saidu, 24 February 1973, Kete-Krachi. It is said that there was no need for a Sarkin Zongo in the early years of the Kete community when it was small (Ibid., Field Note 25, Interview with Malam Musa Zubari, 4 March 1973, Zongo).

19 Ibid., Field Note 18, Interview with Alidu Gazaru, 24 February 1973, Kete-Krachi.

20 PRO CO 96/191: Firminger to Griffith, 20 March 1888, is Firminger's report on his entire journey. The letter describing the case as Firminger heard it is not filed among his other correspondence. Since Governor Griffith meticulously forwarded all other letters which Firminger wrote, it is likely that the former suppressed the affair. Griffith certainly felt that it was not a matter to be brought to the Colonial Office's attention, for whatever reason, because he wrote the Colonial Office in defense of his not informing them: "The murder case . . . must be held to have been dealt with in accordance with the law." (PRO CO 96/127: Griffith to Knutsford, 16 April 1888).

21 BMA D-1, 47 (1887) No. 45: Muller to Basel, Akropong 24 April 1887.

22 PRO CO 96/185, Encl. 1 in 413: Firminger to White, 26 October 1887; Deutsche Kolonial-zeitung (10 November 1894) VII: Herold, "Kratchie und Bismarckburg." See also Maier (1975) II: Field Note 23, Interview with Ma'azu, 27 February 1973, Kete-Krachi, a copy of an authorization note in the possession of Sofo's son.

23 PRO CO 96/185, Encl. 1 in 413: Firminger to White, 26 October 1887.

24 NAG Accra, ADM 11/794: Hodgson to King Kwako Badomagya of Kratchie, Accra 17 November 1888.

25 NAG Accra, ADM 1/9/2: Freeville-Green, for Freeling, to DC Cape Coast, Accra 8 March 1878; Lonsdale (1882) 69.
26 Ibid., 78.
27 NAG Accra, ADM 1/9/4: Griffith to Williams, 3 January 1888, discusses the Ƚ100 of goods left in the keeping of Dente Bosomfo by Firminger for other Gold Coast recruiting Expedition which passed through Kete-Krachi regularly.
28 NAG Accra, ADM 11/1/794: Hodgson to King Kwako Badomagya of Kratchie, Accra 17 November 1888.
29 PRO CO 879/34 African (West) 406, Encl. 1 in No. 27: Herold to Badomgya, Akrosso 10 November 1890.
30 Deutsche Kolonialzeitung (6 February 1892) V: "Das Togogebiet," 19-22. See also Kling (1892) 2-3.
31 Deutsches Kolonialblatt (15 August 1894) VII: Herold, "Kratschi und Bismarckburg."
32 Deutsche Kolonialzeitung (10 November 1894) VII: Herold, "Kratschi und Bismarckburg."
33 Braimah and Goody (1967) provide an excellent narrative of what occurred prior to and during the Salaga Civil War of 1892.
34 PRO CO 879/39 African (West) 458, Encl. 7: Odonkor, Chief of Kpong, to Hull, Kpong 5 June 1893.
35 Idem.
36 Braimah and Goody (1967) 45.
37 Ibid., 50.
38 Ibid., 154, quoting Krause, Yeji 5 September 1894.
39 Klose (1899) 380 and 363.
40 Deutsches Kolonialblatt (15 August 1894) V: "Togo" 426, quoting von Doering.
41 Exchange value is taken here to be the value manifested when commodities or services change hands. It is not necessarily related to the intrinsic value of commodities, but is considered to increase when demand increases.
42 Klose (1899) 362 and 365. Lonsdale expected this of the Krachi authorities as well: see para. 1 of his "Memorandum for the King and Chiefs of Kratshie, and the Chief Priest of Denty," quoted on p. 176-177.
43 Klose (1899) 335; BMA D-1, 63 (1895) No. 153: Rosler to Basel 16 September 1895.
44 Klose (1899) 342.

45 PRO CO 879/39 African (West) 458, Encl. 6 in
    No. 84: Lang, "Notes," 7 March 1894.
46 Klose (1899) 338-339.
47 Maier (1975) II: Field Note 20, Interview with
    Ma'azu, 26 February 1973, Kete-Krachi.
48 Deutsche Kolonialzeitung (10 November 1894)
    VII: Herold, "Kratchi und Bismarckburg."
49 The decision to establish a station at Kete-
    Krachi was opposed at first by the German
    Colonial Society, publisher of Deutsche
    Kolonialzeitung and representative of German
    business interests in the empire, because it
    meant that Bismarckburg Station would have to
    be abandoned. The Society demanded that the
    Government budget more money for the colonies
    rather than abandoning established stations.
    Officers like Herold and Doering however were
    quite persuasive when writing about the
    quantity of trade at Kete-Krachi, and hence the
    importance of having a station there. Bis-
    marckburg, as they pointed out, was in the
    mountains and not on any trade route, and
    indeed was distinguished for very little except
    the view. See Deutsche Kolonialzeitung (1894)
    VII: articles of 8 September, 13 October, and
    10 November. See Deutsches Kolonialblatt (15
    August 1894) V: "Togo," 426, quoting von
    Doering.
50 Deutsche Kolonialzeitung (10 November 1894)
    VII: Herold, "Kratchi und Bismarckburg."
51 BMA D-1, 61 (1894) No. 156: CLerk to Basel,
    Jahresbericht, 1894.
52 Maier (1975) II: Field Note 79, Interview with
    Nana Kwadwo Kumah, 13 July 1973, Genge.
53 Ibid., Field Note 19, Interview with Imam Malam
    Titibrika, 25 February 1973, Kete-Krachi.
54 BMA D-1, 61 (1894) No. 156: Clerk to Basel,
    Worawora 31 December 1894.
55 PRO CO 879/43 African (West) 496, Encl. in No.
    47: Malet to Salisbury, Berlin 10 October
    1895, reporting accounts in the German news-
    papers of a lecture given by Dr. Bruner re-
    calling his experiences on the expedition.
56 Maier (1975) II: Field Note 21, Interview with
    Yaw Atokra, 27 February 1973, Kete-Krachi.
57 PRO CO 879/43 African (West) 496, Encl. in No.
    50: Gruner, "Statement," Berlin 10 October
    1895.

58 Maier (1975) II: Field Note 20, Interview with
    Ma'azu, 26 February 1973, Kete-Krachi; and
    Malam Bello, "History of German Settlement at
    Kete-Krachi," 23 July 1973, given to the author
    3 August 1973.
59 IAS unaccessioned: "Historical Materials
    collected from Mallam al-Hassan Biosama," by
    Kumah, Kete-Krachi 1964.
60 See for example PRO CO 879/43 African (West)
    496, Nos. 50-55. A formal apology was de-
    manded, and received, from the Governor of
    Togoland for the boundary violation: PRO CO
    879/45 African (West) 507, Encl. in No. 14:
    Kohler to Maxwell, Sebbe 10 March 1896.
61 PRO CO 879/41 African (West) 479, Encl. 1 in
    No. 80: Ferguson to Griffith, Christiansborg
    22 February 1895. Ferguson arrived at British
    Krachi across the river from Kete-Krachi on 31
    December 1894 and was able to interview several
    people who had witnessed the arrests.
62 Ibid., Encl. 1 in No. 57:   Ferguson to
    Griffith, Nkoranza 15 December 1894.   What is
    apparently the German order of execution is
    found in NAG Accra ADM 39/1/221:   Legge to
    Senior Political Officer at Lome, Kete-Krachi 9
    February 1916, and is dated "26/11/?" pre-
    sumably 26 November 1894, and this contradicts
    Ferguson's information unless one assumes the
    Germans were writing up the reasons for the
    execution the morning after.   On November 27
    Gruner left Kete-Krachi (Deutsche Kolonial-
    zeitung 19 October 1895), and hence the execu-
    tion occurred prior to that date.
63 PRO CO 879/43 African (West) 496, Encl. in No.
    50:   Gruner, "Statement," Berlin 10 October
    1895.
64 PRO CO 879/41 African (West) 479, Encl. 1 in
    No. 80: Ferguson to Griffith, Christiansborg
    22 February 1895.
65 NAG Accra ADM 39/1/32:   German Kete-Krachi
    District Diary, entry 6 February 1895.
66 PRO CO 879/41 African (West) 479, Encl. 1 in
    No. 80: Ferguson to Griffith, Christiansborg
    22 February 1895.
67 BMA D-1, 63 (1895) No. 131:   Hall, "Report of
    journey to Krakye and Adele," Ntwumuru 17
    September 1895; and Klose (1899) 365.

68 NAG Accra ADM 39/1/32: German Kete-Krachi
    District Diary, entries 31 December 1894, and 2
    January 1895.
69 Ibid., entry 29 January 1895.

Chapter 8: German Colonial Rule

1   Formerly the Asantes had participated in this
    competition and were still involved indirectly,
    given the presence of Nsuta, Atebubu, and
    Dwaben refugees in Kete-Krachi. However, New
    Dwaben was now established deep in the Gold
    Coast Colony. Kumase relinquished plans for
    bringing Krachi again under its authority in
    the 1890s, concentrating on more immediate
    problems such as election disputes and re-
    bellions in Nsuta, Nkroansa and Atebubu. In
    1896 Asantehene Agyeman Prempe I was deported
    by the British, and then Asante ceased entirely
    to pose a threat to Krachi.
2   BMA D-1, 63 (1895) No. 131: Hall, "Report of
    journey to Krakye and Adele," Ntwumuru 17
    September 1895.
3   PRO CO 879/48 African (West) 529: Parmeter,
    "Report from British Krachi," 31 March 1897;
    see Deutsches Kolonialblatt (15 August 1897)
    VIII: 489-490, for an eye-witness account of
    the fire.
4   On forced labor see Great Britain, Foreign
    Office Confidential 9753, Part XII (1910):
    "Report on German Togoland," 1 May 1910, and
    Confidential 10316, Part XIX (1913): Wallis,
    "Report on Togoland," 10 April 1913. on the
    burning of a market place see Braimah and Goody
    (1967) 181-184. For a summary of escalating
    German and British trade restrictions in the
    area see NAG Accra, ADM 56/1/39: Williams to
    Chief Commissioner Northern Territories, 5 June
    1905. On emigration of whole villages to
    British territory, which must surely have been
    caused by many of the same factors which
    effected Kete-Krachi's population drop, see NAG
    Accra, ADM 12/5/149: "Intelligence Report," 31
    December 1908.
5   PRO CO 879/41 African (West) 479, Encl. 1 in
    No. 80: Ferguson to Griffith, Christiansborg 22
    February 1895.

6   See Trierenberg (1913) passim for a complete
    account of German movements from 1888-1900.
    See also Deutsche Kolonialzeitung, (19 October
    1895) for the itinerary of the expedition under
    Gruner that continued on from Kete-Krachi to
    the north in 1894-1895.
7   PRO CO 879/41 African (West) 479, Encl. 1 in
    No. 80: Ferguson to Griffith, Christiansborg
    22 February 1895; and Klose (1899) 384-387.
8   PRO CO 879/45 African (West) 507, Encl. 2 in
    No. 59: "Evidence taken before the District
    Commissioner of Accra relative to the destruc-
    tion of Salaga by German Officials," 17 August
    1896; and PRO CO 879/48 African (west) 529:
    Parmeter to Governor, "Report from British
    Kraki," British Kraki 31 March 1897.
9   Trierenberg (1913) 112-133.
10 PRO CO 879/41 African (West) 479, Encl. 1 in
    No. 89: Ferguson to Griffith, 22 February
    1895.
11 NAG Accra ADM 39/1/32: German Kete-Krachi
    District Diary, entry 8 July 1895.
12 Ramseyer (1886) 74. Binger (1892) II:
    102-103, explains that in 1889 kola nuts,
    depending on their size and quality, could
    retail anywhere from one to thirty cowries a
    piece at Salaga. If one assumes that the price
    was somewhat lower at Kete-Krachi than an
    average value of ten cowries per kola nut seems
    realistic. The Germans however were probably
    being unreasonable to charge a fixed money
    (cowrie) toll on kola which by definition did
    not take into account the size and quality of
    the load.
13 PRO CO 96/215: Ferguson, "Report on Mission to
    Atabubu," 9 January 1891.
14 NAG Accra ADM 39/1/32: German Kete-Krachi
    District Diary, entry 4 January 1895.
15 Ibid., entry 1 March 1895. The 1893 and 1896
    Almanacs show ₤ sterling = 20.43 Marks, so 1
    shilling = 1 Mark was approximately accurate.
16 PRO CO 879/45 African (West 507, Encl. 1 in No.
    15; Leach to Messrs. Swanzy, 17 March 1896;
    and NAG Accra ADM 12/5/149: Sedgwick to Chief
    Commissioner Northern Territories, Gambaga 30
    September 1904.
17 Lome, Bibliotheque Nationale, G6: "Jahres-
    bericht," Kete Krachi Station, 1 July 1900 and
    10 July 1901.

18 Klose (1899) 336 and 383-384; and NAG Accra ADM
    39/1/32: German Kete Krachi District Diary,
    entries 26 January, 31 January, 5 February, 9
    April, and 18 June 1895.
19 Ibid., entry 4 January 1895.
20 PRO CO 879/45 African (West) 506, No. 70:
    Maxwell to Chamberlain, 28 December 1896; and
    PRO CO 879/48 African (West) 529: Parmeter,
    "Report from British Kraki," 31 March 1897.
21 PRO CO 879/45 African (West) 506, No. 70:
    Maxwell to Chamberlain, 28 December 1896; and
    NAG Accra ADM 39/1/32: German Kete Krachi
    District Diary, entry 5 February 1895.
22 See excerpts from Krause's letters in Braimah
    and Goody (1967) 150-156, and Markov and Sebald
    (1963).
23 A summary of the development of these re-
    strictions is found in NAG Accra ADM 56/1/39:
    Williams to Chief Commissioner Northern terri-
    tories, 5 June 1905.
24 Kling (1890) 146 and Kling (1893) 147; Klose
    (1899) 340.
25 Smuggling of powder was a major problem because
    the powder was legal merchandise in German
    territory and was restricted by the British.
    See for example Rhodes House Library, MSS Afr
    s. 470: Ross, "Powder," n.d., which describes
    smuggling powder in a coffin. Ross was the
    Preventative Service officer stationed at
    British Krachi from 1905-1908. See also the
    report on the accidental explosion of smuggled
    gunpowder at British Krachi in NAG Kumase D
    1809: Legge to Chief Commissioner Ashanti, 6
    December 1907.
26 NAG Accra ADM 11/1773: "Palaver Book," 350,
    Kratchi 28 April 1903.
27 NAG Accra ADM 56/1/39: Hood to Colonial
    Secretary 22 Jan. 1904.
28 NAG Accra ADM 56/1/507: Cardinall, "Annual
    Report," Kete-Krachi 31 March 1925.
29 BMA D-1, 63 (1895) No. 153: Rosler, "Reise
    nach Krakye," 16 September 1895.
30 Bosman (1705) 308; Bovill (1958) 84 and 236;
    Kling (1890) 146.
31 Klose (1899) 357.
32 NAG Accra ADM 39/1/32: German Kete Krachi
    District Diary, entry 16 January 1895.
33 Klose (1899) 362.
34 Ibid., 366.

35 NAG Accra ADM 39/1/32: German Kete Krachi
    District Diary, entry 25 March 1895.
36 Ibid., entry 23 March 1895.
37 Ibid., entry 4 April 1895.
38 Ibid., entry 8 April 1895.
39 Ivor Wilks, FN 9: Interview with Malam Abu
    Bakr ibn al-Hajj 'Umar, Kete-Krachi, 21 June
    1962.
40 Braimah and Goody (1967) 152, quoting Krause
    writing to Kreuz-Zeitung a letter dated Salaga
    9 December 1892; and Ivor Wilks FN 63: inter-
    view with al-Hajj Muhammed Limam Thani, Kete-
    Krachi 16 June 1963.
41 Ivor Wilks, FN 8: Interview with Malam Abu
    Bakr ibn al-Hajj 'Umar, Kete-Krachi 15 June
    1963
42 D.E. Ferguson (1973) 24: Interview with Ahmadu
    'dan Limam, Kumase.
43 Maier (1975) II: Field Note 86, Interview with
    Malam Baba Adamu, 27 July 1973, Kete-Krachi;
    and Ivor Wilks, FN 8: Interview with Malam Abu
    Bakr ibn al-Hajj 'Umar, Kete-Krachi 15 June
    1963
44 D.E. Ferguson (1973) 24-25; and Maier (1975)
    II: Field Note 19, Interview with Imam Malam
    Titibrika, 25 February 1973, Kete-Krachi, and
    Field Note 44, Interview with Muhammad
    Majamfula, 7 April 1973, Kete-Krachi.
45 Maier (1975) II: Field Note 43, Interview with
    al-Hajj Bello, 6 April 1973, Kete-Krachi, and
    Field Note 109, Interview with Malam Ibrahima,
    14 August 1973, Kete-Krachi. Mischlisch
    published translations of al-Hajj 'Umar's works
    in Mitteilungen des Seminars fur Orientalische
    Sprachen (1907, 1908, and 1909) and in his Book
    Über die Kulturen im Mittel-Sudan (1942).
    Mischlisch also authored some Hausa Language
    guides (1903, 1906).
46 D.E. Ferguson (1973) is primarily an English
    translation of this document.
47 NAG Tamale, ADM 1/96: Cardinall to Commission-
    er, Kete Krachi 17 June 1926.
48 Lome Bibliotheque Nationale, G6: Jahres-
    bericht, Kete-Kratschi, 1 July 1900; NAG Accra
    ADM 56/1/242: Hutter to District Commissioner,
    Kratchi 10 June 1922.
49 BMA D-1, 61 (1894) No. 153: Clerk to Basel,
    Krakye 28 September 1894.

50 BMA D-1, 63 (1895) No. 131: Hall, "Reise nach Krakye," 17 September 1895.

51 NAG Accra ADM 11/1/794: "History of the Kratchis as related by Head Chief Kuji Dente to the District Political Officer," Kete-Kratchi April 1920.

52 NAG Accra ADM 1/9/4: Griffith to Ferguson, Accra 9 November 1894; PRO CO 879/41 African (West) 479 Encl. in No. 19: Ferguson to Griffith, Yendi 18 August 1894; and Encl. 1 in No. 57: Nkoranza 15 December 1894.

53 NAG Accra ADM 56/1/242: Norris to Provincial Commissioner, Tamale 8 May 1922.

54 PRO CO 879/41 African (West) 479, Encl. 1 in No. 80: Ferguson to Griffith, Christiansborg 22 February 1895; NAG Accra, ADM 12/5/149: "Intelligence Report," 31 December 1908; Maier (1975) II: Field Note 57, Interview with Firao Bosomfo Kofi Brebe, 23 May 1973, Dambae; and Field Note 54, Interview with Nana Kwabena Kobi, 10 May 1973, Kadentwe.

55 Great Britain, Foreign Office Confidential 9753, Part XII (1910): Wallis, "Report on German Togoland," 1 May 1910; and Confidential 10315, Part XIX (1913) Wallis, "Report on Togoland," 10 April 1913.

56 Maier (1975) II: Field Note 32, Interview with Motodiahene Kofi Fusu, 12 March 1973, Osramani.

57 NAG Accra ADM 11/1306: Okuju Dente to Chief Commissioner Ashanti, "A Translation of a Petition from the Head Chiefs of the Kratchi District to the English Government," 26 November 1918.

58 Interview with Malam al-Hasan, Yendi 11 January 1970, recorded by P. Ferguson, Interview 38.

59 Maier (1975) II: Field Note 70, Interview with Tutukpenehene Kwasi Poku II, 14 June 1973, Kete-Krachi.

60 Ibid., Field Note 15, Interview with Malam Momuni, 22 February 1973, Kete-Krachi.

61 Ibid., Field Note 70, Interview with Tutukpenehene Kwasi Poku II, 14 June 1973, Kete-Krachi.

62 NAG Accra ADM 11/572: Messum to Lome, British Krachi 16 November 1914; See also Maier (1975) II: Field NOte 74, Interview with Adontenhene Sreagyema, 10 July 1973, Kete-Krachi; and Field Note 81, Interview with Adua Dente, 16 July 1973, Kete-Krachi.

63 NAG Accra ADM 11/1306: Rattray to Officer
    Commanding British Forces in Togoland, "Memor-
    andum, Appendix B," British Krachi 29 November
    1918.
64 BMA D-1, 75 (1901) No. 87: Awere, "Annual
    Report," Krakye-Kantankofore 30 December 1901.
65 BMA D-1, 77 (1902) No. 58: Awere, "Half Yearly
    Report," Krakye-Kantankofore 30 June 1903; and
    NAG Accra ADM 11/1773: Palaver BOok, 356,
    "Statement of Hutter," Kratchi 28 April 1903.
66 NAG Accra ADM 11/1306: Hobbs to Chief Commis-
    sioner Ashanti, 20 December 1918.
67 BMA D-1, 77 (1902) No. 58: Awere, "Half Yearly
    Report," Krakye-Kantankofore 30 June 1902.
68 NAG Accra ADM 11/1306: Hobbs to Chief Commis-
    sioner Ashanti, 20 December 1918; and ADM
    11/1773: Palaver Book 356-358, Kratchi 28
    April 1903. None of the following Krachiwura
    lists mention Tokuri: NAG Accra ADM 39/1/32:
    Burn, Kete-Krachi 4 September 1932; ADM
    11/1621: Furley, "Notes," Kete-Krachi 18
    February 1918; ADM 11/794: "History of the
    Kratchis as related by Head Chief Kuji Dente,
    Kete-Kratchi April 1920; and NAG Tamale ADM
    1/610: Miller, Kete-Krachi 23 July 1935.
    Interview conducted with Kantankofore elders do
    mention Kwaku Tokuri from Odeafo however
    (Maier, 1975, II: Field Notes 39 and 52,
    Interviews with Kwame Nsia, 2 April and 3 May
    1973, Kantankofore.)
69 NAG Accra ADM 11/603: Furley, "Diary," entry
    10 February 1915.
70 von Rentzell (1922) 53-112 and (1926) 267.
71 Maier (1975) II: Field Note 22, Interview with
    Yaw Atokra, 27 February 1973,Kete-Krachi; von
    Rentzell (1922) 78 and 97-100 states that he
    hanged "Quassikuma" the Oberpriester, and the
    Oberhauptling "Kodjo." It is possible that he
    changed the names for the book, or perhaps he
    really did not know what he was doing.
72 Maier (1975) II: Field Note 49, Interview with
    Nana Kwadwo Kumah, 13 April 1973, Genge; and
    Field Note 22, Interview with Yaw Atokra, 27
    February 1973, Kete-Krachi. Field Note 49,
    Interview with Nana Kwadwo Kumah (13 April
    1973, Genge) and Field Note 59, Interview with
    Akosua Sempoa (29 May 1973, Kete-Krachi) and
    IAS JEK/32: "Krachi Traditions," (recorded by
    Kumah, 1968) 45, all imply that this Kwabena

Okoewane, the same person who became Dente
Bosomfo in 1921, was also sent to prison. His
name is perhaps deleted from some accounts
because of the high position he came to hold.

73 The Gold Coast Leader, 10 November 1912.
74 Maier (1975) II: Field Note 52, Interview with
    Kwame Nsia, 3 May 1973, Kete-Krachi. See also
    Field Note 54, Interview with Nana Kwabena
    Kobi, 10 May 1973, Kadentwe.
75 NAG Accra, ADM 11/603: Furley "Diary," 26
    January 1915; Maier (1975) II: Field Note 52,
    Interview with Kwame Nsia, 3 May 1973, Kete-
    Krachi; Field Note 61, Interview with B.K.
    Mensah, 5 June 1973, Kete-Krachi; Field Note
    90, Interview with Kachipa Kwame, 28 July 1973,
    Kete-Krachi; and others. If Neda did take the
    stool in 1912, and it was not returned until
    after his death, c. 1917, this would explain
    why Okuju Dente, who became Krachiwura c. 1913,
    was accused in 1932 of never having taken the
    formal oath of office. However, Furley, who
    investigated the positions of the various
    chiefs, seems never to have been told that Neda
    had the stool.
76 NAG Accra ADM 11/603: Furley, "Diary," 28
    January 1915. In c. 1917 Krachiwura Neda in
    British Krachi and his ambiguous position of
    Krachiwura-in-exile was taken by Yaw Kumah from
    Odeafo. The latter however was never recog-
    nized as Krachiwura, Okuju Dente being prefer-
    red by Krachis and Brace-Hall, the British
    Officer stationed there, who asserted that Yaw
    Kumah was too old, The war was almost over by
    then anyway and the need of a Krachiwura in
    British territory and one in German territory
    had almost been eliminated. See NAG Accra ADM
    39/1/32: Burn to Duncan-Johnstone, 21 August
    and 4 September 1932; NAG Tamale ADM 1/610:
    Miller to Jones, 23 July 1935; and Maier (1975)
    II: Field NOte 75, Interview with Kwame
    Adotia, 10 July 1973, Kete-Krachi; and Field
    Note 57, Interview with Firao Bosomfo Kofi
    Brebe, 23 May 1973, Dambae.
77 Maier (1975) II: Field Note 52, Interview with
    Kwame Nsia, 3 May 1973, Kete-Krachi.
78 BMA D-1, 71 (1899) No. 120: Awere, "Annual
    Report," Krakye-Kantankofore 29 December 1899.
79 Maier (1975) II: Field Notes 55 and 56,
    Interviews with Nana Kwadwo Kumah, 11 and 18

May, 1973, Genge; NAG Accra ADM 11/751: Norris to Commissioner of Togoland Records, Kete-Krachi 29 December 1920.

80 NAG Accra ADM 11/1621: Armitage, "Memorandum with Reference to the Wishes of the Togoland Natives," 10 January 1918, and Furley, "Notes of statements taken before the Secretary of Native Affairs on his tour of Togoland; NAG Accra ADM 11/1306: Akwasi, Chief of British Kratchis to DC British Kratchi, 27 November 1918; Okugyi Dente to Chief Commissioner Ashanti, 26 November 1918; and Rattray, "Memorandum," British Krachi 29 November 1918.

81 NAG Kumase D 87: Manners to Provincial Commissioner, Eastern Ashanti, Kete-Krachi 8 October 1981.

82 NAG Accra ADM 39/1/64: Page, "Diary," entry on trek 27 January 1934.

Chapter 9: Factionalism

1   Belloni and Beller (1978) 7; Factions have been studied mostly in the setting of village India. See for example Firth (1957), Beals (1959), Lewis (1958) and Nicholas (1963) but Turner (1957) came to some of the same early conclusions working among the Ndembu in Zambia. Nicholas (1965 and 1966) has made excellent efforts towards a comparative analysis, and in his 1965 article even attempts to analyze factions among the Iroquois from historical data.

2   Patron/client relationships are especially emphasized in Foster (1967) studying a Mexican village, Buxton (1958) working among the Mandari, Brass (1965) working in India, Scott (1972) on Southeast Asia, Scalipino and Masumu (1962) looking at Japanese political parties, and Kent (1978) examining the Medici in fifteenth century Florence.

3   Some lodging facilities and traders' services must have been existent at Krachikrom. Bonnat (1876, IV, 5) observed Accras and Adas there, Buss (1879, 34) stayed there in 1878 with an Akropong trader in a house near that of the Dente Bosomfo. Firminger, however, in 1887, could find no place suitable "for Europeans," and hence took up residence in Kete (PRO CO

96/185:   Firminger to White, 26 October 1887, para. 11).

4   Maier (1975) II: Field Note 20, Interview with Ma'azu, 27 February 1973, Kete-Krachi; Ivor Wilks, FN 10, Interview with al-Hajj Idris, Kete-Krachi 21 June 1962;

5   Maier, Interview with al-Hajj Muhammad Baba Bio, Kete-Krachi 11 June 1977.

6   Arhin (1971).

7   Compare for example Maier (1975) II: Field Note 17, Interview with al-Hajj Saidu, 24 February 1973, Kete-Krachi, Field Note 99, Interview with Madam Yaya, 2 August 1973, and Field Note 85, Interview with Malam Karamu Dagomba, 26 July 1973, Kete-Krachi, all Gonja or Dagomba descendants discussing their family occupations, with Field Note 12, Interview with Sarkin Zongo Malam Ladan, 18 February 1973, Field Note 20, and Interview with Ma'azu ibn Sofo, 26 February 1973, Kete-Krachi, of true Hausa families, both trading in kola.

8   Levtzion (1968) 100-101; see also Maier (1975) II: Interview with Asuma Hausa and Isifu Butcher, 8 August 1973, Kete-Krachi.

9   Maier (1975) II: Field Note 103, Interview with Asuma Hausa and Isifu Butcher, 8 August 1973; Maier, Interview with al-Hajj Muhammad Baba Bio, 11 June 1977, Kete-Krachi; and Ivor Wilks FN/8, Interview with malam Abu Bakr, Kete-Krachi, 15 June 1963.

10   NAG Accra, ADM 39/1/64:   Burn, Diary, Kete-Krachi 15 September 1932.

11   Maier, Interview with al-Hajj Muhammad Baba Bio, 11 June 1977, Kete-Kratchi.   See also Maier (1975) II: Field Note 91, Interview with Madam Azumi, 28 July 1973, Kete-Krachi; and Field Note 110, Interview with Muhammad Baba, 16 August 1973, Kete-Krachi.

12   Maier (1975) II: Field Note 19, Interview with Imam Malam Titibrika, 25 February 1973, Kete-Krachi.

13   Ibid., Field Note 56, Interview with Nana Kwadwo Kumah, 18 May 1973, Genge.

14   NAG Accra, ADM 39/1/32:   Burn, "Krachi Stool Conference," 24 October 1932; and Kwaku Kantankofureh to Chief Commissioner, 31 October 1932.

15   Maier (1975) II: Field Note 80, Interview with Nana Kwadwo Kumah, 16 July 1973, Genge.

NOTES FOR PAGES 181-187

16 Kete-Krachi District Office: Kete-Krachi District Record Book.
17 Kete-Krachi District Office: Kete-Krachi District Record Book.
18 Maier (1975) II: Field Note 104, Interview with Horrocks Gyiniso, 8 August 1973; and Field Note 109, Interview with Malam Ibrahima, 14 August 1973, Kete-Krachi.
19 Ibid., Field Note 109, Interview with Malam Ibrahima 14 August 1973, Kete-Krachi.
20 Following the formation of the Volta Lake in 1966, the resettlement town of Kete-Krachi was built immediately adjacent to Kantankofore, with the result that the latter town is even more involved in Kete politics today.
21 NAG Tamale, ADM 1/135: Cooper, Diary, 28 October 1930; NAG Accra, ADM 56/1/343: Court Evidence, 19 December 1930; NAG Tamale, ADM 1/610: Chiefs to Chief Commissioner, 29 August 1935.
22 Maier (1975) II: Field Note 79, Interview with Nana Kwadwo Kumah, 13 July 1973, Genge.
23 Deutsche Kolonialzeitung (10 November 1894) VII: Herold, "Kratchi und Bismarckburg;" Goody (1966) 43.
24 NAG Tamale, ADM 1/135: Cooper, Diary, 28 October 1930; NAG Accra, ADM 56/1/343: Court Evidence, 19 December 1930.
25 Nicholas (1965).
26 Belloni and Beller (1978) 11. Try as Nicholas (1965) does to avoid the negative connotations of factionalism, he still seems to conclude that factions are correlated with "the most intense external pressure," and the breakdown of legitimacy (55).
27 Maier (1975) II: Field Note 110, Interview with Muhammad Baba, 16 August 1973; Ivor Wilks FN/11: Interview with al-Hajj Muhammad Limam Thani, Kete-Krachi 21 June 1962. It is only fair to note however that in the elections of 1954 and 1956 the Kete-Krachi district was overwhelmingly CPP: Daily Graphic, 18 June 1954; Ibid., 1956.
28 Al-Hajj Muhammed Bello, "History of Imam al-Hajj Muhammadu Shani," 21 February 1972, given to the author; Maier (1975) II: Field Note 110, Interview with Muhammad Baba, 16 August 1973; Field Note 100, Interview with Sarkin Zongo Malam Ladan, 3 August 1973, at

Kete-Krachi.   Maier,   Interview   with   B.K.
Mensah, Kete-Krachi, 10 June 1977.

29   Rathbone (1968) 35; Saaka (1978) has also
     suggested   the   persistence   of   traditional
     division in Wa into the post-independence era,
     though with some shifting and "secularization"
     as he calls it.

30   Rathbone (1978) 34-35.

Bibliography

PRINTED WORKS, DISSERTATIONS, ETC.

Allen, W. (1965) The African Husbandman, New York.

Anyane, S. La. (1963) Ghana Agriculture, London.

Arhin, K. (1976) "Market Settlements in Northwestern Ashanti: Kintampo," University of Ghana Institute of African Studies Research Review, Supplement: Ashanti and the North-west, 1, 135-155.

_____. (1970a) "Ashanti and the Northeast," University of Ghana Institute of African Studies Research Review, Supplement: Ashanti and the North-east, 2, 1-14.

_____. (1970b) "Aspects of the Ashanti Northern Trade in the Nineteenth Century," Africa, XL, 4, 363-373.

_____. (1971) "Strangers and Hosts: A Study in the Political Organisation and History of Atebubu Town," Transactions of the Historical Society of Ghana, XII, 61-82.

Arthur, J. (n.d.) Brong Ahafo Handbook, Accra.

Atkins, J. (1735) A Voyage to Guinea, Brasil, and the West-Indies, London.

Austin, D. and Tordoff, W. (1960) "Voting in an African Town," Political Studies, VIII, 2, 130-146.

Banton, M. ed. (1966) Anthropological Approaches to the Study of Religion, London.

Barbot, J. (1746) A Description of the Coasts of North and South Guinea, London.

Beals, A. (1959) "Leadership in a Mysore Village," in R. Lane and I. Tinker, eds. Leadership and Political Institutions in India, Princeton, 427-437.

Beck, G. (1880-1) "Eine neue Route nach den Obern Niger und dem Soudan," Jahresbericht der Geographischen Gesellschaft in Bern, III, 6, 35-53.

Belloni, F. and Beller, D., eds. (1978) Faction Politics, Santa Barbara.

Bevin, H.J. (1960) "M.J. Bonnat: Trader and Mining Promoter," The Economic Bulletin of Ghana, IV, 7, 1-12.

Binger, L.D. (1892) Du Niger au Golfe de Guinee par le Pays de Kong et le Mossi, 2 vols., Paris.

Boahen, A. (1965) "Asante-Dahomey Contacts in the 19th Century," Ghana Notes and Queries, 7, 1-3.

Bonnat, M.J. (1875-6) Letters in L'Explorateur, I, 5-6, 292, 400, 487-8; II, 269-70, 327, 370-1, 460, 543, 565-8, 621-5; III, 1-3, 36-8, 53-5, 82-3, 112-13, 139-41, 238, 375, 409, 456, 587.

_____. (1876) Diary in L'Explorateur, III, 663-8; IV, 3-5, 36-7, 66-7, 87-8.

_____. (1876a) "Salaga," Liverpool Mercury, 12 June.

Bosman, W. (1705) A new and accurate description of the coast of Guinea, divided into the Gold, the Slave, and the Ivory Coasts, London.

Bovill, E.W. (1958) The Golden Trade of the Moors, London.

Bowdich, T.E. (1819) Mission from Cape Coast Castle to Ashantee, London.

_____. (1821) An Essay on the Geography of North-western Africa, Paris.

Braimah, J.A. and Goody, J. (1967) Salaga: The Struggle for Power, London.

Brass, P. (1965) Factional Politics in an Indian State, Berkeley.

Brokensha, D. (1966) Social Change at Larteh, Ghana, London.

Brokensha, D. ed. (1972) Akwapim Handbook, Accra.

Burton, R.F. (1874) "Two Trips on the Gold Coast," Ocean Highways: The Geographical Review I, 448-461.

Buss, P. (1879) "Nach Salaga," Der evangelische Heidenbote, LII, 5, 33-36, and 6, 43-44.

Buttner, R. Dr. (1893) "Bilder aus dem Togohinterlande," Mitteilungen aus den Deutschen Schutzgebieten, VI, 237-254, mit 13 Tafeln.

Buttner, R. Dr. (1911) "Togo," Das Uberseeische Deutschland, II, 2nd ed., Stuttgart.

Buxton, J. (1958) "The Mandari of the Southern Sudan," in J. Middleton and D. Tait, eds. Tribes Without Rulers, London.

Cardinall, A.W. (1920) The Natives of the Northern Territories of the Gold Coast, London.

_____. (1926-7) "The Story of the German Occupation of Togoland," The Gold Coast Review, II, 2, 192-207 and III, 1, 56-72.

_____. (1927) In Ashanti and Beyond, London.

_____. (1931) Tales Told in Togoland, London.

_____. (1932) A Bibliography of the Gold Coast, Accra.

Cattenoz, H.-G. (1961) Tables de Concordance des Eres Chretienne et Hegirienne, Rabat.

Chambers, R., ed. (1970) The Volta Resettlement Experience, London.

Christaller, J.G. (1886) "Eine Reise nach Salaga und Obooso durch die Lander im Osten des mittleren Volta, von dem Negermissionar Dav. Asante," Mitteilungen der Geographische Gesellschaft, Jena, IV, 15-40.

_____. (1887-8) "Die Volta Sprachen-Gruppen," Zeitschrift fur Kolonialsprachen, I, 161-188.

_____. (1890) "Eine Reise in den Hinterlandern von Togo," [including Hall, P. (1890) q.v.] Mitteilungen der Geogrphische Gesellschaft, Jena, VIII, 106-133.

_____. (1933) Dictionary of the Asante and Fante Language, Called Tschi, 2nd. ed., Basel.

Claridge, W.W. (1915) A History of the Gold Coast and Ashanti, 2 vols., London.

Clerk, N. (1891) "Neue Reise in den Hinterlandern von Togo, nach Nkonya, Boem, Obooso, Salaga, Krakye, 2 Dezember 1889 bis 5 Februar 1890," mitgeteilt von J. G. Christaller, Mitteilungen der Geographische Gesellschaft, Jena, IX, 77-98.

Cornevin, R. (1959) Histoire de Togo, Paris.

_____. (1962) Les Bassari du nord Togo, Paris.

Coursey, D.G. (1966) "The Cultivation and use of Yams in West Africa," Ghana Notes and Queries, 9, 45-54.

Croft, J.A. (1874) "Exploration of the River Volta, West Africa," Proceedings of the Royal Geographical Society, XVIII, 2, 183-194.

Danckelman, F. von. (1893) "Bermerkungen zur Ubersichts Skizze des Gebietes zwischen Salaga, Kratye und Bismarcksburg," Mitteilungen aus den Deutschen Schutzbegieten, VI, 66-67.

Dane, Edmund (1919) British Campaigns in Africa and the Pacific 1914-1918, London.

Dapper, O. (1668) Beschreibung von Afrika, Amsterdam.

Davies, O. (1971) The Archaeology of the Flooded Volta Basin, Occasional Papers in Archaeology, No. 1, Department of Archaeology, University of Ghana, Legon.

Debrunner, H.W. (1951) Witchcraft in Ghana, 2nd. ed., Accra.

_____. (1965) A Church between Colonial Powers, London.

_____. (1967) A History of Christianity in Ghana, Accra.

De Graft-Johnson, J.C. (1969) "The Population of Ghana 1846-1967," Transactions of the Historical Society of Ghana, X, 1-12.

Denteh, A.C. (1967) "Ntoro and Nton," University of Ghana Institute of African Studies Research Review, III, 3, 91-96.

Deutscher Kolonialatlas (1918) mit Jahrbuch, Berlin.

Deutsches Kolonial Lexikon (1920) 3 vols., Leipzig.

Dickson, K.B. (1969) A Historical Geography of Ghana, Cambridge.

Dobson, G. (1892) "The River Volta, Gold Coast, West Africa," Journal of the Manchester Geographical Society, VIII, 19-25.

Doering, Lt. von. (1894) "Reise durch die Oti Niederung," Deutsches Kolonialblatt, V, 448-454.

_____. (1895) "Reiseberichte," Mitteilungen aus den Deutschen Schutzgebieten, VIII, 231-271.

Duncan, J. (1847) Travels in Western Africa in 1845 and 1846, 2 Vols., London.

Dupuis, J. (1824) _Journal of a Residence_ in Ashantee, London.

Eine Reise durch die Deutsche Kolonien (1910) Berlin.

Ellis, A.B. (1883) _The Land of Fetish_, London.

_____. (1887) _The Tshi-Speaking Peoples of the Gold Coast of West Africa_, London.

_____. (1893) _A History of the Gold Coast of West Africa_, London.

Ermann, L.W. (1876) "Der Volta-Fluss nach M.J. Bonnat's Forschungen und nach alteren Berichten," _Globus_, XXX, 23, 359-362 and 24, 375-378.

Ferguson, D.E. (1973) "Nineteenth Century Hausaland Being a Description by Imam Imoru of the Land, Economy, and Society of His People," Ph.D. dissertation, University of California, Los Angeles.

Ferguson, P. and Wilks, I. (1970) "Chiefs, Constitutions and the British in Northern Ghana," _West African Chiefs_, eds. M. Crowder and O. Ikime, Ife, 326-369.

Festinger, L., Riecken, H.W., and Schachter, S. (1956) _When Prophecy Fails_, Minneapolis.

Field, M.J. (1937) _Religion and Medicine of the Ga_, London.

_____. (1960) _Search for Security_, Evanston.

_____. (1962) "A Further Note on Burukung," _Ghana Notes and Queries_, 4, 29-30.

Firth, R. (1957) "Introduction to Factions in India and Overseas Indian Societies," _British Journal of Sociology_, 8, 291-295.

Fisch, R. (1911) _Nord Togo und seine westliche Nachbarschaft_, Basle.

Fitzner, R. (1897) _Kolonial Handbuch_, Berlin.

Food and Argiculture Organization of the United
Nations. (1968) Land and Water Survey in the Upper
and Northern Regions: Ghana, 6 vols., Rome.

Foster, G. (1967) "The Dyadic Contract: A Model
for the Social Structure of a Mexican Peasant
Village," in J. Potter, M. Diaz, and G. Foster,
Peasant Society: A Reader, 213-230.

Francois, C. von. (1888) "Bericht des Hauptmann von
Francois uber Reise im Hinterlande des deutschen
Schutzgebiets Togo," Mitteilungen aus den Deutschen
Schutzbegieten, I, 143-182.

_____. (1889) "Bericht von Hauptmann von Francois
uber seine zweite Reise nach Salaga," Mitteilungen
aus den Deutschen Schutzgebieten, II, 33-37.

_____. (1972) Ohne Schuss durch Dick und Dunn,
Esch-Waldems.

Froelich, J.-C., Alexandre, P. and Cornevin, R.
(1963) Les Populations de nord Togo, Paris.

Full, A. (1935) Funfzig Jahre Togo, Berlin.

Gaunt, Mrs. M. (1912) Alone in West Africa, London.

_____. (1913) "A New View of West Africa," The
Scottish Geographical Magazine, XXIX, 113-133.

Gehrts, M. (1915) A Camera Actress in the Wilds of
Togoland, London.

Ghana. Census Office. 1960 Population Census of
Ghana, 6 vols., Accra.

Ghana. Census Office. 1970 Population Census of
Ghana, Accra.

Gifford, P. and Louis, W.R. (1967) Britain and
Germany in Africa, New Haven.

Glover, J. (1874) "Notes on the Country between the
Volta and the Niger," Proceedings of the Royal
Geographical Society, 286-301.

Gold Coast Population Census 1921 (1923) Accra.

Gold Coast Census of Population. 1948 (1950)
London.

Goody, J. (1954) The Ethnography of the Northern
Territories of the Gold Coast, West of the White
Volta, London.

_____. (1963) "Ethnological notes on the distribu-
tion of the Guang languages," Journal of African
Languages, II, 3, 173-189.

_____. (1966a) "Salaga in 1876," Ghana Notes and
Queries, 8, 1-5.

_____. (1966b) "Salaga in 1892," University of
Ghana Institute of African Studies Research Review,
II, 3, 41-53.

_____. (1966c) Succession to High Office, Cam-
bridge.

_____. (1971) Technology, Tradition, and the State
in Africa, Oxford.

Goody, J. and Mustapha, T.M. (1967) "The Caravan
Trade from Kano to Salaga," Journal of the
Historical Society of Nigeria, III, 4, 611-616.

Great Britain. Foreign Office (1920) Togoland,
Handbook Prepared under the Direction of the
Historical Section of the Foreign Office, No. 110,
London.

Gros, J. (1884) Voyages, Aventures et Captivite de
J. Bonnat Chez les Achantis, Paris.

_____. (n.d.) Nos Explorateurs en Afrique, Paris.

Hall, P. (1890) "Bericht uber die Reise nach Nkonya
und Boem vom 4 Januar bis 4 Februar 1887," mit
vorwort und nachwort von J.G. Christaller,
Mitteilungen der Geographische Gesellschaft, Jena,
VIII, 108-132.

Gold Coast Census of Population, 1931 (1932) Accra.
_____. (1965) Autobiography, Accra.

Henty, G.A. (1874) The March to Coomassie, London.

Herold, (1894) "Kratchi und Bismarckburg," Deutsche
Kolonialzeitung, VII, 12, 153-154.

Hill, P. (1966) "Landlords and Brokers: A West
African Trading System," Cahiers d'etudes
Africaines, VI, 3, 349-366.

Hobbs, H.J. (1927) "History of Nkoranza," The Gold
Coast Review, III, 117-121.

Horton, J.A.B. (1870) Letters on the Political
Condition of the Gold Coast, London.

Hupfeld, D. (1900) "Bilder aus den Hinterland der
Togokolonie," Deutsche Kolonialzeitung, 388-395.

Isert, P.E. (1797) Reize van Koppenhagen Naar
Guinea, Amsterdam.

Johnson, M. (1965) "Ashanti East of the Volta,"
Transactions of the Historical Society of Ghana,
VIII, 33-59.

_____. (1966a) Salaga Papers, 2 vols., Institute of
African Studies, Legon.

_____. (1966b) "The Wider Background of the Salaga
Civil War," University of Ghana Institute of
African Studies Research Review, II, 2, 31-39.

_____. (1968) "M. Bonnat on the Volta," Ghana Notes
and Queries, 10, 4-17.

_____. (1970) "The Cowrie Currencies of West
Africa," The Journal of African History, XI, 1,
17-49 and 3, 331-353.

_____. (1971) "Ashanti, Juaben and M. Bonnat,"
Transactions of the Historical Society of Ghana,
XII, 17-41.

Kea, R.A. (1966) "Salt Industries of the Gold
Coast," Institute of African Studies, Legon,
unpublished.

_____. (1969) "Akwamu-Anlo Relations c. 1750-1813,"
Transactions of the Historical Society of Ghana, X,
29-63.

Kent, D. (1978) The Rise of the Medici, Oxford.

Kirby, B. (1884) "A Journey into the Interior of Ashanti," Proceedings of the Royal Geographic Society, VI, 447-452.

Kling, E. (1890) "Bericht des Hauptmann Kling uber seine letzte, von Lome uber Kpandu, Salaga und Naparri nach Bismarckburg ausgefuhrte Reise," Mitteilungen aus den Deutschen Schutzbegieten, III, 137-164.

_____. (1890a) "Uber seine Reise in das Hinterland von Togo," Verhandlungen der Gesellschaft fur Erdkunde zu Berlin, XVII, 348-371.

_____. (1892) "Reise des Hauptmanns Kling von Lome uber Salaga nach Bismarckburg in Sommer 1891," Mitteilungen aus den Deutschen Schutzgebieten, V, 1-6.

_____. (1893) "Auszug aus den Tagebuchern des Hauptmanns Kling 1891 bis 1892," Mitteilungen aus den Deutschen Schutzgebieten, VI, 105-147.

Klose, H. (1896) Togo unter Deutscher Flagge: Reisebilder und Betrachtungen, Berlin.

_____. (1902) "Religiose Anschauungen und Menschen-opfer in Togo," Globus, LXXXI, 190-191.

_____. (1903) "Wohnstatten und Huttenbau im Togo-gebiet," Globus, LXXXII, 165-184.

_____. (1904) "Produktion und Handel Togos," Globus, LXXXVI, 69-73, 145-149, 203-206.

Kopp, J. (1882) "Eine Wolta-Reise auf dem 'Pioneer'," Mitteilungen der Geographische Gesellschaft, Jena, I, 71-78.

Kwamena-Poh, M.A. (1970) "The Emergence of the Akuapem State: 1730-1850," Ghana Notes and Queries, 11, 26-36.

_____. (1972) "History," in Brokensha, D., ed. Akwapim Handbook, Accra.

_____. (1973) Government and Politics in the Akuapem State 1730-1850, London.

Lander, R. and Lander, J. (1832) Journal of an Expedition to Explore the Course and Termination of the Niger, 2 vols., New York.

Lee, Mrs. R. (1835) Stories of Strange Lands, and Fragments from the Notes of a Traveller, London.

Lewis, O. (1958) Village Life in Northern India, New York.

Levtzion, N. (1958) Muslims and Chiefs in West Africa, Oxford.

Lewin, T. (1978) Asante Before the British, Lawrence, Kansas.

Lippert, J. (1907) "Uber die Bedeutung der Hausanation fur unsere Togo und Kamerun Kolonien," Mitteilungen des Seminars fur Orientalische Sprachen, Afrikanische Sprache, III Abt., 193-226.

Lonsdale, R.T. (1882) "Report of his Mission to Coomassie, Salgha, and Yendi, &c." Further Correspondence regarding Affairs of the Gold Coast, C. 3386, 57-101.

Lovejoy, P.E. (1971) "Long-Distance Trade and Islam: The Case of the Nineteenth Century Hausa Kola Trade," Journal of the Historical Society of Nigeria, V, 4, 537-548.

McCaskie, T.C. (1974) "The Paramountcy of Asante-hene Kwaku Dua I (1834-1867)," Ph.D. dissertation, Cambridge.

McKim, W. (1968) "The Organization of Markets in the North-east of Ghana," Yendi Project, Northwestern University and the Institute of African Studies, Legon.

Maier, D. (1975) "Kete-Krachi in the Nineteenth Century: Religious and Commercial Center of the Eastern Asante Borderlands," Ph.D. dissertation, Northwestern University.

Markov, P. (1968) "West African History in German
Archives," Journal of the Historical Society of
Nigeria, III, 602-605.

Markov, P. and Sebald, J. (1967) "Gottlob Adolf
Krause," Journal of the Historical Society of
Nigeria, III, 602-605.

Mathewson, R.D. (1965) "Kitare" A Preliminary
Report," West African Archaeological Newsletter,
III, Oct., 22-25.

Meillassoux, C. ed. (1971) The Development of
Indigenous Trade and Markets in West Africa,
London.

Meyerowitz, E.L.R. (1951) The Sacred State of the
Akan, London.

_____. (1958) The Akan of Ghana, London.

_____. (1960) The Divine Kingship in Ghana and
Ancient Egypt, London.

_____. (1961) "A Further Note on Burukung," Ghana
Notes and Queries, 2, 10.

Mischlisch, A. (1903) "Beitrage zur Geschichte der
Haussastaaten," Mitteilungen des Seminars fur
Orientalische Sprachen, VI, 158-224.

_____. (1906) Worterbuch der Haussasprache, Berlin.

_____. (1907) "Uber Sitten und Gebrauche in
Haussa," Mitteilungen des Seminars fur Orientalische Sprachen, X, 155-181.

_____. (1908) "Uber Sitten und Gebrauche in
Haussa," Mitteilungen des Seminars fur Orientalische Sprachen, XI, 1-81 and XII, 215-274.

_____. (1929) Neue Marchen aus Afrika, Leipzig.

_____. (1942) Uber die Kulturen im Mittel-Sudan,
Berlin.

_____. (1943) "Religiose und Weltliche Gesange der
Mohammedaner aus dem Sudan," Afrika, Studien zur
Auslandskunde, II, 3, 9-198.

Moberly, Brig. Gen. F.J. (1931) History of the Military Operations in Togoland and the Cameroons, 1914-1916, London.

Moxon, J. (1969) Volta: Man's Greatest Lake, London.

Muller, J. (1884) "Die Salagareise," Der evangelische Heidenbote, LVII, 41-42.

Multhauf, R.P. (1978) Neptune's Gift: A History of Common Salt, Baltimore.

Nicholas, R.W. (1963) "Village Factions and Political Parties in Rural West Bengal," Journal of Commonwealth Political Studies, 2: 17-32.

_____. (1965) "Factions: A Comparative Analysis," in M. Banton, ed., Political Systems and the Distribution of Power, London.

_____. (1966) "Segmentary Factional Political Systems," in M. Swartz, et. al., eds., Political Anthropology, Chicago.

Nketia, J.H. (1963) Drumming in Akan Communities of Ghana, London.

Opoku, T. (1878) "Ein Besuch in Salaga," Der evangelische Heidenbote, LI, 9, 66-69.

_____. (1885) "Eines Neger-Pastors Predigtreise durch die Lander am Voltastrom," Evangelisches Missions Magazin, XXIX, 257-272, 305-326, and 353-364.

Painter, C. (1966) "The Guang and West African Historical Reconstruction," Ghana Notes and Queries, 9, 58-66.

_____. (1967) "The distribution of Guang in Ghana and a statistical pre-testing on twenty-five idiolects." Journal of West African Languages, IV, 1, 25-78.

Priestly, M. and Wilks, I. (1960) "The Ashanti Kings in the Eighteenth Century: A Revised Chronology," The Journal of African History, I, 1, 83-96.

Ramseyer, F. (1886) "Eine Reise im Norden von Asante und im Osten vom Volta, von Okwawu nach Bron, Krakye und Boem," Mitteilungen der Geographische Gesellschaft, Jena, IV, 69-87.

_____. (1895) Achtzig Ansichten von der Goldkuste, Neuenburg.

Ramseyer, F., and Kunhe, J. (1875) Four Years in Ashantee, New York.

Ranger, T.O. and Kimambo, I.N. (1972) The Historical Study of African Religion, London.

Rathbone, R. (1968) "Opposition in Ghana: The National Liberation Movement," in Collected Seminar Papers on Opposition in the New African States, University of London Institute of Commonwealth Studies, No. 4.

_____. (1978) "Ghana," in J. Dunn, ed., West African States: Failure and Promise, Cambridge.

Rattray, R.S. (1916) Ashanti Proverbs, Oxford.

_____. (1923) Ashanti, Oxford.

_____. (1927) Religion and Art in Ashanti, Oxford.

_____. (1929) Ashanti Law and Constitution, Oxford.

_____. (1932) The Tribes of the Ashanti Hinterland, 2 vols., Oxford.

_____. (1934) "Hausa Poetry," in Evans-Pritchard, E.E., Essays Presented to C.G. Seligman, London, 255-265.

Reade, W. (1873) The African Sketch-Book, 2 vols., London.

_____. (1874) The Story of the Ashantee Campaign, London.

"Recent Explorations in the Basin of the Volta (Gold Coast) by Missionaries of the Basel Missionary Society," (1886) Proceedings of the Royal Geographic Society, n.s. VIII, 246-256, and map, 288.

Reindorf, C.C. (1895) History of the Gold Coast, Basel.

Rentzell, W. von. (1922) Unvergessenes Land, Hamburg.

_____. (1926) Unvergessenes Lang, Neue Folge, Hamburg.

Riis, A. (1840) "Reise des Missionars A. Riis," Evangelisches Missions Magazin, XXV, 3, 216-235.

Rottman, W. (1894) "Der Gotze Odente, ein Bild aus dem westafrikanischen Heidentum," Evangelisches Missions Magazin, XXXVIII, 367-379.

Saaka, Yakubu (1978) Local Government and Political Change in Northern Ghana, University Press of America.

Scalipino, R. and Masumi, J. (1962) Parties and Politics in Contemporary Japan, Berkeley.

Scott, J. "Patron-Client Politics and Political Change in Southeast Asia," American Political Science Review, 66, 1, 91-113.

Seebald, Peter (1977) "Togo", in Helmuth Stoecker, ed., Drang Nach Afrika, Berlin.

Seeger, M. (1892) "Die Sklaverei im Togoland und der englischen Goldkustkolonie," Deutsche Kolonialzeitung, 54-56.

Seidel, H. (1898) "Salzgewinnung und Salzhandel in Togo," Deutsche Kolonialzeitung, 234 and 251.

_____. (1911a) "Bilder aus Kete-Kratschi in West-Togo," Deutsche Kolonialzeitung, 298-300.

_____. (1911b) "Von Misahohe nach Bimbila," Deutsche Kolonialzeitung, 386-388.

Solken, H. (1970) "Zur Biographie des Imam 'Umaru von Kete-Kratyi," Africana Marburgensia, III, 2, 24-30.

Steemers, J.C.S. (1964) "The Kenekra Tradition of the Kratchis, Part I," Ghana Bulletin of Theology, II, 7, 1-8.

_____. (1970) "The Material Paraphernalia of the Traditional Religious Cults of the Krachi Area," Ghana Notes and Queries, 11, 17-20.

Stewart, J.M. (1966) "Awutu, Larteh, Nkonya and Krachi," Comparative African Wordlists, No. 1, Institute of African Studies, Legon.

Sutton, I.B. (1981) "The Volta River Salt Trade: The survival of an idigenous industry," Journal of African History 22, 1 (1981) 43-61.

Torto, J.O. (1956) "The Cultivation of Yams in the Gold Coast," New Gold Coast Farmer, I, 6-8.

Trierenberg, G. (1914) Togo: Die Aufrichtung der Deutschen Schutzherrschaft und die Erschliessung des Landes, Berlin.

Unwin, A.H. (1912) Report on the Afforestation of Togo with Teak and African Timber Trees, London.

Villault, N. (1670) A Relation of the coasts of Africka called Guinee, London.

Wakkad, M. el- (1961-2) "Qissatu Salga Tarikhu Gonja: The Story of Salaga and the History of Gonja," Ghana Notes and Queries, 3, 8-31 and 4, 6-25.

Wallis, J.R. (1953) "The Kwahus -- Their Connection with the Afram Plain," Transactions of the Gold Coast and Togoland Historical Society, I, 3, 10-26.

Watherston, A.E.C. (1908) "The Northern Territories of the Gold Coast," Journal of the African Society, VIII, 28, 344-373.

Westermann, D. (1914) "Die Verbreitung des Islams in Togo und Kamerun," Die Welt des Islams, II, 202-276.

_____. (1922) Die Sprache der Guang in Togo und auf der Goldkuste und funf andere Togo-Sprachen, Berlin.

_____. (1925) "Das Tschi und Guang," Mitteilungen des Seminars fur Orientalischen Sprachen, XXVIII, 1-85.

_____. (1930) A Study of the Ewe Language, London.

Westermann, D. and Bryan, M.A. (1970) Handbook of African Languages, Part II: Languages of West Africa, International African Institute, London.

White, H.P. (1956) "Internal Exchange of Staple Foods in the Gold Coast," Economic Geography, XXXII, 2, 115-125.

Wilks, I. (1957) "The Rise of the Akwamu Empire, 1650-1710," Transactions of the Historical Society of Ghana, III, 2, 99-136.

_____. (1958) "Akwamu 1650-1750: A Study of the Rise and Fall of a West African Empire," M.A. thesis, University of Wales.

_____. (1961a) The Northern Factor in Ashanti History, University College of Ghana.

_____. (1961b) "Burukung," Ghana Notes and Queries, I, 11-12.

_____. (1963) "The Growth of Islamic Learning in Ghana," Journal of the Historical Society of Nigeria, II, 4, 409-417.

_____. (1966a) "The Position of Muslims in Metopolitan Ashanti in the Early Nineteenth Century," in I. Lewis, ed., Islam in Tropical Africa, London, 318-341.

_____. (1966b) "A Note on the Chronology and Origins of the Gonja Kings," Ghana Notes and Queries, 8, 26-28.

_____. (1968) "The Transmission of Islamic Learning in the Western Sudan," in J. Goody, ed., Literacy in Traditional Societies, Cambridge, 161-197.

_____. (1971) "Asante Policy towards the Hausa Trade in the Nineteenth Century," in C.

Meillassoux, ed., The Development of Indigenous Trade and Markets in West Africa, London, 124-141.

_____. (1975) Asante in the Nineteenth Century: The Structure and Evolution of a Political Order, Cambridge.

Wills, J. ed., (1962) Agriculture and Land Use in Ghana, London.

Wilson, M. (1971) Religion and the Transformation of Society, Cambridge.

Withers-Gill, J. (1924) A Short History of Salaga, Accra.

York, N.R. (1972) "Cowries as Type-Fossils in Ghanaian Archaeology," West African Journal of Archaeology, II, 93-101.

Zech, J. Graf von. (1898) "Vermischte Notizen uber Togo und das Togo Hinterland," Mitteilungen aus den Deutschen Schutzgebieten, XI, 2, 89-147.

_____. (1901) "Ueber Kola in Westafrika," Mitteilungen aus den Deutschen Schutzbegieten, XIV, 8-14.

_____. (1904) "Land und Leute an der Nordwestgrenze von Togo," Mitteilungen aus den Deutschen Schutzgebieten, XVII, 3, 107-135.

Zimmerman, E. (1912) Unsere Kolonien, Berlin.

GREAT BRITAIN PARLIAMENTARY PAPERS

1872: C. 670 Correspondence relative to the Cession by the Netherlands Government to the British Government of the Dutch Settlements on the West Coast of Africa (Accounts and Papers, LXX).

1873: C. 266-I Gold Coast: Part II Despatches from Mr. Pope Hennessy respecting the Transfer of the Dutch Possessions on the Gold Coast, etc. (Accounts and Papers, XLIX).

1873: C. 819 Further Correspondence respecting the Ashanti Invasion (Accounts and Papers, XLIX).

1874: C. 890 Part I: Further papers relating to the Ashanti Invasion.

1874: C. 891 Part II: Further Correspondence re respecting the Ashanti Invasion.

1874: C. 892 Part III: Further Correspondence respecting the Ashanti Invasion.

1874: C. 893 Part IV: Further Correspondence respecting the Ashanti Invasion.

1874: C. 1006 Part IX: Further Correspondence respecting the Ashanti Invasion (Accounts and Papers XLVI).

1875: C. 1139 Correspondence relating to the Queen's Jurisdiction on the Gold Coast, and the Abolition of Slavery within the Protectorate (Accounts and Papers, LII).

1875: C. 1140 Correspondence relating to the Affairs of the Gold Coast (Accounts and Papers, LII).

1876: C. 1343 Papers relating to Her Majesty's Possessions in West Africa (Accounts and Papers, LII).

1876: C. 1402 Papers relating to Her Majesty's Possessions in West Africa (Accounts and Papers, LII).

1876: C. 1409 Correspondence Respecting the Affairs of the Gambia and the Proposed Exchange with France of Possessions on the West Coast of Africa (Accounts and Papers, LII).

1881: C. 3064 Affairs of the Gold Coast and threatened Ashanti Invasion (Accounts and Papers, LXV).

1882: C. 3386 Further Correspondence regarding Affairs of the Gold Coast (Accounts and Papers, XLVI)

1883: C. 3387 Further Correspondence regarding Affairs of the Gold Coast (Accounts and Papers, XLVIII).

1884: C. 4052 Further Correspondence regarding
Affairs of the Gold Coast (Accounts and Papers,
XLVI).

1885: C. 4477 Further Correspondence regarding
Affairs of the Gold Coast (Accounts and Papers, LV)

1886: C. 4906 Further Correspondence regarding
Affairs of the Gold Coast (Accounts and Papers,
XLVII).

1888: C. 5357 Further Correspondence regarding
Affairs of the Gold Coast (Accounts and Papers,
LXXV).

1888: C. 5615 Further Correspondence regarding
Affairs of the Gold Coast (Accounts and Papers,
LXXV).

1896: C. 7917 Further Correspondence relating to
Affairs in Ashanti (Accounts and Papers, LVIII).

1896: C. 7918 Further Correspondence relating to
Affairs in Ashanti (Accounts and Papers, LVIII).

1901: C. 501 Correspondence relating to the
Ashanti War 1900 (Accounts and Papers, XLVIII).

1902: C. 933 Further Correspondence relating to
Ashanti.

ARCHIVES, FIELD MATERIALS, NEWSPAPERS ETC.

All sources in this classification have been cited
in full in the footnotes. The major classes of
materials however are listed below with the
abreviations used.

United Kindgom

PRO: Public Record Office, London:
CO 879/- Colonial Office Confidential Print
      African West.
CO 96/- Colonial Office, Original Correspondence,
      Gold Coast.
FO - Foreign Office Papers.

Rhodes House, Oxford.

Switzerland

BMA: Basel Mission Archives, Basel.

Ghana

NAG: National Archives of Ghana; Accra, Kumase,
Tamale, Ho. The following are the major though not
exclusive units examined in the Accra archives:

ADM 1/1/-Correspondence, Secretary of State to
      Governor
ADM 1/2/- Correspondence, Governor to Secretary
      of State
ADM 1/7/- Miscellaneous letters
ADM 1/9/- Letters to Officials
ADM 11/1/- Secretary of Native Affairs
ADM 12/3/- Confidential to Secretary of State
ADM 12/5/- Confidential to Officials
ADM 38/1-6/- Regional Records, Ho
ADM 39/1-5/- District Commissioner Records, Ho
ADM 42/1/- Kete-Krachi Records
ADM 56/1/- Chief Commissioner Northern
      Territories Record
MFA 4/- Ministry of Foreign Affairs, Treaties and
      Agreements

In Kumase, the D series was used; in Ho the C and D
series were used. In Tamale, all documents are
under simply one classification, ADM 1/-.

IAS: Institute of African Studies, University of
Ghana, Legon:

IASAS/- Asante Stool Histories, recorded by J.
      Agyeman-Duah.
IASAR/- Arabic Manuscript Collection
IASAM/- Traditions from the Afram Plains, recorded
      by K. Ameyaw.
IASJEK/- Traditions from Krachi, recorded by
      J. Kumah

Kete-Krachi District Office: The District Record
Book has been consulted extensively and cited
accordingly in the text.

Togo

Bibliotheque Nationale, Lome. The more than 5,000
items available in this archive are uncataloged.
Most of them have letter and number identification,
usually D- or S-, assigned apparently by the
Germans. Almost the entire collection is in German
schrift, though there is also a 2,000 volume German
colonial library in the Bibliotheque. The British
occupied Lome in 1914 and examined all the records
then. Before turning over Lome to the French they
apparently removed most of the material to Accra
that pertained to Yendi and Kete-Krachi, although
some annual reports and letters remain.

Field Materials

Field work was done by the author in Ghana, 1972-
1973, 1977 and 1979. The 1973 field notes constitute Volume II of the author's dissertation, "Kete-
Krachi in the Nineteenth Century," Northwestern
Univeristy, 1975, and are referred to in the
present text as Maier (1975) II. They are available from the University Microfilms International,
Ann Arbor, Michigan.

The field notes of I. Wilks (FN/-) are on deposit
in the Herskovits Memorial Library, Northwestern
University, Evanston.

The field notes of P. Ferguson and D. Warren are on
deposit in the African Oral Data Archives, Indiana
University, Bloomington.

Newspapers

Numerous articles from the following newpapers are
essential for an understanding of much material in
this book and have not necessarily been quoted.

The African Times (London)

The Daily Graphic (Accra)

Deutsche Kolonialzeitung (Berlin)

Deutsches Kolonialblatt (Berlin)

Index